Stripping Off the Labels

REESY NEFF

Year of the Book
135 Glen Avenue
Glen Rock, PA 17327

ISBN: 978-1-64649-199-5 (print)
ISBN: 978-1-64649-200-8 (ebook)

This book is memoir. It reflects the author's present recollections of experiences over time. Some names and characteristics have been changed, some events have been compressed, and some dialogue has been recreated. If you remember them differently, bless your heart, write your own book.

Dedication

In loving memory of my mama, Gladys,
or Happy, as her friends knew her.

She taught me so many lessons in life.
She taught me to be a survivor.
She taught me that "It's going to be okay."
Most importantly, she taught me love.

1 | The Why Behind the What

And Certain Not Necessarily Needed Disclaimers

Six years ago at Thanksgiving, my cousin Greg asked, "What would you do if money wasn't an issue?" I thought about it and answered something like, "I'd help people, add beauty... I don't know. Maybe I'd design shoes!"

After everyone left, I continued to think about Greg's question. If money wasn't an issue I landed on the answer that I would become a motivational speaker. As you get to know me, you will find I am very candid. You will also learn about my character flaws and potty mouth. For the most part I have learned to embrace these traits. Hopefully you will, too!

I love to inspire people to do things, to believe in themselves. I also love to be on stage and captivate an audience. My imagined new career prompted me to reflect on experiences of love, tragedy, and devastation... and how everything somehow turned out all right. Considering the struggles and challenges endured, I'm a fucking rock star!

My biggest life lesson is that you can't let other people place labels on you. You may also discover that you've been labeling yourself. It's time to find the real you behind all those fake classifications and characterizations. People may try to force you into boxes, but you weren't made that way—you're not veal!

"Sassy" is a label I acquired young. My daddy was a Marine (with quite the potty mouth himself) and recalls when I was three years old and walked into the living room saying, "I'm getting tired of this shit. I'm gonna pack my stuff and leave." Guess I must have heard that somewhere before.

As I share my journey to strip the labels, I want you to meet the authentic me. Not some fancy pants fake person who has skipped along in life without adversity. My hope is that after learning of my struggles, you will be inspired and see that you too can accomplish anything you put your mind to—even when you're starting at a disadvantage.

We all have a story to tell. And the most powerful ones come from a place of being vulnerable enough to share.

It's time to strip off those labels, one by one!

2 | Family History Runs Deep

My daddy was from Detroit, Michigan. His mother was one of the meanest people I have ever known, probably because her husband left her when my daddy was just two years old. I am quite sure it was difficult being a divorced, single mother in the early '50s, but let me tell you, if she was on earth, I'm not sure who was running hell.

Daddy was verbally and physically abused. If he was five minutes late getting home, she would lock him out of the house—and Detroit gets really, really cold. When she was pissed at him, she would kneel in front of the picture of Jesus and pray not to kill him. Then she would beat him mercilessly all over his body.

Daddy was raised Catholic and went to Catholic school. He used to talk about the nuns beating his hands with rulers, although he spoke of it as a good memory. Perhaps it was at least more caring than his own home.

At age 17, Daddy joined the Marines. He was an only son, so his mother had to "sign off" on it. This was during Vietnam, so enlisting meant the sure possibility of death, not to mention the after-effects of exposure to Agent Orange. Things must have been pretty bad for him to risk leaving the "relative" safety of home for a foreign country where death loomed.

My mama's story is also one of challenges and tribulations. "Reesy, we are survivors," she would tell me, "and it will get better. It may take time, but it will get better." She had a gift of making me believe no matter the circumstances, that everything would be all right. I wish I could hear those words from her once more.

Mama was raised in Chocowinity, North Carolina, the middle child of six—five girls and one boy. Her parents had married young and both came from large families of 12 or 13 siblings. When Mama was a baby, Granddaddy got drafted for World War II at age 28. He left my grandmama with three children and was gone for four years. He did write home every week—romantic and funny letters—ending in, "Tell Pig (my mama) I love her." I wonder if he felt guilty for being away in those most important years.

During the war, one of the things that was rationed were shoes. Somehow my grandmother had more pairs than anyone else. She used to hide them so no one would know. Even as she aged, she particularly loved gold, glitzy shoes. I believe it's hereditary because when I first met my husband, I had 85 pairs. We now have a rule that if I buy a pair, I have to get rid of one first. Except for the occasional sneaking of a pair, which I may or may not have been known to do. I plead the Fifth.

Before Granddaddy came back from the war, he found himself in a situation where he had to kill two young boys. Whatever really happened, it messed him up. He arrived home when Mama was four. When she was seven, my grandparents had their next child—a boy, Adolph Jr. Mama was upset as she had been the baby and didn't want any competition. Then came two other children, Betty Jane and my namesake Recie.

My understanding is that Granddaddy would binge drink, lying in bed all day for weeks on end. Then he would decide to sober up, admit himself to the Veterans Hospital, go through withdrawal and then come home. He did this several times. Grandmama even left him once. I'm sure the neighbors talked about that, too. After all, it was a small town and everyone knew everyone else's business.

One day all that changed. He was sitting praying by the river and a man came up to him to see what was wrong. My granddaddy explained that he had no money; he was a drinker and had a family to support and didn't know what he was going to do. That man gave him $100, which was a lot of money back then. Granddaddy quit drinking and got a job. Aunt Jane says that she and the two younger children had a "different" daddy—he became a changed man.

Granddaddy became a fish salesman and Grandmama stayed home raising babies, though she worked in tobacco in the summer to earn extra money. She was also a wonderful seamstress. On Sunday at church, she would see young girls' lovely dresses and then go home and make her own patterns to sew them for her girls. Sometimes there wasn't enough material to make the same dress for all the sisters, so she would make my mama's from a different fabric. Boy, did that piss off my mama, as evidenced in funny family pictures, all because those dresses didn't match. But Grandmama did the best she could.

The five girls were Alma (known as "Tootsie"), Toby, then my mama (Gladys), followed by Betty Jane and then Recie. All were family names passed down from generations. My name is Theresia, like my Aunt Recie, however my kindergarten teacher taught me to spell it R-e-e-s-y, which really annoyed my daddy. He never once spelled it R-e-e-s-y. Always Recie.

Aunt Toby got married first. She was 15 and Grandmama had to sign for it to be okay. Toby got pregnant quickly and was told not to pick up the baby every time it cried. One day she laid the baby girl down and, as she had been told, ignored the crying. When she went back to check on the child, the infant had gotten caught between the mattress and the crib bars and was dead. This marked the beginning of many tragedies that haunted the Sadler family. Needless to say, Toby was inconsolable and turned to alcohol for comfort, like others in my family.

My mama was the biggest of the girls—not fat, just more voluptuous. She married at 17, to a man who hit her and brought home venereal diseases, not once but twice. She got pregnant and had my brother Troy in 1958, then had a second pregnancy, but in one of her husband's violent moments, he pushed her and she lost the baby.

When he cheated on her with her best friend, Mama took her five-year-old son and moved back with her parents. It was the early '60s and divorce was still frowned upon. But in relative terms, it was a pretty good time in my mother's life. She became sort of a "second mama" to her younger three siblings, especially Jane and Recie. Apparently, Granddaddy would let them go out if my mama went with them. Mama still had to have a curfew even though she was a grown woman with a child. It was a rule that she had to be home by 11:00. And of course, any dates had to come and meet the parents just as if she was still a teenager.

Mama worked at a sewing factory to make ends meet. She spent a lot of time with her best friend Shirley. One night they went together to a drive-in movie theater in New Bern, probably to get away from the small town where everyone knew everyone, and all of their "business," too.

While Mama had some dates, I don't think boys came lining up at my grandparents' door to date a divorced woman, not to mention one with a child. But on one of those nights out, Mama met my daddy. I picture him with a Marine buzzcut. He had just gotten back from California so he was super tan, especially since his father's mother was a full-blooded Cherokee. He was seven years younger than Mama, but that didn't stop him, or her.

The first time she brought him home to meet her parents, they thought he was African-American because he was so tan. And in 1967 in the South... that was not acceptable. She was also dating another man who was quite a bit older. Apparently both men wanted to marry her. Though the older man offered a lot more stability, I believe she chose love, and on June 11, 1967, she married my daddy in her parents' living room. She wore a light blue tea-length dress with a small laced veil. He wore his khaki military uniform.

I am not 100% sure what made them move back to Michigan but my guess is that there weren't many jobs in Chocowinity. Plus not only was my mother labeled as a divorced single mom, but now she was marrying a Yankee. They moved to Detroit and in with the Devil... I mean my grandmother. Mama went to work as a waitress and Daddy got a really good job at GM.

I can't imagine how difficult it was for Mama to pick up her little boy and move that far away from family. Then to top things off, to move in with her mother-in-law under such extreme rules. It must have felt like living on pins and needles.

My older brother Troy took a lot of weird shit like, "You can only have two cookies." He was a growing boy. What the hell would be wrong with three cookies? It was also one of those houses with plastic on the furniture. No dirt allowed. Man, that had to be uncomfortable. Daddy didn't know what to do with my brother, since the closest thing Daddy had to a father figure was one uncle. Troy's daddy wasn't exactly father of the year, but how would the child ever get to see him living in Detroit?

Mama got pregnant and I was born January 14, 1969. The story goes that my Daddy was at work that day and when he got the call he went running with his toolbelt still on. They had to stop him to retrieve those tools before he could leave.

As so many folks have told me, I was the apple of my daddy's eye. I am sure this did not help Troy feel any better, although my older brother took great care of me and would quickly become my hero.

I am not sure exactly what happened next, but my understanding is that there were lots of disagreements between Daddy and his mother. I think she treated Mama pretty shitty too. It was so bad that my daddy was on the verge of a nervous breakdown. The doctor said he had to get away from his mother, so when I was nine months old we moved back to Chocowinity.

At first we rented a house. Daddy got a job at a factory and Mama took a job waitressing. Then she got pregnant again with my little brother, Jerry Jr., and he was born June 11, 1970, only 18 months after me. It was a rough pregnancy and delivery. It almost killed my mama. When Jerry Jr. came out, the doctors and nurses thought he was dead. They even laid him to the side presuming his death until a nurse saw him move. He was so bruised from the delivery by forceps—aka vagina ruiners—that he could barely be held. I think Daddy resented Jerry Jr. for all the pain and suffering Mama went through.

We eventually bought a little brick house in Washington, a small town right next to Chocowinity. Finally things were good. Daddy worked at a place called National Spinning Mill and Mama was waitressing.

From my little girl perspective, all was well. Nice little family in a nice little house. But happily-ever-afters only happen in storybooks, and this ain't no fairytale.

3 | *Little Recie vs. Adult Reesy*

I believe there are some personality traits that spark into existence. I was born sassy, outspoken and a thinker. Personally, I believe these are early signs of leadership skills, but others often labeled them something less flattering.

One time, Mama gave me a bath in the sink and afterward I ran around the house naked—which is surprising as I am really not much of a naked person. Now, there are naked people and not-naked people. I am in the second category. I am confident in many ways, but acquired lots of body image labels that I'm still stripping off.

My husband sleeps naked. He has tried to get me to do the same, saying it feels so good... "You don't get all tangled up with pajamas." But if I lay in the bed naked, all I think about is how weird I will feel getting up in the middle of the night to pee. What if a burglar breaks in? Should I run out naked to the neighbor's house for help? Or should I just hide under the covers and pretend not to hear him? Poor body image sucks. Needless to say, my husband is disappointed by my PJs.

Back at two years old though, I didn't have these issues. Mama said, "You better get in here before your granddaddy sees your bum." As my naked little body ran out of the room, I looked over my shoulder, stuck my heiny in the air, and wiggled it at him. Yep, no body images then. Granddaddy loved to tell that story.

One time after I got some sort of shot from the doctor, I was walking around the drugstore holding my heiny when a sweet old lady asked, "Honey, what's the matter?" Being open and honest, I told her, "I just got a shot in my ass and it hurts." Because we are from the South, Mama—embarrassed like crazy—walked completely away from me. Of course she came back... but not until the lady left. These days you wouldn't think of walking away from your child. Back then and being in the South, it wasn't a big deal at all. Much better than being embarrassed by your child's potty mouth.

When I was six I decided to cure myself of being scared of the dark. I put on a scary Halloween record and turned off all the lights. That lasted about ten seconds before I raced back to the light.

When I was six, we had to change babysitters and my brother and I started going to a nursery. It smelled weird and the walls were concrete block painted "institutional" green. I didn't know anyone there, but eventually I made a friend. We bonded over the fact that she hated the nursery as much as I did. Being a thinker, I devised a plan to get us both out. I thought if we ran away from daycare, our parents would understand how much we hated it and would never make us go again. I decided we would walk to my new friend's mother's work—which I thought was close, but what the hell did I know? After all, I was only six.

We... I mean I... planned our great escape. We picked a specific time to ask to go get a drink of water in the hall. My little friend stood back as I bravely and ever so stealthily started toward the exit. After what seemed like a very long walk, I made it. There I stood right in front of the double glass doors. I looked back at my friend and slowly put my six-year-old hand on the door. Just as I was about to open it... *boom!* I chickened out. I was too scared of getting my ass beat to open that door and escape.

I remember playing Barbie dolls near our front door. I also distinctly recall getting a pixie cut. It's basically a boy's haircut, kind of like a mullet only whispier in the back. I hated it! I read that if you brush your hair it helps it grow. I brushed the shit out of that hair every day to make it grow after that. Some memories are best left behind.

4 | Adults Can Be So Complicated

From my perspective, things were good. Daddy and Mama both worked, and my younger brother and I had plenty of toys, bikes, books, and a big console television. What I did not know was that Daddy was having an affair with the neighbor—another of Mama's best friends. Apparently, she really should have chosen her best friends a little more carefully. Mama actually caught them playing footsy under the table while they were all four together playing cards.

I didn't know what happened. But suddenly my younger brother and I were no longer allowed to play with the neighbor's children. We were also not allowed to go to their house anymore. It made no sense to us that, without explanation, we couldn't be their friends. Then one day, Daddy took this lady and together they left us all... her children, me and my brothers, and Mama. He went off to find his own father after probably years of searching for answers to his own abandonment issues.

The good news was that the grandfather I'd never met learned some lessons. He advised my daddy not to do like he had done. "Go back and take care of your children," he said. "They are your responsibility even if you no longer want to be with their mother."

They came back. I'm not sure where Daddy lived, I just knew that I missed him terribly. During his absence, I got really sick so Mama took me to the doctor. After the examination, the doctor said there was not anything physically wrong with me. I believe I had a little broken heart. In place of medicine, Mama started taking me to see Daddy at his nighttime job while he was on break. Just like that, I got better!

Things were hard for Mama. She worked but didn't make enough money to pay all the bills, raising three children on her own. When she asked why my father had strayed, his answer was a painful one—he told her he left because of her weight. Mama was never a small woman, however, she never really lost any of her baby weight. I know how badly this must have hurt. I can imagine the labels she assigned to herself, in addition to the ones Daddy added.

I don't know what got them back together—perhaps us kids, or maybe he really loved her—and I don't know how she forgave him. Probably she didn't want to get divorced a second time, now with three children to raise. My hope is that it also had to do with love. Mama used to tell me how she and Daddy could sit for hours and just talk. She said he was the only one she could do that with.

My older brother Troy never bonded with my daddy. For me though, Troy was the one I always thought of as my hero. In fact, whenever I would get picked on, I wouldn't say, "I'm gonna tell my daddy on you." No, I would say, "I'm gonna tell my big brother on you." He would always protect me.

Once when I was being stubborn and Mama spanked me for the same thing several times, she came after me with hell fire in her eyes. Hell fire is an awesome Southern term. I went running on my little four-year-old legs to my room and hid under the bed as far back against the wall as I could get. I clearly recall her angry arm flailing under that bed with a fly swatter to whoop my ass. My heart raced. Then in came my hero brother. "Mama, let me get her," Troy said. "I'll take care of her." Mama retreated and calmed down. One more reason he was my hero.

My brother got married at age seventeen. All I remember about the girl is that she was older, blonde and pretty, and once again I didn't get to see him much. He met her at work. What I did not realize then was that he was giving most of his pay to my parents to help with the bills. Of course, there was always the promise to pay him back... but the time never came, a lesson I personally learned later.

It was hard when Troy left. I would stand at the sliding back doors and cry for him. I felt less safe. That was the second time in my life I learned men could just leave you and somehow it's your fault. So many things impact how we feel about ourselves. That being said, it really is up to you to fix that shit and work on yourself. Otherwise, you will be left living the lies that never even belonged to you.

Around that same time, Daddy's mother—aka the devil's right hand woman—came to visit for two weeks. Two years later, she was still there. My parents didn't say much about it as she helped to take care of me and my younger brother, and worked part time to help pay the bills.

Since she had done such a stellar job with my daddy, her disciplinarian tactics followed her to North Carolina. She particularly seemed to dislike me. But she did do one special thing for me. I loved the show *Police Woman*. It came on at 10:00 P.M., way past my bedtime. Some nights she would allow me to watch it, "because you get up so good." I found out years later that she did that for my brother as well.

There was lots of fighting though. Once she even climbed on the bus to return to Michigan, only to come back and stay longer. Whatever was happening in the house, unbeknownst to five-year-old me, was not healthy. Haunted by money issues, the affair, and now his own mother, Daddy had a nervous breakdown and was put in the hospital.

One day Mama found me crying and upset. I said, "Grandmama told me it was my fault that Daddy's in the hospital." (See, I told you she was the devil.) Mama was pissed. She told Grandma, "If you ever say anything like that again to my child I will stomp your goddamn ass in the ground." (Exact words, by the way, and not something you would normally hear come out of a Southern woman's mouth.)

Grandma slept in the same room with me. Sadly, I peed the bed. I don't know the thing that finally convinced Grandma to go back to Michigan, however, the glorious day arrived. Ironically, I quit peeing the bed as soon as she left.

When I turned seven, Mama discovered alcohol. She had never had a drink of liquor until she was 38 and went out with my Aunt Recie. Well, she must have liked it. Remember, it was in her blood. I am sure she was trying to bury feelings from all the shit she had been through.

One day when I was in second grade she was supposed to pick me up from school. I stood there holding the hand of my awesome teacher, patiently waiting as all the other children left until it was just me and the teacher. Confusion began to set in... and then fear. Where was Mama? Finally, when we were just about to go back inside the building, she showed up. It took at least a year for me to trust that she wouldn't forget again. Every time she dropped me off, I would obsessively make her promise to pick me up. It was not good enough for her to just agree that she would remember. I would literally beg her to say it out loud.

While I might not have known she was a drunk, I knew something was wrong. I also knew that Daddy left me once and so had Troy. What if Mama would leave me, too?

5 | Moving Fixes Everything—Not

Life's path has frequently presented a fork in my road. The other way may have been a better choice, yet those paths chosen ultimately made me stronger.

The summer between second and third grade, my parents decided to move us to Arizona for my mother's health. She had gotten sick with bronchitis and asthma. I am sure smoking a pack of cigarettes a day didn't help. Or maybe it was really to get away from that "other woman."

They put our cute little brick house on the market, packed our stuff in a moving van, and began the cross-country drive. First stop was Hickory, NC, where Aunt Tootsie and Uncle Lyndsey lived in a magnificent A-frame house. They had this huge bear rug in the middle of the room. All the adults told me to feel how soft it was, and despite my fear, I touched it. Curiosity has always been one of my weaknesses—or strengths, depending on how you look at it. It was soft and furry but still scared the shit out of me.

We left all of our stuff in storage in Hickory, including my brand new banana bike, with a purple sparkly seat and streamers on the handlebars, my collectible dolls that I was only allowed to look at and not play with, Daddy's elaborate collection of beautiful books, and our console television, beds, and living room furniture. My younger brother and I were allowed to take a few toys to entertain us on the drive.

Next stop was an amusement park called Carawins. This trip seemed awesome. We stayed in hotels and visited all the sites on the way to Arizona. Our first local stay there was with Mama's ex-brother-in-law... Weird, right?

From what I understood, anywhere we could find a place to live, Daddy couldn't find a job. But where Daddy could find a job, we couldn't find a place to live. We were down to the last of the money from the equity in the house. With no place to live and no place to work, my parents decided to return to North Carolina.

They hocked their wedding rings at a pawn shop along the way. Mama hid her tears and told me the kindness of strangers saved us. Apparently small motel owners would let us stay for free and feed us. What pity they must have had on this family trying to get back across the country to safety and security.

We eventually made it back to North Carolina and temporarily moved in with Mama's best friend and her husband Roy in a three-bedroom trailer in Chocowinity. Roy was not attractive. And by *not attractive*, I mean he was ugly. He had wild, curly, almost kinky, blonde hair, beady little eyes and lots of pock marks on his face from the terrible acne he must have suffered with as a teenager. However, in those years he was my "boyfriend." He would bring me Nutty Buddies—ice cream—and he would always play with me. He would lift me up and put me on the top bar of my swing set. We would play hide and seek with a bunch of the kids in the neighborhood. I even gave him a little Valentine's Day card that he carried in his wallet.

One time we were playing hide and seek in the dark. He was my partner. We hid together in the pump house, which is a small utility room that has various things I know nothing about that helps support the water system. He said, "I have a knife. Would you like to feel it?" Being the curious little girl that I was, I said yes. He took my little hand and pushed it down his pants. There it was. Something I had never felt before—his erect penis. I instinctively yanked my hand out of his pants and beat a quick exit.

Not a word was ever spoken about that incident. Luckily, he never tried anything like that again. I knew it was wrong, yet he was my friend. He played with me and brought me presents. Still, there was an awkwardness that would never go away even though he continued to act as if nothing had happened.

What would my parents say? It would break my mother's heart that her best friend's husband was a pervert. My father would have broken the man's face. I couldn't tell anyone. My young mind could not comprehend what happened. This was someone I was supposed to trust. He wouldn't hurt me, right? Yet the comfort he once gave was completely gone.

When I was 32, Mama called me, upset. She said Roy's niece was claiming he had tried to make her give him a blow job. Mama commenced to defend him. That's the moment when I had to tell her what happened to me. She was shocked, angry and confused. My grown mind now wished I had told someone back then. Who knows how many other little girls he molested. Oh, how the men in my life taught me not to trust them!

But there was a bright light to the move. My brother and I started at Chocowinity Elementary. I had a wonderful third-grade teacher and really enjoyed school. I met my best friend Dayna, who is still my best friend to this day.

She and I quickly bonded. One time we decided to catch the attention of this boy in our neighborhood. He wasn't that cute, but he was close to our age and we wanted to impress him. We decided to stuff our bras with toilet paper and prance around his house. We must have really put on a show.

Little did I know, trying to impress a boy with either something I had or didn't have would become an obsession. Was I already learning to be someone other than who I was at the ripe old age of eight?

6 | Moving Again... and Again

As it goes, when living in tight quarters with so many different personalities, things were not all peaches and cream back at the trailer. My brother caught the grass on fire... he was obsessed with fire then. In addition, my father had a disagreement with Roy. To preserve the relationship, we moved to the lovely Fountain Lodge—or as some like to call it, the Roach Motel.

This is where I began to become attached to the labels people can place upon you. Chocowinity was like most small towns, and if you were living in the Fountain Lodge, you were definitely considered poor and possibly white trash.

Our first "apartment," a room really, was two beds plus a bathroom and some sort of kitchen. I was embarrassed... I mean, who lives in a motel? Apparently, more people than you might think.

The good news was that I went to third grade in a small elementary school where not many had money. It was mostly a farming community growing good ol' tobacco. Back in the '70s everyone smoked cigarettes, but especially if you lived in the tobacco belt. In fact our school was part of the "tobacco belt conference" and had a smoking area for the students.

My family got the opportunity to move into one of the larger rooms at the motel. It had a second bedroom. If you turned on all the lights in the kitchen you could sometimes catch a glimpse of roaches running to hide. An extermination company came. Right after one of their lovely treatments, I walked in without shoes but wearing pantyhose. Whatever they had sprayed on the floor ate the bottoms of the hose right off my feet!

A few weeks can be a lifetime for an eight-year-old. Soon we moved into a trailer park that didn't have roaches and was less embarrassing than the motel. Still kind of shitty though. Now I just needed all my toys, my bike and the other stuff we'd left in storage in Hickory. But how would we get this stuff back without any money? Mama said she bargained with my uncle that if he paid the bill and shipped our things, he could keep the brand new console television.

Every day after school I excitedly got off the bus in anticipation of finding all of our stuff returned. I couldn't wait to ride my sparkly-seated purple banana bike. The day came. The boxes arrived. But... there were only two large boxes, certainly not enough for all that stuff. My bike was nowhere to be found. Mama was upset but my father was downright pissed. I didn't understand what happened.

Then I bravely looked into those boxes. No dolls, no bike, no toys, no books, no furniture. It looked like trash to me. I didn't hardly recognize any of it. The tears came. There had to be a mistake! Where was my beautiful bike?

As I was about to give up hope, I saw a tiny blonde head... my very favorite baby doll. She was a sparkle in my little world that gave me hope that perhaps our other things would return. But they never did.

The sad truth was that our very own family—an aunt and uncle and nephew—had taken our stuff and sold it. Who does that to their loved ones? My most prized possessions were gone. Gone forever. My little heart was broken.

Daddy wanted to confront them. After all, it wasn't just my toys that were missing. But Mama seemed hellbent on not letting him. I now believe this stole a bit of his manhood that he would never regain.

Daddy would get a job, get pissed for some reason and then leave without having another one lined up. The timing was always just when things were almost looking up. I acquired a new label of "your Dad is a poor provider." Mama still waitressed and cooked.

When necessary, she begged and borrowed. And it was often necessary.

When I was in fourth grade, Daddy found a good job and we moved into a nicer trailer park. It was clean and my room was much larger than anything I had since the little brick house in Washington. Life seemed to be going okay.

"Okay" meant I had my own room, there weren't any roaches, and Daddy was working. It also meant we could have some of the "luxuries" in life like ham instead of bologna. We might even be able to buy a bag of real Doritos or a candy bar at the grocery store. I'm quite sure my fourth-grade perspective of "okay" was very different than most of my friends. And yet, I'm also quite sure it was better than others.

7 | Death and Tragedy Strike Hard

Aunt Recie was absolutely the most charming, outgoing, live-out-loud, sexy ladies you could meet. From the moment I was born, she adored me. And I equally adored her. She was larger than life and I wanted to be just like her.

Her auburn hair was curly. She had green eyes and stood 5'2". Boy, did she love to party! Aunt Recie had a natural sexiness that can't be learned. All the Sadler women had this amazing charm. Mama used to say Recie could put on a potato sack and still look good. There is a difference between being pretty and being sexy. If you can't have both, I believe sexy is better.

When she was 17, she married a handsome man. He joined the military and she left little Chocowinity to follow him—New Jersey and then Germany. Upon her return, she got pregnant and had an amazing little boy.

One midnight in September when I was 11 years old, the phone rang. No call at midnight is ever good news. I was half asleep but heard Mama crying. Somehow I knew it was about Aunt Recie. I decided she had probably broken a leg or something. Unable to stay awake, I fell back to sleep.

The next morning Daddy somberly came into my room and told me Aunt Recie had died in a car accident. She was just 29 years old. I guess my parents thought I would handle that news just fine. They sent me to school in a state of shock and disbelief. By the time I got to my first classroom, I could not stop crying. Luckily, my teacher recognized that I needed to go home.

I later found out things had not been going well with Aunt Recie's husband. They were separated. Being the party girl that she was, she had gone out to a bar that night, mixing booze with recreational drugs. From what the police could figure out, she was driving over the Pamlico River bridge and reached down to the passenger floorboard for her purse. She lost control of the car. Witnesses said the vehicle sort of jumped the sidewalk and then came back as if she had regained control. But then the car dramatically increased speed. As she exited the bridge she ran into a telephone poll.

Despite that, my parents sent me to school immediately after learning of Aunt Recie's death, I wasn't allowed to go to the funeral. It was one of the largest events the town had ever seen. Standing room only with over 500 in attendance.

I'm sure Aunt Recie carried quite a few labels herself—"party girl" and "separated woman." Men loved her, even those who weren't single. I believe she was doing her best to be her true authentic self. Whatever the case, she managed to positively impact many people. Especially me. Whenever things were not going so well, I imagined she would have let me come to live with her had she not died so young.

8 | Boy Crazy

Around this time I became completely and utterly "boy crazy." I already had boobs and my period, and looked much older than 11. In fifth grade, I got my first boyfriend. I thought Michael was the cat's meow. The "thing" back then was to meet your boyfriend by the buses before leaving school and give him a big kiss, tongue and all. We "went together" for about six months.

I wound up in trouble for sneaking out on my bike to get a kiss from Michael. Mama once got a call from my teacher that a group of us were playing spin the bottle in the back of the classroom. I'm sure that teacher just knew I was going to be a slut. That's how she made my mama feel. I quickly learned to hide what went on with boys.

Once again, Daddy lost his job, we got behind in the rent, and had to move back to Washington. Their car was also repossessed. The good news was that we moved into a neighborhood completely full of teenage boys. I was in heaven. The other good news was that Mama made sure my brother and I stayed in the same school, using my grandmother's Chocowinity address.

I became best friends with the boy across the street. His dad happened to be our landlord and childhood friend of my mom. All the neighborhood boys had dirt bikes. Some even had go-carts and a few had trampolines, including my new best guy friend. Pure, innocent friendship. I adored him. We hung out every day. His name was Mark.

We would spend hours in my front yard making up dance routines. Another benefit of being his best friend was that he had lots and lots of cute cousins. Most everyone in the neighborhood was related. Because we weren't romantically involved, he was always willing to support my pursuits. I was 12 though I looked

15, wearing makeup really dark and walking around in short shorts and halter tops.

My first neighborhood boyfriend was Ryan. He was a year older and had the most gorgeous curly white-blond hair and steel blue eyes. We would hold hands and steal kisses now and again.

Then I noticed his brother. Paul was older, 15, with sandy brown hair and big brown eyes. Because it was summer and he worked in tobacco, as a lot of kids did back in NC, he had the most gorgeous bronze tan along with rippling muscles—quite the Adonis.

I did everything I could to catch his attention. I would go over to his house when I saw him outside and ask to jump on their trampoline with him. In one of my attempts to catch Paul's attention, I wore a strapless halter top and short shorts to get my first lesson from my best friend Mark on steering and driving a dirt bike. Switching gears was my biggest challenge. When my best friend said, "Hit it," I thought he meant to step on the gas, but what he really meant was to change gears. The sand made the bike's wheels spin out. Somehow we both flew over the steering wheel. While bodies and legs were flying ass over tin cup, my cute strapless halter came down, exposing my pubescent boobs to my true love and whomever else was watching.

I skinned my knee, but I could have broken an arm for all I cared. The embarrassment of exposing my boobs was far more painful. Of course, my best friend thought it was the funniest thing ever.

My parents were going through yet another rough financial time and did not have the money to hire a babysitter, so they left me in charge of my 11-year-old brother. Not a great idea with so many boys in the neighborhood and my hormones blazing.

We were assigned chores and weren't allowed to leave the house. Summer was filled with emptying ashtrays—both parents smoked, of course—plus dusting and vacuuming. I even learned how to make spaghetti and tacos. Television was our only entertainment.

One summer day, a knock came at the back door. It was Paul! My heart was about to beat out of my chest. He had gotten off work. His parents weren't home so he decided to pay me a visit. I guess my hormones weren't the only ones blazing.

He suggested we go into my room and "talk." I eagerly agreed and swore my brother to secrecy. Thus our summer romance began. Every afternoon I would watch for the truck to drop Paul off from working in tobacco. Things heated up over time, from kissing to heavy petting to just about everything but actual intercourse.

Paul wanted to keep our summer romance a secret. Was he ashamed? Was it my age? Was it me? While he didn't want to tell anyone about our romance, he did want to "go all the way." He would give me the old "If you cared about me you would do it with me" line. I did believe I loved him. In my immature mind I thought that if I did it with him, he would finally become my boyfriend, out in the open for all to see.

In a weak moment, I decided I was going to do it. We met over in his grandmother's barn. I lost my virginity on a cot in a barn filled with hay. In my diary I wrote, "Something very special happened today." We did it one more time at his parents' house when they weren't home. But that was it. No more knocks on the back door and no more invites to meet.

Can you believe it? It was over! All I wanted was for him to love me the way I loved him. My heart was broken. It wasn't special. It was stupid. He made his conquest and he was done.

Mama used to tell me, "A hard dick has no conscience." It's particularly true with boys in the throes of puberty.

The best part? He told his friends. Great! Label: slut.

9 | How Much Tragedy Can One Family Take

For as long as I can remember and whenever I felt there was no hope, Mama would say, "Recie, we Sadler women are survivors."

I don't remember much about Aunt Tootsie and her husband other than the few visits they made back to Chocowinity, but after the non-return of our stuff, I did know for sure that Uncle Lyndsey was a real asshole.

Their relationship was abusive—physical, verbal, plus drugs and alcohol. They would get drunk just about every night and that is when the fights and abuse would begin. It's difficult to hide a black eye. The call came in the middle of the night as they always seemed to. It ended in one of the worse ways possible... murder-suicide. The police reported that the husband shot his wife and then turned the gun on himself.

I'm not sure how my grandparents survived one death of a child, let alone another. Mom would later tell me that when my grandmother heard the news, she said, "Well at least he won't beat her tonight."

Somehow we all went on breathing.

10 | Boys, Friends, and Boyfriends

Par for the course, something happened and we moved again, this time into an old farmhouse that Daddy was going to "fix up." There was only one bathroom, which was fine, except in the winter because it was really cold in there. There wasn't a shower either. You had to take a tub bath. At least this house was big, but there wasn't air conditioning or heat. Spend one summer in Eastern North Carolina and you'll know why A/C is important. When it got cold, we used a kerosene heater in the living room at the back of the house and small space heaters in our bedrooms at night.

When we first moved in, the upstairs was a real mess. My brother and I were promised that space for our bedrooms once they were repaired. In the meantime, I used a large room on the first floor which had probably been some sort of parlor.

The outside was painted white and had a circular dirt driveway surrounded by trees, like an old Southern plantation. There was the promise of how beautiful it would all be when renovated. There was also the promise that the owner would work with us on buying it. Here comes the hope. Again.

Daddy started his own painting business. He decided he was smarter than the last boss and this was the way to our financial security. Painting was great when Daddy had clients. He was meticulous and very good at it. Sometimes I think he was too meticulous and took too much time. Mama kept working at the diner.

We had a terrible car. It was old and a nasty shade of faded olive green. It didn't even have seatbelts. Not what you wanted to be seen in when your mom drops you off at school. We would buy one piece of shit car and replace it with another. Because of all of their financial problems, my parents were not credit worthy. No one would finance a car for them.

Once, my mom and I were going somewhere in the faded olive green POS, down this small hill. The brakes began to fail. Sunday church had let out and cross-traffic was heavy at the intersection ahead. Mama panicked and so did I. The light hadn't turned green. Terror welled in my throat.

Mama pumped the brakes, then tried to put the car in park, anything to stop the vehicle. Luckily she was a pretty smart cookie. Instead of plowing us straight into traffic, she took the lesser of two evils and ran up over the curb and hit the light pole. My body flung forward, because of course I wasn't wearing a seatbelt. My face hit the dashboard hard. Luckily, no teeth were broken. Mama was shaking like a leaf, but she was safe and no one else got hurt.

She got a ticket for driving a piece of shit, something like "faulty equipment." Mama felt horrible about my face. A little over the top considering I wasn't seriously injured. Then again, I was bleeding and she was my mom. There were moments where I think she cared more about how I looked than I did.

During this time, Mama drank quite often. She would get off work around 2:00 P.M. and start with the alcohol. McDonald's used to give away glasses with Looney Tunes characters on them, and she would fill the vodka to Tweety Bird's feet and the rest with Kool-Aid. Then she would clean the house.

She was not in the best shape. She had taken a fall out of one of the trailers we lived in and hurt her back so she was in pain every day. Extremely overweight, she also suffered from asthma. Add to that all the stress she dealt with on a daily basis—alcohol was her coping method.

I hated it. I would come home and she would be blasted. One of the worse parts for me was that no one else seemed to notice. Family would visit. Daddy would come home from whatever paint job he was doing. Not one word was spoken. How could I be the only one who noticed how drunk she was?

I would literally beg Mama not to drink. It was not good for her. I still carried with me the memory of her forgetting me at school. On more than one occasion, I grabbed the liquor bottle and poured it down the sink. What was she going to do since no one else seemed to know this secret? I was stressed, confused and most of all, I felt alone. I was 14 years old.

I spent most of my time in my room doing latch hook rugs and reading. Daddy always encouraged reading, especially the classics. I enjoyed books by Jane Austen and anything by the Bronte sisters. He would give me book after book. When he gave me Socrates, I decided to find books of my own liking. Stephen King became one of my many new favorites.

Money was not flowing at the Roop house. Salvation Army provided Christmas presents for my brother and me. You know... one generic set of toys for girls and one for boys. At least I would have something to tell my friends when I went back to school after Christmas break. I just wouldn't mention where the presents came from. Truly I was thankful. It wouldn't be the last Christmas there wasn't much under the tree.

At age 14 I knew how poor we really were. I didn't actually label us as "poor"... I guess I just thought we didn't have money. I watched Daddy quit job after job while Mama worked hard with bad health at the restaurant. I saw her borrow money from family, friends, anyone who would lend it. By the time the next check came, she had to pay them back and start asking again.

I watched her dig in her purse, literally, to scrape together enough money just to buy a loaf of bread. Growing up poor brings a heavy weight. So much worry that I carried around with me. Would my dad keep his job this time? Would we have enough to eat? Would we have electricity or a phone? That kind of worry steals something from a child.

When there's not enough money for Christmas, there's certainly not enough for name-brand clothing. As a teenager, fashion became important to me. All of my friends had Levi jeans and Polo shirts. I wore hand-me-down corduroy bell bottoms from my cousins. Not exactly cool. I clung to the fact that at least they said "Levi" on the pocket.

Things seemed different for my younger brother. Brought up in the same household with the same value systems, we chose such different paths. I believe Mama did not think my brother was very capable. He didn't exhibit a lot of ambition, and had no desire to work. Somehow he ended up with a few pairs of Levi's. But because I was willing and driven to work for what I wanted, she left me to fend for myself.

When I wanted a pair of Gloria Vanderbilt jeans, Mama said that not only did she not have the money, but she was not going to pay forty dollars for a pair of pants that would probably not fit me in a year. This was the real beginning of my understanding that if I wanted something I was going to have to work for it. I discovered that when I wanted something badly enough, I was an unstoppable force. My determination to get what I wanted began to sprout. This was the moment when I had to make a decision. Accept mediocrity or do something about it?

I believed I couldn't really count on anyone except myself. If I wanted something it was going to have to be on me. How was I going to get those jeans? The neighbor, who was also our landlord, said he would pay me ten dollars a week to mow his lawn. Dreaming of just how cute those Vanderbilts were going to look, I took the job. Four weeks later I was wearing those jeans.

Our farmhouse wasn't in a neighborhood, hence no one to hang out with. I was in eighth grade and upset to have moved away from my friends, still in Washington, too far for a bike ride to Chocowinity. Somehow, Mama knew a man who had a daughter a grade ahead of me. She asked if I wanted to meet this girl. Out of desperation I said yes. Mama drove me over to my soon-to-be new friend's house and left me there.

Mama would later regret that move. Tammy gave me courage to do things I surely would not have tried without her support. Historically, I had been the daredevil. Perhaps even an instigator. Now I prefer to say that I was developing leadership skills. It was a different story with Tammy. I don't know what it was about that girl, but I would have followed her through the gates of hell.

There we were in Tammy's room. She had curly permed brown hair as most did in the '80s. A little taller than me, she was lanky with pretty green eyes. She was also a gymnast with a super flat stomach... something I very much wanted. She had this way of looking at you as if checking out each detail. It was creepy at first but I got used to it. She was also a habitual liar. Luckily I could always tell. Being the person that I was, I would call her out on it. I think that is one of the reasons she liked me so much. She couldn't bullshit me. We quickly became best friends.

Tammy introduced me to a whole group of boys from her school. That's when I met Teddy, my real "first love." Way better than Paul, Teddy liked me back. Tall, with sandy brown hair, hazel eyes and a great sense of humor, he was the first boy I was allowed to go with on an actual "car date." We had a lovely romance. Whatever labels the situation with Paul had caused, they had not followed me into my relationship with Teddy.

Sometimes when I played hooky from school, he would too. He would come over while my mother was at work. He told me he loved me and I loved him. I was sure he was the one for me forever. He even gave me his class ring. I wrapped it in plenty of tape and proudly wore it on my pointer finger. Because I loved Teddy and Teddy loved me, I decided he would be my real first. I would erase the experience with Paul and start over. We even used condoms.

One day I was at Tammy's house, hanging out and having fun. The phone rang. It was Mama. "Get home now!" From the sound of her voice I knew I was in trouble. Trying to sound innocent I asked, "What's wrong?" She repeated, "Just get home."

There was no fucking way I was going home without knowing something more. If I was going to get an ass beating, I wanted to be prepared. Finally she said, "Stinker (our dog) was playing with a rubber. Now get your ass home!"

Oh my God! My heart was racing so fast. What was I going to say?

Tammy, being the friend that she was, suggested saying that Teddy and I were having water balloon fights with condoms. I got on my bicycle and raced the mile home thinking every minute of the way that Mama was going to kill me! Would the condom balloon fight thing work? That was one very long mile, but it was also the fastest my little ass ever biked.

I walked in the door, red faced and tearing up. Mama was in the kitchen watching dishes. "Sorry," I told her. "We were having water balloon fights with condoms..." I started, and then something gave me the courage to tell her the truth. I still held onto the story around the water balloon thing, but I added that we were having sex, crying and blubbering apologies.

Mama told me the story of how she had been washing dishes and looked down and saw the dog playing with something. *"Whatcha got there, Stinker?"* Luckily the dog had cleaned it up pretty good before she picked it up. At least that's what I tell myself. She had accused my poor brother, sure it was his. But as always, a mother's intuition realized who it belonged to. That damn dog had been in my trash can. Another angel was watching out for me that day because if it had been my dad who found out, I would probably not be here right now.

Mama calmed me down and said she was not going to let me get pregnant. *Boom!* Just like that an appointment with the gynecologist was made.

That experience was worse than her finding the condom. Coming from a small town, the worst part was while the doctor was doing that wonderful exam, he started asking about my grandfather.

Then he started singing "On Top of Old Smokey." At least two levels of hell.

But good news for Teddy, no more condoms.

Forever after that, my Mom was the one who helped many of my friends get on the pill. I think I would be pretty pissed if I found out another parent had helped my child with such a decision and yet thank God she did. Most of these girls were sexually active and deathly afraid to talk with their parents. So good or bad, my friends were thankful.

In addition to Teddy being my true first love, he was also another first. Yep, the big "O."

Teddy's mom, along with another single mom, wanted to take their sons and their sons' girlfriends to the beach. How in the world was I going to get my parents, mostly my dad, to agree to me going on a (albeit chaperoned) beach trip? The other guy's girlfriend had already gotten approval so I built up the courage to ask. There it was... a big fat NO. I began to cry. I wanted to go so badly. As would become a pattern, I got my mom alone and began the challenge of convincing her it would be fine for me to go. After all, two parents would be there with us. We would not be sleeping in the same room... yeah, that's not really true. More tears and more begging. In another pattern, she got my dad alone and started the convincing. Finally, after what seemed like a lifetime, Daddy gave in. Phew! I was psyched.

At the beach on a Saturday night in bed with Teddy, while the other couple was in the bed next to us doing, I'm quite sure, exactly what we were doing, I had the big "O." Giving a girl an orgasm didn't seem to be most boys' priority at that age. In fact, I am not sure they even knew about it. Quite honestly when it happened, I didn't know what it was, but it was *awesome*! I'm not sure if I was embarrassed or what, but I never told him. Guess he's gonna know now. Good for you, Teddy... or rather, good for me.

Prior to the orgasm, I thought sex was mostly for the happiness of the guy. I certainly had that all wrong. My friends didn't discuss that part and Mama had failed to mention it.

Sadly, Teddy broke my heart after nine months of dating. He told me over the phone as I lay on the living room floor (because that's where the phone was). I cried a lot. I literally begged Teddy not to do it. All the tears had zero effect though. He had found another girl.

Getting over Teddy was challenging. Good thing I had Tammy. We developed an obsession with Marines, or basically any boy in uniform. We found them a little "dangerous." Taboo, if you will. Boys in the military seemed so tough and afraid of nothing. They usually had large egos, probably due to learning how to kill people at age 19. And let's not forget about those uniforms... a complete turn-on. We became known as the girls who liked Marines. More labels.

I had also continued to look older than I was. I didn't date boys my own age. At 135 pounds, I wasn't fat. I was just bigger than most of my 100-pound skinny friends. Really just more developed. But the label came anyway: "She has a pretty face but she's chubby."

I hated feeling that way about myself. I joke now, saying I have been on a diet since I was 12. That label created a battle for a positive body self-image. Older boys were much easier to attract as they didn't think I was fat. They thought I was cute and really rather sexy.

In addition to my desire to have a boyfriend in the military, there were some logistics involved. First, we were less than a hundred miles from four different military bases—so there were plenty of choices. The two Marine bases were less than 50 miles away, near the beach where my friends and I would always go. These boys also didn't seem to think I was chubby.

Perhaps, I had built Marines up in my mind because of Daddy's stories about his time in the service. I loved the big egos and cockiness that went along with those uniforms. Since I have a strong personality (I am sure you have figured that out by now), I needed a strong man or I got bored. Really bored.

And Reesy bored is never a good thing. Bored Reesy will find some shit to get into.

11 | It Was the Best of Times, the Worst of Times. It Was High School

At the end of eighth grade we were allowed to try out for the high school cheerleading squad. They cheered for two sports, football and basketball. A friend of mine was staying with us to finish out the year in school after her mom had moved. But this friend would be going to a different school the next year. Still, we both decided to try out, along with three of my best friends—Dayna, Becky and Tracy.

In a group, we were taught cheers, chants, and a dance routine to use for try-outs. The big day came. We picked numbers, as that was how the judges would identify us. I was number 2. It was pinned on my shorts.

I did my best to control my rapid heartbeat and the shaking of my legs. In my teenage mind, becoming a cheerleader would make everything better. It had the power to make me super cool and popular... everything a teenage girls wants. Perhaps it could even take away some labels, giving me confidence about my body.

What I did not know then was that I was already awesome. Those boys I thought weren't paying attention... they were just scared of an outspoken gal like me. I lived out loud and with not much of a filter. Outspoken, opinionated and daring equals a lot of immaturity and sometimes a perception of being a bitch.

A lot of girls tried out for cheerleading that year, the highest percentage being future freshmen. Once your number is called, you rush into the gym with as much "school spirit" as possible, adding perhaps a cartwheel, back handspring, and yells of "Go team, go!" You stop right in front of a panel of judges, three to five individuals seated at a table with paper in front of them. They are often previous cheerleaders from your school or college cheerleaders or coaches, sitting with great posture and smiles on their faces. They've all "been there" and have an idea of how you are feeling.

After your grand entrance, you stand straight and give the signal, usually a nod, that you are ready for them to start the music. You do the dance first, then the chant, and lastly the cheer, smiling your ass off and doing your best to make every move perfect. One mistake can really take you off course. You are allowed to start over once, which can be even worse. I have seen girls simply break down and cry.

My turn came and went in a blur. After that, it's like you've been holding your breath for approximately a week and you can finally exhale. But the pressure is not over. Once everyone is done, the judges do their thing and calculate the numbers. All girls are called back into the gym. Typically you sit on the floor clutching your best friend's hands and holding your breath once again while your heart beats out of your chest.

They called a name, then another and then it happened. I couldn't believe it! "Number 2, Reesy Roop." I jumped up screaming and ran to the group of girls who had already been chosen. I was psyched out of my mind, crying tears of joy. More names were called—Tracey, Becky, Dayna... all three of my best friends.

They finished up the names and there left in the circle were the very sad girls who had not made the team. It was such a wave of emotions. I was delirious with happiness and yet there were those girls who were absolutely devastated. Some were even sobbing. Being from the South—and also thanks to cheer etiquette—you have to contain your joy so as not to show too much happiness in front of those other girls.

The worst part for me was that the girl who was staying with us did not get chosen. What an awful ride home. I wanted to scream at the top of my lungs that I made it. Meanwhile, the car was filled with silence. Other than her horrible sobbing.

It should've been my moment... one of the happiest for a teenage girl like me. I know there are many negative labels applied to cheerleaders, but I was bursting with pride! I couldn't stop smiling! Then I would look at her puffy eyes and feel horrible. She said her congratulations through tears and sobs. The school year ended and she moved with her mother, which had been the plan from the beginning. Had she thought that if she made the team she would be allowed to stay?

As a cheerleader I felt instantly cool. I freakin' loved it! I was also pretty good at it, if I do say so myself. Once you make the team in May, it is immediately time for practice to get ready for cheerleading camp. Usually held at a college in mid-July, it teaches you the latest and greatest in cheers and dances to prepare you for games and future competitions.

Midsummer in North Carolina is sunny with 90-degree days and 100% humidity, doing gymnastics, special jumps, yelling and dancing. Holy shit, it was hotter than standing on the sun. The camp started at 8:00 A.M. and didn't end until 9:00 at night. Anyone who says that cheerleading is not a real sport needs a throat punch.

I was running on a high for quite a while. I told everyone I made the team, and my friend Tammy bragged me up to her friends, too. Then reality set in... Like any sport, you need money for cheerleading. Everyone wears the same shoes, the same everything, ordered from a specific store. You have to buy the specially made matching shorts and t-shirts for camp. And let's not forget about the cost of camp itself. Never mind the "extras" like ice cream or snacks. The worries began. How would I get money for all of that? My parents certainly didn't have it.

Mama still worked at a restaurant and was able to get me a few hours a week as a waitress. Since I could not get my worker's permit until age 15 ½, the pay was under the table. I didn't care... no taxes, it was money. I was able to help buy shoes, socks, and briefs, the underwear cheerleaders wear under their skirts and over their real underwear because it's a lot better than showing your ass.

I also was a pretty good fundraiser. The more I raised, the less I would have to pay for. We sold donuts, held yard sales, anything to raise the money. Not many of the girls were well off so we all seemed to push pretty good at the fundraising. And let's admit it—it's tough to say no to a cute cheerleader in a short skirt.

As would continue all through my high school years, my parents would "borrow" some of my money and say they would pay me back. Payback never really happened. It was stressful for me. I couldn't say no to Mama because I knew she needed it for groceries and the light bill. Yet how could I say yes to giving the fundraising money away? It was not my money to give. What if someone found out? I would have been humiliated. The guilt always won out though, and I would give the money. Between Mom and me, we would replace the cash. Often at the last minute. It was like raising money twice.

Parties were also a big part of high school. I did my fair share, trying alcohol and weed... don't judge. A North Carolina child of the '80s pretty much always smoked a little home-grown marijuana. But as a cheerleader, if you were caught drinking you would be kicked off the squad. Even so, in ninth grade, all the cheerleaders decided we would get drunk together. If we all did it, no one would be able to tattle.

At the time, I was living in the big house and had plenty of room for nine girls to come over. The Saturday night arrived. We had gotten older kids to buy us the alcohol. It was some sort of nasty whiskey. Not the best choice. The more we drank, the louder we got. Also, the more we drank, the more the girls started taking off their clothes. For any of you perverts out there, we were not "experimenting" with each other. We just all stripped down to our sleeping shirts... a big t-shirt that hung low.

Of course when you are drinking like that, you have to pee, and often. The bathroom was at the bottom of the stairs and, much to my younger brother's delight, right across from his room. He would just stand at the bottom of the steps and watch half-naked cheerleaders go up and down the stairs in twos, as everyone needed a little help. I am sure it was one of the happiest times of his youth.

Loudness continued to grow. Not one of us was sober. Then it happened. Mom's voice came from downstairs. "Reesy Ann, can you please come here?"

Oh no. She used my middle name. That usually had multiple meanings. Somehow, I was supposed to navigate my way down those stairs without assistance and pretend to be sober. This was going to be tough.

Carefully I maneuvered, doing my best to walk straight, and more importantly not fall down. Mama was waiting for me in the bathroom. I decided it would be best if I sat on the end of the bathtub.

"Are you drunk? Are the girls drunk?" she asked.

"No, M-mama," I slurred as I swayed back and forth holding onto the tub so as not to just fall on the floor. That was some powerful whiskey.

"We'll just see about that. Let's go upstairs."

Now I was going to have to make that trek back up the stairs, not fall, not stumble, all while my mama followed close behind. We walked in, me first. I did not trip over my friend's foot who was sprawled half-naked on my beanbag chair, and I did not projectile vomit across the room as I fell on my face. (I refuse to acknowledge that actually happened.)

The other girls just froze. Some freaked out because of the vomiting but mostly because my mama was right there looking at nine half-naked, drunk-off-their-asses cheerleaders. Being the "cool" mom that she was, she said, "You girls need to quiet down and get in bed... Party's over."

The next morning everyone wanted to leave as early as possible to avoid further embarrassment. Once again, Mama saved my ass and did not tell Daddy. As the girls were leaving, my parents stood at the door. Daddy was eager to make everyone a lovely, greasy breakfast... not appealing as we held back our own vomit.

As each girl did the exit of shame, they hugged my dad and then my mom. "Sorry, Ms. Gladys," they all whispered in Mama's ear.

After everyone left, I got my mom alone and gave the most sincere apology along with all the justification as to why she had drunk cheerleaders in her house the night before. I explained that we all wanted to try it and we wanted to do it safely at home. We were actually being responsible. Safety first.

Did she buy that shit? I mean it was true. I begged her not to call the other girls' parents. "Well, at least you had sense enough to do it here." She never told anyone. Just one more reason my friends all loved my mama.

Another infamous party was held at my dear friend Dayna's house. Her mom was a nurse and worked at night. More math— parents not at home all night + teenagers = party time. Plus her older siblings were away at college, so we had the whole house to ourselves.

What an awesome party! So many people came, it was crazy. The problem with a big party is that a neighbor just might call your parents and tell them there's a shit-ton of vehicles at your house and it looks like a party's going on.

The phone rang at 11:00 P.M. Uh-oh! Dayna's mom was on the other end of the line and Dayna was far from sober. She got off the call in tears. Drunk girl tears are the worst. Once they start, it is impossible to get them under control. First, she screamed at all our friends to leave, then started some coffee and climbed in the shower with all of her clothes on.

I was spending the night, so in the midst of trying to calm her down, I remembered that I was completely stoned. Someone had brought some really good weed to the party. My attempts to hold my laughter back were not exactly soothing to Dayna.

She climbed out of the shower and changed into dry clothes. I was suddenly fascinated by her braces... another reaction to the weed. Then the munchies hit. I found these delicious cookies. Dayna became concerned that I was going to throw up because I'd never been able to handle my alcohol. Yet another reason weed should be legalized—one of marijuana's medicinal purposes is to help calm the stomach.

Meanwhile, I had these delicious cookies in hand. Dayna chased me around the kitchen table trying to get them away from me. She was becoming sober. Now it was her turn to get me to sober up, or at least lay down. Unbeknownst to me, there was more math. Weed + alcohol is a recipe for the spins and nausea.

Finally, I laid down and sometime during the night I vomited all over Dayna's comforter. The good news was I had zero remembrance the next day, but the comforter was obvious evidence. Even though I did my fair share of partying, I think the one label I never got was "party girl."

Or maybe I did.

But at least I didn't label myself that.

12 | My True Reality

My reality at age 15 was that Mama had drinking problems and Daddy couldn't keep a job. I don't think he didn't want to work. I think he just thought he was smarter than everyone else. Although he had an above-average IQ, his military tour in Vietnam exposed him to Agent Orange which caused many health issues. I also believe he was so hurt mentally from the war (and my batshit crazy grandmother) that he just wanted the pain to stop.

Dysfunction and codependency ran amuck in our house. Mama felt Daddy would only listen to me. When they had arguments she would often ask me to talk to him. I thought it was kind of cool then. But I was way too young for the responsibility of my parents' marriage. What saved me from self-destruction was knowing that I always felt loved.

Ninth grade was so exciting! With all the high school grades in the same building, there were older boys to go crazy for. It was quite ridiculous. I hung out with the "popular girls" who in turn hung out with the "popular boys." Several of my friends were dating seniors. Shouldn't I be dating a senior too? But I didn't have much luck. I would like one and he wouldn't like me back.

Even though I excelled academically, education was not my focus. It was all about the social aspect.

I also missed a lot of school. Mama was pretty lenient. If I kept good grades and helped around the house, she didn't argue much if I wanted to take a day off. I wouldn't have admitted at the time that I was smart and easily bored. Once in Geometry class, I raised my hand and asked, "Can you please tell me one place in life that I am going to use this again?" I was super frustrated. The teacher's response was to completely ignore me. Yep. No answer at all. He could have made such a difference in that moment with a couple of examples. Instead he chose to label me as "smartass" instead of a student with a gifted mind that needed to be inspired. Too bad for him. Too bad for me too.

Cheering became a big part of my life. My junior year I was co-captain with Tracey. She certainly came from a more "appropriate" family. They went to church whenever the doors were open, didn't cuss, and she was generally always on her best behavior. No one's perfect though.

In February of 1984 on a Sunday, I started getting this pain in my side. Not too terrible. Just a dull ache that wouldn't go away. Mama gave me a Darvocet for the pain and I laid down. Finally, late in the afternoon, they took me to the emergency room.

When you are a girl and you have pain below your belly button, doctors are going to ask if you've ever had sex. Luckily they quietly asked my mother without my daddy hearing. Guess they realized daddies don't like sex questions about their "little girls." They did a pregnancy test just in case. Thank goodness that was a big fat *negative*!

Then came the internal exam. I was mortified. I threw up. Next came x-rays with the dye stuff. They found a blockage in my left ureter, saying I was probably born with it, but now it had closed up, blocking that kidney. I had to see a urologist. He drew me pictures and explained what was going on. It would require surgery to fix the blockage.

I can't imagine what went through Mama's mind—no insurance, she already owed people money. Daddy was doing his "painting business" which was not going well. Now I had to have surgery. The doctors agreed it could wait until summer after cheerleading camp. I *had* to go to cheerleading camp. That's where you learn the new stuff. I was adamant that I was not going to be behind with the new cheers and dance routines. I had football games, basketball games, and cheerleading competitions that were at the very top of my priority list. Not this annoying major kidney surgery stuff.

As God and angels have always watched over me, Daddy got a great job right before my surgery that was scheduled for late July, working for what was considered one of the best companies in our small town. This company even gave out college scholarships, which meant I might eventually have the opportunity to go. On top of all of the benefits, they gave my family the greatest gift ever—though Dad had not been on the job for the allotted 30 days for insurance to kick in, they made sure my surgery would be covered. It was truly a miracle!

As a teenage girl, I was already self-conscious about my body and in no way ready for the invasion of privacy that happens with surgery. First, some male nurse came in to shave my stomach, pretty much down to my pubic area. Next I had to wear a gown without any underwear or bra. I wasn't happy with my boobs, and in particular I thought I had larger than normal nipples. Obviously, I had little to compare them to. Luckily they give you some "I don't give a shit about my nipples or anything else" drugs right beforehand.

After that, I gladly gave up my gown and found humor in the colorful hat my doctor wore. In my drug-induced state I said, "You really look funny in that hat." That's the story he shared with my parents when I came out of surgery. Typical Reesy. Thank goodness for that Sadler Southern charm.

The next thing I remember was being wakened by the worst pain I ever felt, like a knife ripping through my side. I cried and moaned in agony, sure they had done something that was going to kill me. The nurse came with a shot of morphine. Hallelujah!

I remained in the hospital for nine days with a six-inch incision on my left side. I had tubes coming out of me and a lovely catheter—which thankfully had been installed while I was under anesthesia. The surgery was a success. The doctor said my kidneys were rather high so he'd had to cut out part of one of my ribs and two inches of muscle in my back. "She has more muscle than most boys her age." *Hell yeah, don't tell me cheerleading isn't a sport!* Short story, the blockage was fixed and the tubes would come out before I went home.

My poor mother had to go to work at 5:00 in the morning, get off at 2:00, go home, shower and then come spend the night with me at the hospital sleeping on a cot. That's a mama's love.

I had lots of visitors, which I am sure the hospital hated—particularly when my buddy Mark came before Mama arrived and drove me all around the hospital in a wheelchair... might've gotten in a little trouble for that one!

Nine days later I was begging my mother to let me go to cheerleading practice "just to watch." I finally got her to agree. She dropped me off at school. After she drove away, I thought I could do some of the moves if I was careful. As soon as I got out there, she drove by and yelled, "Recie Ann, get your ass in this car. What do you think you're doing?"

Turns out she was right. I had lots of pain that night. Eventually I did heal with nothing more than a scar that looks like I was in a knife fight.

13 | The Army Guy that Scared My Mom

My search was on. I needed a boyfriend, wanted a boyfriend, dreamed of some romance right out of a fairytale. The good news was that I did not have to be limited to the boys at my school, or even Tammy's school. The beach was only 50 miles away, and so were all those Marines.

A male friend went into the Army—82nd airborne, to be exact—and often brought friends home. Lucky for me and Tammy! Meeting boys who literally jumped out of airplanes was one of the coolest things ever! We were introduced to two such crazy plane-jumping paratroopers. Because I would follow Tammy through the gates of hell, when she suggested, "Let's sneak out in the middle of the night and hang out with them," I said yes without hesitation.

Tammy arranged to sleep over at my house. We were still living in the two-story farmhouse, and my bedroom was now on the top floor. How were we going to sneak out? Already labeled the "wild one" with the "smart mouth," I locked the bedroom door so my parents couldn't get in, and took the phone "off the hook." This meant no calls could ring in the middle of the night.

Tammy was slightly taller than me, so she climbed out the bedroom window and hopped down to the next level. Then I shimmied out the window and she grabbed my waist to help me slide to where we could both jump to the ground. After all of that, we ran down the road about a quarter mile, hiding in ditches when cars would pass.

We made it down the road unharmed. The guys were waiting in my date's red Chevette. My heart started beating a mile a minute. I could not believe this guy liked me... I still held the label of "chubby girl with the pretty face," but John seemed genuinely enamored. My whole body told me this was real. He was so handsome, with sandy blond hair and green eyes. He was originally from California, which to this small town gal made him even cooler. He was tall and quite muscular. You really can't be a guy who jumps out of planes and not be in shape. He also had what I thought was a very cool west-coast accent. To me he was a California dreamboat.

We spent what I thought was the most romantic night at Havens Garden, a park by the river, listening to Billy Squire and The Cars. No attempts at sex, but we totally made out. He was quite the gentleman. Everything I ever dreamed in my Cinderella fantasy.

Tammy and I snuck back in by 5:00 A.M. When we finally got up late that morning, Mama said, "Wow, you girls must have really been sleeping hard last night. The woods behind the house caught on fire and the neighbor came to use the phone. It must have been off the hook because we couldn't call the fire department. We knocked on your door and you wouldn't answer." Once again, God had saved my life because Daddy would have totally killed me if we got caught.

John and I had several more dates. I became increasingly positive that he was my soulmate. He was the first boy my mother was "afraid" of. She was sure I might run away and marry this guy. Unfortunately, I believed the labels that followed me around kept that from happening. John quit calling and didn't want to see me.

I wrote him an emotional love letter confessing my feelings. My heart was so broken. What happened? He had seemed to be just as in love as I was. I wondered if someone had told him something about me. Later I learned he had tried to call me once. Mama talked me into going to my cousin's recital to get my mind off of John. When I did not answer the phone that night, he never tried again. I will always remember him though and I hope he found happiness.

Since my bestie Tammy was still dating John's friend, we had to find a new boy for me. It was really quite easy. All I had to do was call the barracks and ask for John. When he didn't come to the phone, I would just talk to whoever answered. Desperate times brought desperate behaviors. I began a long-distance phone relationship with someone I had never met. I thought maybe this would make John jealous.

It led to the most daring thing Tammy and I did. She was so good at lying... and she had a plan. We told our parents we were going with the other person to the beach when, in fact, we were going to hop a bus to Fort Bragg, home of the 82nd Airborne. It was such a stupid, dangerous thing to do.

Tammy told some lie to a guy friend to get a ride to the bus station. We were not scared at all, which of course tells you how *stupid* we were. This trip was yet another reason I believe in God and angels. Someone was watching over us so that we didn't die. The bus stopped at McDonald's halfway there for food. The bus driver asked us to stay in the front seat while he placed our order. Somehow he knew we were up to no good. God's guardian angel.

We finally made it to Fort Bragg, where at least three guys were waiting for us. The boy I had been talking with was in no way as cute as I had built him up in my head. He also was rather feminine. *Lucky me—slight reduction in rape scenario.* We checked into a hotel... more scary rape possibilities. Add some alcohol... it just kept getting stupid here. And *poof*, we had a party going. Thank goodness the guy was a real gentlemen or perhaps gay. Either way, I made it through the night, rape and death free.

The next day, Tammy and I rode the bus back. I totally thought we had gotten away with it. I strolled into the house. Mama was in the bathroom and I walked in to talk with her. For some weird reason that's where lots of our conversations happened... I guess because my dad was in the living room and we needed privacy.

"So how was your trip?" she asked.

My mouth flew open. "How did you know?"

The smart woman replied, "Well, you just told me."

Oh my God... she totally got me to confess. She was so good at that. She was also excellent at making me feel guilty. For the next thirty minutes she told me all the horrible things that could have happened to me... how I could have been hurt or even could have died. She told me her mother's intuition knew I'd gone to Ft. Bragg. Finally, I asked her to just beat me. I could not take the guilt any longer.

Just so we are clear, I may have been "wild and crazy" but I was not a "slut." Unfortunately, some adults thought the terms were interchangeable. While I did have sex at an early age, it was always with someone I "loved." As most folks do not seek the truth, I was stuck wearing those labels. "Wild and crazy" fit me almost as well as my Levi's and Gloria Vanderbilt's.

14 | Beach Party

A lot of my friends were dating seriously. I longed for romance and true love while never really knowing exactly what that was. Being much smarter than me, Dayna dated a lot more without sleeping with anyone. That was such a better way to go.

In the Spring of ninth grade, I got inducted into the Beta Club at school for maintaining an A average—finally a positive label: "She's smart."

Every year, the weekend before Memorial Day, there was a music festival on the beach at Emerald Isle, NC. I was invited to go with another friend, Paige, and her sister. Cars started to line up at 8:00 A.M. just to get in the park. People brought kegs and all kinds of coolers, because alcohol was allowed as long as it wasn't in glass containers. We, of course, were not old enough to buy alcohol. I would later find out that if you were a cute girl in a bikini, you didn't have to bring your own.

People were everywhere—beach blankets, bathing suits, coolers and kegs. Awesome bands started to play and the drinking began. There was a small path to walk to the bathroom. Everyone was super friendly... well, we were in the South and most everyone was intoxicated.

I was wearing a two-piece hot pink bikini. Paige and her sister were clad in super cute bathing suits as well. More math... Three cute girls in bikinis plus guys with alcohol equals free drinks wherever we went. It started when we were sitting there on our blanket soaking in the sun. This guy turned around with a beer and started to pour it on my leg. Unsure whether I should be angry, he started explaining that beer is the best suntan lotion. He then filled up three cups and handed them to us.

Another math equation... lots of beer equals lots of potty breaks. The bathrooms were not nearby. The trek to the restroom was quite interesting. There were beach towels, beach blankets and bathing suit clad (often inebriated) people everywhere. You could barely take a step without walking on someone's blanket or towel. No one cared though. Everyone was having the best time.

On our many trips back and forth to the potty, there were lots of cat calls from the aforementioned inebriated men. Then I saw him—a Marine who looked exactly like Tom Cruise from *Top Gun*. Unfortunately he was passed out under a tree. Did that stop this Marine-crazy girl? I nudged him a little with my foot to wake him. Too light. A little harder kick. He sleepily, or drunkenly, looked up. Because he was half leaning against the tree, his face was pretty much directly in front of my hot pink bikini bottoms. "Have I died and gone to heaven?" he asked.

Once he realized he wasn't imagining a gal in a hot pink bikini waking him, he sat straight up. I introduced myself. His name was Michael. I spent the rest of that day going back and forth between the boys we met at our blanket and back to the bathroom to see Michael. While the blanket boy was cute, Michael won day. I mean, he was a Marine.

He was fit, around 5'7", with puppy dog brown eyes and dark brown hair. His mischievous smile lifted slightly to the side. I was hoping to get to see him in a bomber jacket, riding a motorcycle, so I could confirm the likeness to Tom Cruise. I gave him my number. With one last very long kiss and Paige and Kim yelling, I left Michael the Marine at the beach and wondered if he would actually call me.

Oddly enough, I somehow had a thing for boys named Michael. At the time, there were three different Michaels that I liked... don't judge. Back in the 1980s there was no Caller ID and no way to identify which Michael was calling. I had to rely on voice recognition.

One summer day a Michael called. Not the Marine. I enjoyed chatting with him and had not completely taken him out of the running for my next boyfriend, but after beach Marine Michael, this one had definitely moved down a notch.

That same day, the phone rang. "Hey, it's Michael."

Uh-oh. I couldn't tell which one. *Keep him talking!* My heart started beating faster as I realized it was him... *the* Michael, Michael the Marine. I couldn't believe it! It had been less than a week and he was calling! Holy shit! Now what?

I thought he was so cool. He was from Roanoke, Virginia. He had what I thought was a bit of a Northern accent. Just so you know, most folks from Virginia don't really consider themselves Southern, and most people from the South don't think of them as Southern either. Sort of like Florida. Hardly anyone from Florida is actually from Florida... so therefore no accent, not really Southern. As far as I was concerned, Michael the Marine was a Northern boy. The slight bit of Southern accent he had, he worked hard to cover up.

I was thrilled. Then I found out he was 23... Of course, I saw absolutely nothing wrong with an almost 16-year-old dating a 23-year-old, but I was absolutely sure that my father would feel differently. Being of sound mind and afraid of either dying or worse, I said he was 21, though I did tell the truth to my mother.

Once again, she helped to keep my secret. She should have said no. I have a feeling that she recognized my determination and realized it would be much more difficult to fight me. If I wanted something badly enough, I would not give up. Typically, I would eventually get my way. That sounds really selfish and it probably was. As I had already learned, if you want something, it will not be handed to you. You have to go for it. And I wanted Michael the Marine no matter how old he was.

15 | Moving On

We moved two more times and wound up living at an apartment in the back of a motel. Mama ran the motel and Daddy was still at the new job, thank goodness. He also worked nights which made my life easier as far as dating was concerned. Michael was stationed at Camp Lejeune and did not have a car. Somehow between the two of us, we rounded up enough money for him to catch a bus to see me.

Ironically, he found a way to visit about every other weekend. Once again, I was in love. Once again, I gave that special part of me to him whenever I could. At some point he bought a little Le Car. He invited me to his hometown once. My parents let me go, as long as my friend Paige went with us. She happened to be dating his friend that we met at the beach. Michael's parents were away. We had the house to ourselves. It was at a lake and the view was breathtaking. The water was so crystal clear, you could see all the way to the bottom. I was in awe. Surrounded by woods and cliffs, it was the most romantic place I had ever been. I really thought this was it—the forever boyfriend. We would get married, have children. He had to be the one, right? But oddly I began to realize he never came to visit me on pay weeks.

I never believed in breaking up with a boy and then going back with him, as I saw many of my friends do. Pretty mature behavior, considering my age. If things were going poorly, I would give "the talk" and discuss my grievances. If things didn't change, then the "love switch" would just go "off." After that, I was done. I never once broke up with a boyfriend and got back together with him.

As time went by, Michael's visits became fewer. His excuses always seemed to be about not having enough money. I had already been giving my parents money, and now I had to give him money if I wanted to see him. His phone calls were always collect, which caused real problems at home with the phone bill. I had to pay those as well, so this was really starting to be bullshit.

I was finally old enough to get my work permit, so I landed my first "real" job at McDonald's with Dayna and Becky. I had cheerleading practice three days a week right after school from 3:15 until 5:00. Mama would then drive me to McDonald's where I would work until 8:00 or sometimes as late as 10:00. I worked weekends as well. In the fall, I had one football game to cheer at on Friday nights. If we had a competition, practices were more. I was still keeping my grades up.

There were a lot of great things about that job. I got to work with two of my best friends. In addition, this particular McDonald's had a great location, across from our only very small mall. On Friday and Saturday nights, it was a "thing" to make the "loop" around the mall, cross the street and circle McDonald's, perhaps even stop for a bite to eat. I met a lot of cute boys that way. It was also on the main highway that led to the military bases at Cherry Point and Camp Lejeune. Many Marines would stop for food. I brazenly admit to doing a lot of flirting with those hungry boys since I wasn't getting much attention from Michael.

I don't need fancy presents or romantic getaways. I do, however, need attention. No attention equals boredom for me. No good has ever come from Reesy being bored.

One day at work, a very sweet boy I worked with named Greg made me a soda. We were about the same age. I will never forget this little encounter. He mixed Sprite and Orange soda together and said, "Try this."

It was yummy. As I stood by the soda machine sipping on that delicious nectar, my favorite manager said to me, "You know that boy likes you, don't you?" *What?* Of course I was oblivious that he had a crush on me. I had never dated a boy my age. I hadn't really ever found one that liked me. Most, at least in my mind, had that chubby-with-a-pretty-face label slapped all over me. Amongst others, I'm sure. Greg went to a different school and lived an hour away. McDonald's was a halfway point between our houses. Still challenged to believe this boy liked me, I started to investigate the situation. After all, I hadn't really had much luck with boys my own age. As I started to search for cues and clues, I began to notice a few things. He was looking at me all the time. He would find ways to conveniently share break time with me. I'm sure the same favorite manager helped with that. In fact, it seemed upon investigation, everyone knew this guy liked me. How had I missed it? Too much Michael the no-attention-paying Marine on the brain, I guess.

Another interesting thing began to happen. The more I checked Greg out, the cuter he got. He had these really gorgeous green eyes with gold flecks, and dark brown hair parted in the middle, a little longer in the back. He had that fresh boy-next-door face. He continued flirting with me. I flirted back. He would be in the back flipping burgers. I would be up front working the cash register. Whenever I would get a chance to catch his eye, I gave him a little wink. I never met a boy who was so nice to me. He knew about Michael the Marine, however that knowledge never stopped him from his pursuit.

Speaking of Michael, things were progressively getting worse. Like I mentioned, he only visited when he didn't have money.

School started and Greg's adoration just kept growing while Michael's seemed to fade by the day. Truth be told, I wasn't being fair to Greg. I was getting all the attention I needed from him while maintaining my boyfriend status with Michael. Those around us could tell that sweet Greg was really in serious "like" with me. Maybe even a bit in love.

In December, Greg invited me to go to the movies on Christmas Eve—a great time since there weren't very many people there. It was an extra bonus for me because there wasn't exactly a lot of holiday spirit at my house. For Greg, it was just him and his dad. I had never cheated on any boyfriends before. I thought going to the movies with Greg as "friends" would be perfectly fine. Right?

We went to see *Ferris Bueller's Day Off*, an iconic 1986 flick. I am not sure if it was the hormones building up from all that flirting or what. We decided to leave the movie early. We felt it wasn't very good. (I know, I know. Opinions.) We decided to go somewhere to "talk." He drove a red 1969 Plymouth Barracuda with a black stripe down the middle that he had fixed up. Even though it was an older car, it was a pretty cool ride. It made a loud noise when you revved the engine and had that old car smell and leather bucket seats.

The talking was short lived. We totally made out for hours... kissing only! I was completely impressed by his kissing abilities. He was so sweet and not attempting any business of trying to get into my pants. He didn't even try and feel up my boobs as almost all teenage boys did.

What was I doing? What about Michael? At that moment, all thoughts of Michael faded behind Greg's sweet kisses. Oh no! I had broken my streak of never cheating. No matter how I tried, there was no justifying kissing for hours with another boy. That was definitely cheating. I needed to tell Michael. Greg was amazing! He made me feel special. I even felt a bit tingly after our make-out session. I was so confused.

I have learned that when push comes to shove, someone is going to push or someone is going to shove. This love triangle was not going to be any different. Things got more complicated. Along came a new girl at McDonald's who was absolutely crazy about Greg. Apparently, they had been having little talks about me. She suggested I was just using him in some way. She definitely tried to plant doubt in his mind to cause the kind of drama that a girl who wants a boy would do to get him away from that other girl.

I wasn't using him. Was I? I liked Greg. Yet, I still hadn't broken up with Michael. I was really just confused. Well, she straightened that confusion shit right out of me. One day at McDonald's while I was on break, she came to me in tears, baring her soul to me and confessing her undying love of Greg. Basically she said, "If you do not like him, then please let him go. That is the only way he will be with me." She was almost as good as my mom at handing out guilt.

She was right. It wasn't fair to anyone, especially Greg. I really didn't think Michael gave a shit. Here came the push... I decided to become Greg's girlfriend. Sorry, girl at McDonald's. I wasn't going to let this guy go.

How exactly would I break up with the Marine? I reminded myself that I'd had the talks with him. No changes. I was not happy in this one-sided relationship. He didn't seem to give a shit about me unless he needed a booty call on the weekends when he didn't have money. He had to know how unhappy I was, right?

So I quit calling him as a first step. After a few days, the phone rang. "This is the operator. Will you accept the charges for a collect call from Michael?"

My heart was racing. I quickly said, "No," and hung up.

It only took a few minutes for him to miraculously find enough money to call me back. Mama knew the whole story. She was also familiar with my "switch." She knew I was done with this guy. Love switch *off*. Michael became the first of many boys who would try to talk with her about why I broke up with them. They would always ask what they could do to get me back. Mama, being the "cool" mom that she was, would always talk to them. She would always try to ease the pain.

She answered the phone this time. "Reesy doesn't want to talk to you, Michael." He was dumbfounded. Did he think I was kidding when I talked with him about my concerns? Did he think because I was young I was going to keep putting up with his shit? Guess what... I was done. Mama kindly reminded him of our conversations then she essentially broke up with Michael for me. She really saved me a lot of hassle. He was not a happy guy.

Meanwhile, I had absolutely found the sweetest guy in the world. Greg was funny, kind and he absolutely adored me. It was also good that he went to another school. That way, I could still spend time with my female friends at my school and spend time with him on the weekends or see him at work.

16 | The Marine's Crazy and Greg Isn't

After away football or basketball games, our team would ride in the school bus and the cheerleaders would follow in a van. One Friday night, Greg was going to pick me up. When we arrived at the school, the cheerleading van pulled in first with the bus directly behind us, blocking the entrance to the back parking lot. That's where Greg was waiting for me. As our van parked, I looked out the window and what did I see... Le Car. Oh shit! What was Michael doing there?

Greg and his very red Barracuda were in the parking lot. He had arrived early and was waiting. Remember, not a big school. Not a lot of extra parking. There I was sitting in the van, heart racing, knowing Greg was expecting his new girlfriend in her cute little cheerleading outfit and pompoms. Then there was Michael, presumably looking for his ex-girlfriend. Talk about being between a rock and a hard place. I was shaking on the inside while my heart felt like it was going to pound out of my chest. Truthfully, I was freaking the fuck out!

What was I going to do? I hadn't told Michael that I had a new boyfriend. I had quit taking his calls. My sweet mother had confirmed that I no longer wanted anything to do with him. He should have gotten the message.

What would he do if he knew about Greg? Michael was a fully trained Marine. Greg was just a still developing junior in high school. Michael could kill him... for real. Maybe I was being dramatic, but I was pretty sure he was going to kill Greg and kidnap me, never to be seen again. As you recall, one of the reasons I liked military boys was the crazy wildness they all seem to have. But that was the old me. This was the new me—finally dating a boy my own age who lived nearby, trying to get rid of wild and crazy labels.

My friend and peer cheerleader, Gail, had met Michael and shared my concerns. I had to get off that van without Michael seeing me, then get to Greg's car and leave as quickly as possible. We let the other girls know what was going on, and when my opportunity came, I darted out of that van as parents and students all swarmed around. I ran to Greg's car as if I was some sort of gold medal Olympic sprinter. I did not look back once. I did not want Michael to recognize my very frightened face.

I jumped in and said, "Let's go," as if nothing was wrong. I did not want to alarm Greg. I certainly didn't want any type of confrontation between my new sweetheart and Le Asshole in Le Car. Especially in front of half the school. Michael did stop Gail on her way out of the van asking for me. She innocently said I must have already left.

Greg drove me home to the apartment behind the motel. We were just hanging out. Dad was at work when the motel doorbell rang. It wasn't unusual for folks to check in late. Mom went up front to presumably check in the customer. It took a while and I started getting worried. Just as I was about to go up front to make sure everything was okay she came back with that holy shit look in her eyes. "Michael's here."

Oh my God! I should have known it wasn't over when he did not find me at the school. I should have remembered the motel was on the same major highway back to his barracks. He had driven over 75 miles to find me. He wasn't going to leave without the satisfaction. Apparently, he had added a few beers to his usual brazenness. He was also not alone. He had brought a Marine buddy with him. Great! There were two of them to contend with.

My mom could handle a crisis. She had been doing so her whole life. She knew how to keep calm back in those days. She advised me and Greg to stay put. She said she would tell Michael that I was not home. Back she went to deal with Michael the now drunk Marine. She was going to have to explain to him once again that my "switch" was off and there was nothing he could do to change my mind. That particular night, she spent two hours convincing Michael that I was done. It took extra explaining since he was drunk. I think he kept stalling in hopes that I would eventually come home.

Michael told Mama he had even bought me an engagement ring... Really? I was only 16 still. He also confessed that he had a girlfriend in Virginia. So that's where his time and money had been going. He professed that he was going to give up the girlfriend and his terrible ways, all for me. My poor mother had to keep telling him it was over. He had screwed up too many times. After what seemed like a lifetime, he drove off screeching his tires... well, as much as a Le Car will screech. In his final act of kindness he threw a beer bottle out of the window and busted it all over the parking lot. Really mature.

I presume he made it back to the barracks okay as that was the last time I ever heard from him. I wouldn't be surprised if he got himself into trouble. He was a bit wild and crazy. Or maybe those were just the labels I had given him. So sorry, Michael the Marine. You lose, and the high school sweetheart wins.

17 | Love At Last

Greg and I were having quite the romance. Did I mention his sweetness? Not something I had ever really experienced.

Basketball cheerleading started in January for both the girls' and boys' teams. They played back to back games every Tuesday and Friday nights. That meant cheerleading practice on Mondays, Wednesdays and Thursdays. I was busy, but at least I got to see Greg at work. If the manager was nice, we were placed on the same schedule and break times.

After his parents divorced, Greg lived with his dad in Pinetown and his brother lived with their mother in Greenville. Greg's dad had a nice brick house, but I don't think decorating or cleaning were top priorities. It looked like a bachelor pad.

Mom was so happy I was dating a boy my own age. While Daddy was never happy about me dating anyone, he was glad I wasn't dating someone in the military anymore.

Greg's dad worked out of town a lot though, and we decided to spend a weekend together. His dad didn't seem to care if I stayed overnight, so I just had to convince Mom without telling Daddy. He would never have allowed that. But Mom lied for me and said I was over at a girlfriend's house. This became a pretty regular thing for me to spend the night, especially since he lived an hour away. It was safer than being out on some swamp road making out. Which, by the way, we had done plenty.

Mom once told me the reason she allowed me to do so much was because her dad had not let her do anything. She always had to be home earlier than the rest of her friends and rarely was allowed out for activities. Of course when she was home, a lot of the responsibility for her younger siblings fell on her shoulders.

This made her want me to be able to do as many things as I could. And I did.

During junior and senior year, I got to go to two different proms. Before you start judging, remember Greg went to a different school. Junior prom was most memorable. I was "in love" again and this time it was "real." My friend Tammy went with me to pick out the dress—white with a sash that tied in a big bow in the back, with cap sleeves and a sweetheart neckline. I had to wear crinoline underneath. If you are not familiar, it is a slip-like skirt worn under the dress to puff it out. Smaller than a hoopskirt others wore under their dresses at that time, it still gave that '80's prom gown look.

Much to my surprise, the dress looked really nice on me. It was perfect. But it cost $185. How was I going to pay for that? I had always given much of my earnings to my parents, but this time Mom helped. We put the dress on lay-away. Every paycheck, I would pay some money toward it. The only problem was that the dress needed alterations, and that could not happen until it was paid for. Luckily Mom knew how important this was to me. Between the two of us, we barely made it, but we did! I would wear my dream dress with my dream guy.

The evening of the dance, I curled my hair and pinned back the sides. I had asked Greg to wear a white dinner jacket like James Bond... my favorite type of tuxedo. And with me sporting long white gloves, I must say we looked adorable!

Tradition dictated dinner before the dance. For the first time I felt like a princess in a real love story. It was also tradition at our school that right after prom everyone went to the beach for the rest of the weekend. It was about an hour and a half drive. My friend Gail, who was a grade below me, was dating one of my favorite guy friends who was also named Greg. We went to the beach together for a magical night and weekend. Perfect dress, perfect guy and great friends.

When it came time for Greg's prom, I got to wear the dress again. At that time, our schools were sports rivals, so I felt pretty awkward. Maybe there was a little hate going on, but Greg was sweet and we sat with his best friend to ease my nervousness.

Our romance was exactly what I had always dreamed of. He was sweet, kind and attentive. He even had a license plate made for the front of his car that said "Reesy and Greg." I thought it was one of the most romantic things in the world that he would put my name on his car for everyone to see.

It was way more like love than any of my other relationships. We even talked of it being forever. For Christmas, Greg got me a "promise" ring—which signifies that one day we would get engaged. It seems ridiculous now, but I wore it proudly. We were sweet, innocent and experiencing the purest kind of love. The kind of love that can usually only happen once, before you become all jaded from heartbreak.

When we were 17, he wrote a sort of love letter in my yearbook.[1] Before I share it, I want you to understand I am a forever romantic. I believe in love. I also believe you have to look hard to find it. To me his words epitomize the very nature of innocent and pure young love. Everyone deserves to have someone write them a love letter. If you don't have someone to write you one, then perhaps you should be the one writing.

It's my offering to anyone who may not believe in love and happiness. Whatever the outcome of our relationship, Greg showed me how I should be treated and adored. He showed me that I deserved better. I am forever thankful. He came to me in some of my darkest times. Every person should experience such love.

> My dearest Reesy, I'm not sure what I should write. I'm sure you realize how much I love you! I'm so glad I finally met you "the girl of my dreams"! When I think of you my heart skips a beat! I truly love you! Although we've been dating only a short while, I feel as if I've known you for years. I can honestly say I want to spend

---

[1] Shared here with his permission.

the rest of my life with you. I am a very lucky guy. I've finally found someone that cares as much for me as I care for you! I really could not live without you. You make it worth getting up in the morning. I am so much looking forward to all the special moments we will share together. And the moments we have spent together have been so tender. You will never know how fast my heart beat the first time we danced together when I looked into your eyes that night... I saw my future with the girl I love. I guess you can tell by now that I am not good at writing this stuff. But what it comes down to is I love you with every bit of my soul! You have captured my heart... Be gentle! I love you, Greg

Can you even stand all the sweetness from this? He says he wasn't good at writing but it was the best stuff a 17-year-old gal like me could have asked for. You can ask for that too. Or you can offer it as a gift to someone. Even if you have to write the love letter to yourself!

This was a light in my life when I didn't have much of it anywhere else. Thank you, Greg, for helping me believe there was such a thing as love.

18 | More Financial Troubles, Moves and Parties

Daddy kept his great job, but we were still living at the motel. I had high hopes of getting a scholarship from his workplace, since my grades and extracurricular activities would qualify, because it would be the only way I would be able to afford college. At least in my mind. Not all guidance counselors go the extra mile to help students understand the opportunities. Plus I had been able to keep more of my own paychecks while he was working regularly. But when Daddy started calling in sick and complaining all the time, I knew things were going downhill. I was all too familiar with the pattern.

We had just gotten what I considered to be a half decent car—a 1974 Datsun 240. It was blue and not nearly as embarrassing as the many other POS's we had. There was only one problem. It was a stick shift.

With my usual determination, and some general directions from Mom, I practiced shifting gears in the motel parking lot. Filled with an I-can-do-this attitude, my determination was quickly replaced with super frustration. It was way harder than anticipated. It was also more challenging in older cars than the ones today. I stalled out every time. That frustration grew. But if I did not learn how to drive that car, I would not be going anywhere. My social life would be squashed. Fear of losing my freedom led to my head on the steering wheel with tears streaming down my face.

Then I pulled up my big girl panties and shouted, "I can and will do this!" This was one of those times that tested my determination. I dried my eyes and started talking myself through the steps.

Again. Stall, stall, and then I went a little. Stall. I went a little further and switched gears. Stall.

And then, after so many stalls, it happened. I got the feel. If you have ever learned to drive a stick shift, you know what I mean. My mind shouted, *My life is not over!*

I was only able to drive the car when daddy or mama didn't need it. It's hard to imagine a household these days with just one car. But that's all we ever had. On the very first day of conquering the stick shift, I was able to drive myself to work. I did stall out going across a bridge—which scared the shit out of me as well as the drivers around me—but I stayed calm, restarted the car and off I went. Success!

Sometimes because of Daddy's work schedule, Greg would drive me home after work. That helped a lot. Otherwise, I would have had to find a ride some other way. While my parents didn't seem to mind asking others for help, I struggled with it. I actually found it slightly embarrassing. Luckily Greg helped. It gave us time together since we often worked on the weekends and during the week.

Daddy's complaining over work continued to worsen. I just kept thinking to myself, *Please keep this job, please keep this job. I need you to keep this job.* I knew I could get that scholarship. Why couldn't he get over himself and hold onto that job? Apparently, he felt he knew more than his boss. Which he probably did—my daddy was smart. However, he wasn't the supervisor. He needed to just put on his big boy pants and deal with it. He needed to keep that job for his family. At least that was how I felt.

One of the nights that daddy had the car for work, Greg gave me a ride home. We pulled around the back to our apartment's entrance. There it was... the stick-shift Datsun. My heart started racing. That could only mean one thing—Daddy had either quit his job or gotten fired and was home.

I sat in the car with Greg for a minute. I felt frozen to that bucket seat. I did not want to go in. I just knew what was waiting.

When I walked in the back door, I saw Mom in the kitchen with that look of worry on her face. Probably she dreaded telling me more than I dreaded hearing it. She knew what it meant to me. I had really thought his job was my ticket to college.

I asked the question I already knew the answer to. Daddy had gotten mad at his manager, who had wanted him to do something Daddy didn't think was necessary. He had walked off the job. I was infuriated! How could he do this to us? Why could he not swallow his fucking pride for his family for once? I was mad and sad and scared all at the same time. Literally shaking. Then anger turned to fear and I started to sob.

My father, of course, was "hiding" in his room. I am sure he did not want to face me. I kept asking my Mom, "How could he do this?" She tried to get me to calm down while poor Greg just sort of stood there sliding closer to the corner.

Once again, a lesson was reiterated—I couldn't trust anyone. It taught me that I was not important enough for Daddy to stick it out at a job. Nothing was ever going to change. This incident played a huge role in my struggle for self-worth and to feel secure. I know he loved me, but when it came to keeping a job, he was just fucked up. I feel guilty for thinking these things, but guilt has been a big issue for me as well.

Mom finally got me calmed down. She told me to go with Greg and stay with him for the night. I think she was truly afraid of what I might say to Dad. At that moment, I didn't even want to look at him. A sense of total and utter defeat crept over me, like all the air had been taken out of my body. How was I ever going to be able to afford college? How would I ever be able to leave home?

Plus once again, Mom would need more of my help financially.

The motel was not what you would call fancy, but it wasn't terrible either. There were basically two types of clientele—folks who rented a room for a few hours (ahem), and customers who traveled from other places for work, mostly construction. They would stay for a few months and then move on to the next job. It was not difficult work, but it was physically demanding on my mother to clean the rooms. I helped when I could.

Now that Daddy didn't have a job, Mom would sometimes "borrow" the money from the short-stay customers. Her health issues continued, and so did Dad's effects from Agent Orange. He had a couple of surgeries, neck and hernia, and though he filed for disability, he kept being turned down. Mom, however, filed for disability and actually got it. At that point, things started going downhill at the motel. Maybe the owner began to suspect that he was not getting all of his rent. The details were not shared. I just knew that we had to move. Again.

Back in Chocowinity, we got a small three-bedroom house. My mother had known the family who owned it and her parents had known their parents. When we couldn't pay the rent on time, the owners were understanding and worked with us.

Dad had always wanted to work at the Post Office, so he applied often. Meanwhile, he kept filing and refiling for disability from Veterans Affairs. He finally got what they called "Zero Disability," that was for some reason better than no disability. It was also supposed to be one step toward the actual disability assistance. He received some medical benefits, but no money.

By this time, he was hooked on prescription drugs. He took valium for his nerves and always had pain medication. Mom did too. With all the genetic addiction factors and personal issues they both wanted to escape, it wasn't hard to imagine why they wanted relief from the emotional pain.

How was I doing, you might wonder? I wondered too. I had been on that roller coaster my whole short life. I couldn't talk to anyone about it. How could I? I was embarrassed. I couldn't even tell Greg.

On the inside, I was worried about, well, everything. My heart still ached from my daddy's willingness to walk off of the best job he'd ever had, leaving his family in such need once again. If I sat too still, too many questions would swirl in mind. *How would I ever be able to go to college? What could I do about my parents' situation? How could I make more money so I could get a car?*

The responsibility of my home life weighed heavily. No one knew the depths of my stress and worry. So I did what I had learned to do long ago. I put on a smiling face and happy demeanor. I did everything I could to stay busy so I could bury those looming questions. There was no sitting still for me. Not for a minute... or all those worries would creep up and swallow me whole.

19 | Being 17 Was So Much Fun

I was going to school, cheering, working and had a great boyfriend. Money, as always, was still an issue at my house. I made good grades without much effort, and was involved in several clubs at school. Staying busy and never being home helped to keep the mental demons away.

In addition to cheering, the drama club was my next favorite activity. I began trying out and getting parts in ninth grade. By Junior year I landed leading roles. In fact, that year the drama teacher decided to do a serious play rather than our normal comedies. Thank goodness we did not do any musicals... as I can't sing unless I have had too much to drink, at which point I think I sound real good. I even won "Best Leading Actress" for the part I played in Chocowinity High School's first production. I was so proud. I loved being on stage.

My friend Tracy and I were co-captain and Ruth Ann was captain of our cheerleading squad, which historically won competitions including the "Tobacco Belt Conference Cheerleading Competition." These days you would never hear that title, but back then tobacco was a top money producer in our part of North Carolina.

My squad was not about to lose that title. We won regionals and were off to the State competition. It was such an exciting time. We were going to be staying at a hotel and competing on Saturday. Eleven nervous cheerleaders traveled to Fayetteville, NC, competing for the first time at a state level. We had practiced and practiced. We were ready. Our performance was outstanding!

It came time for the announcement of the winners. My heart was beating a mile a minute. My palms were sweaty. We stood together holding hands. Thank goodness everyone's hands were sweaty. "Third place ... Second Place ... and in First Place— Chocowinity High School Indians!" OH MY GOD, WE DID IT! I am sure they heard our screaming two hours away in Chocowinity.

The only sad part was that my parents did not have the money to attend. In fact, I don't think Mom ever saw me cheer. Certainly, never in competition. I wasn't sad then, however, later in life I now really wish she would have seen it. I think she would have been proud.

You can't imagine the ride back from that competition. Eleven winning State Championship cheerleaders in one vehicle was quite the celebration. I don't know how our coach handled it. She had to drive for over two hours listening to us scream, sing, and dance. I am pretty sure we literally rocked that van. And then it got better.

As we neared the school, we saw more than the normal number of vehicles. In fact, there was a shit-ton of cars there. And a news van! It was the culmination of a cheerleader's life. We went on to win State Championship again my Senior year. However, it would never feel the same as that magical night.

As a team we were named "Athlete of the Week" by the news. Each of the Seniors were interviewed... I am so glad I don't have a copy of that tape. I have cheered in front of hundreds, had starring roles in plays, and that little camera scared the shit out of me. I completely sounded like some sort of valley girl by saying "so" and "totally" so many times most would have assumed I was a "typical" dumb cheerleader. By the way, none of those girls were dumb. In fact, a certain grade point average was required. Most of the girls were top of their class.

Talk about labels. When I tell someone I was a cheerleader in high school, I first get the "of course you were" look, then comes all the teasing labels... dumb, slutty, etc. I was proud of being a cheerleader. It was one of the things that I was really good at. It was also the best escape from my home life. I seemed to be able to conceal what was happening behind the scenes of my life whenever I was out there cheering.

Fall of my Senior year, I was still madly in love with Greg. My family was living in an okay house. Our car wasn't breaking down every other day. However, financial woes always haunted us. I worked as much as I could to try and save for a car. I would get up at 5:00 A.M., do an opening shift at McDonald's, work until 7:30 then go home and dress for school, go to cheerleading practice afterward, and then go back to McDonald's from 8:00 to 10:00 at night depending upon the schedule.

All that working and still I couldn't save enough for a car. Something would happen at home and Mom would need to "borrow" money from me. I couldn't say no. "Hey Reesy, I need to borrow some money or the lights are going to get shut off." I have watched my mother dig in her purse to find enough change to buy a loaf of bread on more than one occasion. I didn't think I would ever be able to save enough for a car, but I still kept working at it.

Senior year is always busy. Kids apply for colleges and try to figure out who they are and what they want to do with the rest of their lives. Really, that is such bullshit. When they don't even really know who they are, how the hell are they supposed to figure out who they want to be?

At the time, I thought I wanted to be a court judge. That would mean a lot of school. But I didn't have any money, and my parents had not gone to college and didn't know what was possible with financial aid. The guidance counselor wasn't any help either. I really couldn't see how I was going to do this without loads of money.

I scored pretty well on the SAT. Well enough that I did not have to take it again. I was sixth in my class. The class was small but that was still good. Especially considering I really did not put all my effort into studying. It was much more of a social event for me. I remember visiting my English teacher two years after I had graduated. She said to me, "You know you could have been valedictorian if you wanted to." That was one label I didn't expect to hear. I was too busy having fun.

Fall 1986, the start of my Senior year, I had one little bucket list item I wanted—to be on the homecoming court. I did not necessarily want to win. I just wanted to be on the court. Two of my aunts had been crowned homecoming queen so it was a bit of a Sadler tradition.

In the South, the football team used to pick the court—four girls from each grade, ninth through twelfth. As a further sign of the times and location, two white girls and two black girls were chosen to represent their respective classes. Two homecoming queens were crowned, one white and one black. I know, I know. It's really hard to comprehend the school did it that way. However, it was 1986 in the South and there wasn't a lot of diversity at Chocowinity High School. And why did the football team get to pick? Weird, right?

The day came and the football team met early in the morning. A good friend on the team secretly told me that I had been picked. I was so pumped! It was supposed to be me and Dayna as the "white" representatives for the Seniors. I was pretty sure Dayna was going to win though. She was much nicer and more well behaved than me. Other than, of course, the times I would lead her astray. I didn't care. I just wanted to be on the court. Dayna was also one of my best friends. I would be happy for her to win.

The daily announcements came over the intercom. Wait. They didn't announce the court per the usual. Here came those labels. Apparently, the football coach decided he didn't like the team's choice of me. I was a wild child. I did not fit his criteria. He actually made them meet again at lunch and pick someone else. When the announcements finally came later that day, I was devastated! I went home and cried to my mom. She really wanted to go to the school and have a talk with him. I begged her not to. It would have only made things worse. Thinking back, I should have let her.

A new bucket list item was created to one day see that coach in person and let him know that I found out what he did. He had no right to judge me. Yet, this adult—a teacher, someone we were supposed to trust to make good decisions—thought I did not deserve to be on the homecoming court. I was captain of the cheerleading squad, participated in five different clubs, was named "Who's Who" in my class, and had top grades, but somehow his label for me said I did not deserve to be on the court. I really should be over this. The teenage girl in me wants to tell him, *"Fuck you, asshole!"* The mature woman merely wishes for him to get what he has given.

Senior year was bittersweet. Everything was a "last time." Final homecoming dance, last game to cheer at, last school play. I did it all!

I was accepted at East Carolina University for the following year, but had no idea how I was going to pay for it, or even how I would physically get there. The school was only thirty minutes away, but as you know, I didn't have a car and I couldn't pay for a dorm.

Money was tight for Greg, too. With his parents divorcing, he had to pay for a lot of things himself, including replacing the motor in his car. Which, by the way, I waited and watched him do many a "date night." He asked me for help with gas money since he did most of the driving. It started to feel like I was drowning. The pressure was intense. How was I ever going to do anything or be anything? The stress crashed down hard.

As Spring came, things got even scarier, and prompted years of therapy later on. The life lesson was: Never make important life changes when you are an emotional wreck. I decided nothing was working for me. I was turned down for an assistant manager job at McDonald's. In reality, because I had started calling in sick way more often than in the past, they probably should have been nervous to promote me.

But my parents were asking for money every time I got paid and I knew Greg needed or wanted gas money from me as well. I had to gain some kind of control. So I started with a diet. I often joke that I have been on a diet since I was 12, but I now wish I was as fat as I thought I was then!

One night on the cheerleading bus we stopped at McDonald's to eat after the game. I would usually share a twenty-piece Chicken McNuggets with one of the other cheerleaders. Ten nuggets with hot mustard and a Coke. But I was tired of being the chubby girl with the pretty face. I was tired of all of my friends being smaller than me. In a light-switch moment, I said to myself... *Enough!*

I started a 1,000-calorie per day diet. I counted everything. I ran extra laps at cheerleading practice. When there was a carry-out order waiting at McDonald's, I would run it out to the car. I was determined, a woman obsessed. And it worked! How couldn't it? A thousand calories a day is not much. I think I got down to about a size 6. We did not have a scale at our house... that would have been a luxury, but I probably lost twenty pounds. I began to turn heads. People finally began to notice after all that hard work. Even Greg noticed. He had his arms around my waist and said, "Wow, you are starting to get tiny." Needless to say, he got extra make-out time.

I also decided that a new job was in order. I had not gotten the promotion and both of my best friends, Becky and Dayna, were not working there anymore. So I went to work at a department store with another of my very good friends. It was going to be great! No more midnight hours or 5:00 A.M. openings. And I would be able to dress up!

But wait... that would mean I had to buy new clothes.

How was I going to do that?

20 | So Much Responsibility

When I was working at McDonald's there was a man who would come in every day to get coffee. He worked for the telephone company and was always very nice to me. In conversation, I learned he had a son who went to a different school and was my age—the same birthday, even. This man often mentioned how he wanted me to date his son. When my birthday came, he offered me a present. Since he was a telephone man, he came to my house while Mom was home and installed an extra telephone line in my room. As a teenage girl, I was psyched to have that bit of privacy!

I thought it was nice of him. Then as Christmas approached the next year, he said, "You better tell me what you want, or I'll give you a picture of Ben Franklin,"...aka $100.00. Not quite sure what to say, I told the truth. I needed new clothes. He told me to go pick them out and he would pay for them. *Wow*, I thought. *This is a really nice man.*

Remember, not one time was I ever alone with this 40-something man. Not once did he make any moves on me or make me feel uncomfortable. I truly thought he was buying me presents to be nice. I was also desperate for new clothing as saving my own money wasn't happening due to always having to help out at home.

At the department store I tried on clothes and made my choices. As is the Southern way, one of the ladies who worked there began chatting with me. I was so excited about my new wardrobe, I told her all about the man who was buying clothes for me. When I mentioned his name though, she gave me the strangest look. I knew something was wrong. What had I missed?

Well, she knew his wife. No big deal. However, I'm pretty sure this lady told the wife about her husband's generosity... and I didn't see him much after that. I put those clothes on layaway, eventually paying them off. Yeah, no picture of Ben Franklin or new clothes from this man.

I am sure I gained a few new labels from this experience that were absolutely untrue. I was so naïve and desperate for help. Had I put some weird signal out there? I was under so much pressure that I failed to see anything other than a nice person buying me something, rather than the other way around. This would not be the last time I misunderstood someone's intentions.

I felt the weight of the world on my shoulders. How was I ever going to go to college, buy a car, do something other than take care of everyone else? There seemed to be no end in sight of giving my parents a lot of my paycheck without being paid back. No wonder I accepted that man's gifts without a thought.

I had been given a parental role far before it was time. It was me that Mama would come to when she was fighting with Daddy. It was me she would ask to talk to him when he was being an asshole. She said I was the only one he would listen to. I think her spirit was broken. Hence, she looked to me, the over-responsible teenager life had made me. I did whatever she asked to keep the peace.

Mother shared all her worries of the world with me. Way too much for any child to have to handle or know about. When you are a teenager you think it is kind of cool being in this "adult world" and being asked to help with "adult problems." The reality is you completely miss your childhood. You lose your innocence. Because your world is so small and the adults around you are putting all their shit on you, you become the *responsible* one. Who else was going to take care of things?

Clearly, my parents were struggling with life. I had already been told at the ripe old age of five that I was responsible for my father's nervous breakdown. I must be responsible for everything else, too. Based on my childhood, I instinctively took on the responsibility for everything and everyone. The pressure to keep everything okay just mounted and mounted. I started to have stomachaches. I might have been developing an ulcer.

Even though I didn't realize it, more than anything I wanted to run away from it all. I desired relief from my pressure cooker life. It was about to pop. I wanted someone to take care of me for once. I was exhausted from taking care of everyone else.

I think Greg was in need of the same thing. His parents were divorcing and he was trying to figure out his own way to college. Both of our "buckets" were empty and neither of us had the maturity or ability to fulfill that order. We needed our parents. Maybe in different ways, but we needed them. No wonder I did what I did.

Because of not having a car and no way that I knew of to go to college, I thought perhaps I could start at a community college. It would be cheaper. I could always transfer once I figured things out. One of my best friends, Becky, was going there too, to study some sort of criminal justice. Since I wanted to go into law, our classes for the first semester would be the same. We could commute together. Not exactly perfect but it was a beginning.

I was still having all those feelings of being taken for granted by Greg. Things started to occur that seemed to reinforce the theory. First, his car's engine broke. It was going to take a lot of money to replace. He decided that he and his friend would do the work to reduce costs. I spent many a night in his living room watching TV alone while he and his buddy worked on the car. It was so boring. He was never in a good mood either. I guess working on that car took a toll on him. When he was behind with things at school, I even wrote his senior term paper. I felt very unappreciated.

Before we get to me and my crossroads, let's talk about the influences on a girl in the '80s. *Officer and a Gentleman* was popular at the movie theater. I was a poor girl living near a military base, looking for love and someone to rescue her. So many parallels to my life... or at least it felt like it. *Top Gun* with Tom Cruise at his sexiest once again was about saving the girl and all that romantic stuff. But every female on television was skinny. You could practically read their vaginas through those Jordache jeans. And their hair had to be big and permed—an expensive proposition for someone like me with straight hair. Aerobics and being in shape were super important. And while having sex before marriage was rampant, you still needed to be a good girl to win the guy. Lots of pressure to be perfect.

Where was my rescuer? Where was my perfect body?

21 | High School Heartbreak and Another Marine

Every year at Easter it was a tradition to go to the beach. Some years were pretty warm and other times you froze your ass off. If it was cold, we would sink into the sand as far as possible and let the warmth of the sun bake us, creating the very first glimpse of that awesome tan we sought out every year. If it was warm... bonus!

That April Easter was fairly nice. I traveled with Dayna and a manager from work who was over 21. Of course, we had to have some lovely Boone's Farm Strawberry Wine to warm us.

The closest beach was Atlantic—with all the Marines. When soldiers get bored, they head to the beach to check out the bikini-clad scenery. I remember it so vividly, down to the bathing suit I was wearing—a monokini. They should bring those back. It's sort of like a one-piece bathing suit with part of it missing. The bottoms were black and the top was hot pink and attached by a black piece of material that went down the side. I would buy that bathing suit today it was so cute. It was also quite flattering thanks to my new weight loss. And it covered the scar from my kidney surgery.

Dayna and I were slightly tipsy from the Boone's Farm and went for a walk down the beach. I spotted two hunky Marines walking toward us. I was particularly drawn to the shorter, dark-haired full-of-muscles one. Dayna, who would never normally do this, yelled out, "Hey, this girl likes you." The guys laughed along, contemplating our ages. The taller one kept saying, "Under 18 will get you 10 to 20." I presume he meant jail time for messing with a minor. Lucky for him, I was over 18. Just not by much, mind you.

They came over and chatted with us. By the time the conversation was done, Lance Corporal Todd S. had my number. I really didn't expect him to call. But what about Greg? My 18-year-old self was still upset that he'd been taking me for granted.

I hadn't even given Greg the "talk" about how I felt. Truth be told, I now realize we were not doing a very good job communicating at all. Too bad we were immature and scared, not understanding what we were both going through on the inside that had nothing to do with each other. No one really knew the depths of my stress. It was too embarrassing to share how much I did to support things at home. I hid that pressure and pain well with my big smile and bubbly personality. Only my closest friends had somewhat of a clue. However, I could never share it all. How could I? In my mind, their lives seemed perfect. Most had cars, nice clothes and were all set to go to college. I was just doing my best to survive. I'm not sure I even realized the full impact of all that adult pressure until too many mistakes later.

The Marine called right away. He was from Pennsylvania, had a cool accent and seemed nice. He had these dark brown eyes, was really built and a little shy. He wanted to take me out on a date. Would I break off my fairytale-gone-bad high school romance? Was it that bad? All I knew was I was unhappy and scared of an uncertain future. I didn't want to hurt Greg no matter how things were going.

If I was going to go out with Todd the Marine, I had to break up with Greg. Considering I had already said yes to the date, I was left with few choices. I either had to cheat, cancel the date, or break up with Greg. I kept telling myself Greg was going to move past me anyway. Rumors were floating that he had cheated on me with a girl at his school. Then there was the gas money thing. And most of all, the once over the top generosity of attention and affection seemed to be fading. I believe his "empty bucket" hadn't left much for him to contribute to my "empty bucket."

I remember the moment—like all crossroads—very well. We were having the Beta Club dinner. Greg knew something was up because I was acting strange. Over the phone, on a whim, right before dinner, I did it. I told him I thought we should break up. It almost felt like someone else was talking. I didn't think, I just did it, so I could go out with Todd without actually cheating on Greg. I broke his heart, and honestly, I broke mine too. I just didn't know it at the time.

Greg and I kept in touch. He grew up to be quite handsome, married with two children. He moved far away from Eastern North Carolina. As the next few years passed, I often wondered if I had made the wrong choice. The sad truth for both of us was that we needed someone to rescue us... which meant we couldn't do it for each other.

Even though we were broken up, Greg and I decided to still go to prom together. It was a little awkward. I had this lacy red dress with a broad white cummerbund accenting my then-small waist, while Greg wore a white tuxedo with a matching red tie and cummerbund. The dress was gorgeous. I was gorgeous. Greg was gorgeous.

It was the same year the song "Lady in Red" came out. When that tune played, Greg and I slow danced. He sang in my ear. I had a moment of regret for breaking up with him. I quickly pushed that thought away to remember that Todd the Marine was going to take me away from that small town and give me all the things I never had. *Boy, was I delusional.*

The night ended with a kiss and a goodbye. When I look at those prom pictures I can see the sadness in Greg's eyes. My high school sweetheart was gone forever.

After prom, Greg made one more attempt to reach me. He came over to my house on his motorcycle. My parents were not home. Guess what happens when parents aren't home? We had one last make-out session. Another moment of regret. But Greg was going to leave me and move on anyway. That strong Marine from somewhere other than my small town was waiting with open arms. Maybe he could still save me.

Thank goodness I was working at the department store. I could remove myself from Greg's presence. I couldn't look at him. Somewhere inside I knew I had made a mistake and yet I had to keep going. I had to find a way to get away. Had I stayed at McDonald's where I would have seen Greg every day, I may have broken my never-break-up-and-get-back-together rule. The overwhelming urge to run overpowered every other rational thought.

Years later I learned that Greg too was suffering. He had pushed me away because of stress at home and school, and by the time he realized it, it was too late. He was and will always be my very first true love. He took the cake on that one.

22 | Graduation and Everything Changes

Graduation neared. I applied for a Pell grant for college but had not heard anything. I had to pay for my own senior pictures and class ring, although Mom helped pay for my prom dress. Stress was mounting. Stomachaches continued. I put all my hope in Todd the Marine. He had to fall in love with me and take me away from all of this.

Graduation was surreal. I can't describe the sadness and happiness occurring at the same time. A lot of people say they hated high school... Well, I loved it! Mostly due to the social aspect, however, I had a great high school experience.

Todd attended my Baccalaureate along with his best Marine friend, Smitty. I was ranked sixth in my class. Not bad considering I liked boys and friends way more than school. We graduated June 6, 1987. I cried a lot. All my friends did too. One of the saddest parts was that Dayna's Mom got divorced and they were going to move back to Tennessee where her family was from originally. So we decided to go to the beach for one last week of shenanigans. We rented a huge house right on the shore with three others.

Todd told some of his Marine friends about our little trip and they were more than happy to visit a beach house full of pretty girls. One night, Todd and I decided to go out to dinner while the others stayed behind. As we were driving back we could tell something was going on. There was yelling and screaming and people running around. Apparently the male neighbors had a run-in with the visiting Marines. It was quite scary to this naïve 18-year-old. We got out of the car just in time to see one of Todd's friends get hit in the middle of his back with a heavy beer mug. Needless to say, a fight ensued.

Todd and I went inside. He told me to get down on the floor behind the bed while he went into what I would call "MP Marine mode," crouching and working his way toward the door. I begged him not to leave me in there alone. I had seen typical fights at school that lasted about two minutes, but this was way different—trained Marines going at it with big grown-ass men.

Todd left the room. There I was hiding behind the bed scared to death when I heard a loud crash and the sound of breaking glass. My heart was about to pound out of my chest. Todd came back as the police arrived. One of the neighbors had thrown that same heavy beer mug through our front glass door. Oh no! My parents had signed for the rental. They were going to be so pissed.

Everything got quiet. Other than the gals being scared shitless, there were no injuries except one Marine getting a cut hand. We explained to the police that the neighbors truly were the ones who started the whole thing. The cops went next door and we heard not another word from police or neighbors.

While out of physical danger, I was going to have to tell my parents what happened... and we were going to have to pay for the damages. I was sure my security deposit was going to be gone—$425, which was a lot of money in 1987.

I found myself facing my parents the next day as we were laying on the beach. When I looked up the sand dune, there they were. Apparently, they had already gotten a call since they were the ones who signed for the rental. My plan had been not to tell them until we got home. But two things saved my ass. Todd and I had been at dinner and had nothing to do with the situation. Also, my friends helped to pay for the repairs. My parents were placated and left with a stern message of no more parties.

At that point, I had been seeing Todd for about a month. I thought surely he must be in love with me by then. I certainly had convinced myself I was in love with him. So one night I told him that I loved him. He didn't say it back. I became confused. He acted like he loved me... because, of course, I knew exactly what that looked like. I started to cry and ask probing questions.

Finally, after the tears and interrogation, he said, "I love you, too."

Great! But then he started to cry. What the...? Now I was not only confused, but I had no idea what to say. At the time I thought it was just hard for him to express his feelings. Why would I even begin to question his emotional health? If I looked at that, I might find a red flag. I didn't want to see any red flags. I wanted to see a knight in shining armor. So I chose to focus on the fact that he had said the words. He loved me. Yeah, right!

The summer of fun continued, dating Todd, taking lots of weekend beach trips and having fun. I enrolled at Pitt Community College and received The Clyde Harding scholarship from my school. Mr. Harding was an icon of a teacher. He even taught my mom and drove the bus for all the sporting events. The scholarship was enough for me to attend the first and second semester. I could commute with Becky for the first term. I don't know what I would have done without her.

The good news was that Todd knew nothing of my "labels" so I had the rest of the summer to coax him to ask me to marry him. That's right. I wanted to be engaged and get married. Time was of the essence. All my friends were getting engaged to their high school sweethearts. I felt the pressure, albeit self-inflicted. In addition, Todd was due to get out of the Marines in November. If he decided to "re-up" for another four years, he would be shipped off somewhere other than North Carolina. If he didn't do that, he would either stay in North Carolina if he could find a job or he would head back home to Pennsylvania. For me, all of these choices meant I had to have that ring before November.

As I look back, so many signs told me to go one way while my immature mind led me another. There were crossroads that would have changed my life forever. We feel so smart when we are young, but with every passing year, we realize how dumb we were. We will never be "smarter" than we were at 18.

23 | Will He Rescue Me? And What's Up with His Family?

I thought Todd was exactly what I was looking for, my knight in shining armor, my Marine who would take me away and provide the happily ever after I always wanted. Boy, was I wrong.

He came to pick me up for our first date in a canary yellow Corvette. I was super impressed. I have come to realize that a fancy car is a sign of low self-esteem or inadequacies in a man. But he was quite the gentleman. He would drive from the base about 50 miles away, take me to dinner, then drive all the way back. Sometimes we would get a hotel room and spend the night together. My father knew none of the overnight stuff though I always kept Mom up to speed on where I was. Always my confidante.

Todd was 24—quite a bit older. Outside of the Marines, he was not very "worldly." In fact, he had only been stationed at one base, Cherry Point. It was like a scene from the movie *Officer and a Gentleman* where Todd, like Richard Gere, didn't feel he deserved love. I was a mixture of Debra Wenger and her friend. I wouldn't try to get pregnant on purpose, but I was desperate to find someone to take care of me.

He was wonderful, taking me to dinner and paying for everything. He also took me clothes shopping at a store near the base with really great deals. It had irregulars and seconds, but none of that mattered to me. He bought me tons of clothing. I was so impressed. No one had ever done anything like that for me before. He wined and dined me. I was blinded by the vision of security and getting away from the stress.

He was also sweet in bed. He had never been with anyone before me, but with my limited experience, I couldn't tell. He seemed to know what he was doing. Perhaps he had watched a lot of porn. What I did know was that he was a real virgin and wouldn't compare me to anyone.

While our first kiss and sexual relationship weren't exactly memorable, I will always recall that sad first "I love you" at the beach. I'd expected it to be nothing less than hearing the Prince song "When Doves Fly" as the boy whispers, "I love you," in my ear.

Later, in one of the darkest parts of my life, I made the mistake of asking him exactly why he was with me. He actually replied, "I'm with you because you are the best that I can get." What a label that was. What a box he put me in! I didn't know that I was so much better than his "as good as he could get" comment. Maybe he came from a fucked-up family that never said "I love you" to each other. Perhaps he just loved the sex and felt guilty. If his struggle was something other than an excuse I came up with, it meant something different—something I probably wouldn't like. It could mean that I had broken up with Greg, the greatest boyfriend ever, to be with this guy. That couldn't be it. That would have killed me. Or so I thought... Actually I didn't think at all. I just kept going, running toward a way out.

He took me to Pennsylvania in July to meet his parents. It was so beautiful. I came from one of the flattest places on earth to those lovely, lush mountains, which were really just rolling hills. We stayed for three weeks, sleeping on the floor in his old room.

Todd's parents were gracious hosts. Looking back, I think they were just super happy Todd had found a girl. We visited local attractions like Gettysburg, some car shows, and Hershey. I remember standing at the kitchen sink, looking out the window at the beautiful scenery. I remember thinking, "I will probably never see this again." Little did I know what the future would bring. Life is funny that way. One day you are looking out a window thinking it is the last time you will see a place and the next you may be standing at that same window crying and wishing to see the beautiful flat fields of tobacco and gorgeous beaches where you came from.

Something was off though. Todd's dad was particularly attentive. In the South it's normal to be hugged on a regular basis. Todd's dad hugged me often. He liked to sit beside me too. I noticed his mom seemed to be "uncomfortable" with hugging and "uncomfortable" with the dad sitting beside me. Was I misreading her? I decided all was normal. After all, what did I know about being in the North? My dad hugged my friends.

Todd also had a weird, not so pretty... and I am being nice here... sister. When I say unattractive... wow. Don't judge me. I try to find beauty in everyone and, well I got nothing. She was, however, engaged to a handsome man. I think he was gay. He was definitely feminine. It confused me. She wasn't mean, but she wasn't nice. She just sort of stayed in her room, yelling at her mom about something occasionally. Not sure of her mental capacity, but she was "special."

The three-week vacation ended as a success as far as I was concerned. We got back to NC and things continued nicely. Dinners, calls, overnight stays at hotels for which he always paid. He even met my grandmother and went with me to my niece's wedding in his uniform. I was so proud.

There were signs along the way that I apparently refused to see. My vision was completely blocked by my desire to get married and escape my home life.

Todd loved to hunt. I grew up with lots of guys who loved to hunt, so no big deal. I surely wasn't paying attention. My thoughts were all about making him fall deeply, madly in love with me and ask me to marry him. I wanted that fairy tale. I needed that fairy tale!

Todd was so happy when I introduced him to one of my best friends' fiancé... of course another of my friends was engaged... so Todd could go deer hunting. Apparently, in North Carolina, there were so many deer that there wasn't a limit on how many you could shoot during deer season. Todd was invited to go along for a deer hunt and he was thrilled.

They headed out. Both of them killed a deer. Todd got two. He was pumped. I was so happy he was happy. But according to hunting etiquette, something politically incorrect happened while they were out. Apparently, my friend's fiancé was close to a deer. It should have been his kill. Instead Todd took aim and shot. I, of course, thought, "*Whatever.*" Not only was I the girl who liked Marines but also the girl who liked Marines who were asshole hunters.

North Carolina also had other hunting laws that were less stringent than Pennsylvania's. In North Carolina you were allowed to use lure to get the animals to come to you. I think it is quite unfair for the animals. However, Todd thought this was just great. One day he asked if we could go to this open field at night where he was going to set up a tape recorder (remember this was the '80s) with screaming baby rabbits playing. He was going to turn on this recording so a fox, hearing the cry for supper—aka screaming baby rabbits—was going to come out of the woods and Todd would shoot it. All I heard was "alone at night with my boyfriend." I was sure it was code for "let's go make out in the woods." I mean, who would believe a fox would actually come out of the woods because of some tape recording of screaming rabbits? I surely didn't.

Off we went one November night. It was a little chilly in the field. It was so dark. But dark doesn't really do it justice. It was pitch black. Todd had some sort of red light on his gun... apparently foxes can't see this light. It was the only illumination we had on that dark night. I was really starting to get creeped out. Then he asked me to sit by the tape recorder. *Hello, Reesy. Isn't this where the fox is going to be headed?* Todd perched himself up with his gun several feet away from me.

As I was sitting there in the dark by myself, shivering, a light bulb went off in my head. Mind you, not a light bulb bright enough to pierce that darkness or give me warmth, nonetheless, a thought began to grow. It occurred to me that if the fox really came out of the woods searching for the not-really-there baby rabbits to eat, and if Todd missed his shot, the fox could potentially, yep, get me. Oh my God! First of all, this was the second sign that this man really didn't give a shit about my feelings. He hadn't asked if I was scared, and didn't care if I was cold. He just wanted to shoot that fucking fox.

Yet, there I was, one of the prissiest girls you will ever meet, sitting in the pitch black on a cold rock listening to baby rabbits scream. As my brain pondered that fox coming out of the woods, my hormones began to realize that there would be no making out. The fullness of that light bulb finally illuminated my brain. I realized all Todd really wanted to do was shoot this fox.

Time slowed. I became increasingly nervous and scared. Weren't most adventures with boys just ways for them to get you alone? That had been my experience. I guess you have to be a hunter to understand. I was no hunter.

Okay Reesy, calm down, I said to myself. *A fox really isn't going to come out of those woods. Any minute now Todd is going to say, "Come on, honey, let's go make out."*

I was attempting to calm my breathing and reassure myself that there was not going to be any fox. Then I saw it... There he was! A little red fox slowly skulked out of the woods. I could not believe my eyes. I was frozen scared. *Holy shit, that recording thing actually worked.* My heart was beating so fast. I tried to sit still because that was what Todd wanted. The recurring thought, "What if he misses, what if he misses?" kept getting louder.

I had already been super uncomfortable in so many ways. Mama always said I was much more of a Southern gal sipping mint juleps on a veranda than one who enjoyed communing with nature. I mean I don't mind the outdoors as long as I'm relatively comfortable. But at that moment, I was beyond uncomfortable. I was petrified. What should I do? Should I run? What if the fox chased me? I had no idea what that fox would do should he reach me and find no rabbit stew for his dinner. Where had I gone wrong? This was supposed to have been a fun date. Well, Todd was having fun, I guess. But my plan had been to lure a husband, not a fox.

The animal kept coming toward me. It didn't turn around to go back into the woods. Just as Todd was about to shoot, I couldn't help myself. I couldn't control it. I screamed louder than I probably have or had since then. The noise of the gun firing was painfully loud. This encouraged another scream from me. The fox ran back into the woods. Thank goodness.

I was shaking like a leaf and tears began to form. As Todd approached I could tell he wasn't happy. "Why did you do that!" he yelled. He was actually mad at me for screaming and scaring his fox away. Are you fucking kidding me? I could no longer hold back the tears. As far as I was concerned, he had just put my life in danger. I still couldn't believe that shit.

At least when he saw how upset I was, it reined in his anger. He put an arm around me and told me everything was all right. I said I just wanted to leave. He reluctantly agreed. Had I not been so upset, I actually think he would have tried again.

See what I mean about signs? What boyfriend takes his girl out in the woods at night to sit beside a recorder of screaming baby rabbits so he can shoot a fox? I should have punched him in the face and demanded him to take me home. But with hugs and an "I'm sorry" I quickly forgave him and continued my quest for the engagement ring.

24 | Gotta Close This Deal

Todd's enlistment finished at the beginning of November. He couldn't find a job in North Carolina, where land was much cheaper than his home state. I was learning he was rather frugal or perhaps cheap. He was upset about this, but also had a good paying job waiting for him in Pennsylvania as a brick mason. He had no real choice, so I needed to move up my plan.

One night while I was working at the department store, he came by. "What are you doing here?" I asked. He pulled out a little box from his pocket and opened it. Inside was a shiny half-carat diamond ring. He just stood there holding this box open and looking at me. No bent knee. No romantic anything. Finally, I broke the silence. "What does this mean?" He sort of mumbled something that might have been "Will you marry me?" There I was in the middle of hosiery with this man holding a box open and saying nothing.

As the bible says: "There is none so blind as those that *will not see.*"

But wait... now I had that engagement ring! Did it really matter that it felt kind of wrong? Did it really matter that it was not the romantic proposal of my dreams? In that moment, I gained hope for my security and my happily ever after.

Interestingly enough Daddy didn't seem to like Todd. Mama said that Daddy didn't think he was smart enough for me. But I wasn't about to let a little intelligence keep me away from my escape. I liked being the smarter one. Or so I thought. A person can justify just about anything when they are desperate enough.

In December, Todd went home to Pennsylvania to that brick mason job. I was hopeful he would move me up there as soon as things were all set. Christmas came and it was the same old story at our house. No money. In fact, I did not get one gift from my parents that year. They did buy my brother a boom box. However, that was all they could spare. I bought myself a watch and told friends it had been a Christmas present. I will never forget that feeling—like I didn't matter to my parents other than my paycheck. I mean not even a pair of socks or new underwear. Nothing.

It was a tough pill to swallow, but I downed it whole. I decided I would never let this happen to my children. I was engaged and soon to be rescued. It was just a matter of time.

Second semester started. I didn't have classes with my dear friend. Everything got tougher. Daddy still wasn't working. There was definitely no way I was going to be able to save money for a car or school. All of my friends were in college and doing their own thing as tends to happen after graduation. I was lonely. I missed Todd so much.

In the meantime, Todd found us a place to live in Pennsylvania. We would have a room in a house with his best friend and the friend's fiancée until we could afford our own place. Todd would qualify for a VA loan for a house, so the plan was for me to join him in February and find a job so we could buy a house together.

Two days after I quit school I received a letter stating I had qualified for a PEL grant—essentially a full scholarship. But I thought it was too late. Plus I had to get away from my parents. I felt like they were sucking me dry. I first told my mother my plans to leave, and she told my dad. He walked around all pissed off and ready to explode at any minute. I'm sure he felt helpless to change the situation. After all, I was 19, an adult. Yeah, right.

It became so awkward at home. Daddy wouldn't speak to me. I felt like I was walking on eggshells the whole time. Mama finally explained to him that if he ever wanted to see his daughter again, he would need to start acting better. Years later, I reflect that my mother pretty much took away my father's manhood... just like his own mother had done before.

No one even attempted to sit me down and discuss this huge decision I was about to make. My mother just let me go. Nineteen, moving 400 miles away with a guy I had only met six months earlier. Perhaps she knew the money thing would never stop, and hoped this would save me... that Todd would save me. It might not have changed my actions then, but it matters to me now.

Todd showed up in his new Honda CRX on a rainy February day. He had traded his canary yellow Corvette for something more practical. Plus, he already got the girl, so who did he need to impress with a Corvette? We packed my belongings in his car. There wasn't much. Mostly clothes and some china I had bought when I was 16 to go in my hope chest. I hugged my parents and got in the car. Mama went directly into the house, not looking back. I know because I did turn and look back. There on the porch stood my father, both hands in his pockets, head slightly down, staring at his only daughter driving away, surrounded by a cloud of sadness.

I swallowed the lump in my throat. How could I let Todd see me sob? I quit looking back because every time I did Daddy was still standing there, almost like he thought I was going to turn around and come home. I stared forward and let the tears silently fall down my cheeks.

We decided to stay in a hotel in Greenville for the night. We hadn't seen each other in two months so hormones were raging. But Todd looked different now. And by *different*, I don't mean good. He wore glasses. Where had the contacts gone? He was much smaller. Where had the muscles gone? His hair was longer—not that Marine cut I found so attractive. I told myself it didn't matter. All that mattered was I was engaged and getting out of town.

So there we were at the hotel, the beginning of my fairy tale. I was thirsty so Todd went to go get us a couple of sodas. Alone in the hotel room, I pondered the olive green phone with the black push buttons. I wondered if leaving home had been the right thing. That phone taunted me. *"All you have to do, Reesy, is pick me up and call your parents. They will be here in a flash to take you back home. You can stop this. Just pick me up and dial."*

Wait a minute, Mr. Olive Green Phone. I can't do that! Todd should be back any moment with those sodas. He loved me, right? Other thoughts slammed into my 19-year-old brain. *It's too late! I am too far down this road. I quit college. I broke up with the high school boyfriend. My parents are going to keep taking money from me. I will never be able to find someone to take care of me in North Carolina. This is the only way.*

Finally the door opened and Todd returned with the sodas. I pushed as hard as I could to get those thoughts out of my head and never looked at that phone again. You lose, green phone.

25 | New Apartment, New Job, and Hell

We arrived at the house we would share with Todd's best friend, and apparently only friend, Darin and his fiancée Anne. We had one room to ourselves with a sheet for a door. But I had lived in worse conditions. Darin and Anne were welcoming. Not Southern welcoming though. Todd and I just had to bide our time until we could get our own place.

The next day they all left for work. There wasn't even a television for me to watch. I tried reading. Outside it was much colder than I was used to, so I stayed in. It was so quiet. I really felt lonely. I couldn't even make any phone calls as back then there was no such thing as a cell phone. It would have been a long distance call that cost money—Todd wouldn't like that. We had to save all our money for our own place. I had to find a job and quick. This alone thing would kill me.

Obviously, I didn't have a lot of qualifications. I did, however, know how to type and I had taken accounting classes in high school. I applied for a receptionist position at a car dealership that required a good personality and light typing. I also had a few assets I wasn't aware of... apparently northerners were quite taken by my accent. In particular, northern men. I had also entered a whole new grownup world where weighing 125 pounds wasn't considered fat. I had a "woman's body." With my self-esteem already in the ditch I had no idea how this asset would help me get a job.

I went for the interview. I met with a very nice man with a beard and pretty blue eyes who oversaw the service department and body shop. I found it odd that the receptionist would sit out in the showroom. A day later I got the job offer—$5.35 an hour, almost $2.00 more than what I made at McDonald's. I thought I was rich. I immediately accepted. Now I just needed a car.

We applied for a loan at a local community bank. Todd had excellent credit so we were approved rather quickly. Todd's grandmother had a used 1984 Mazda 626 she sold to us. She gave us a deal. And it was in great condition. It was the quintessential "old lady's" car... low mileage and in great condition. My first car! It was a grey four-door sedan with grey cloth interior, better than any car my parents ever owned!

I would also need nice business casual clothes for this job. Todd's mother worked at a consignment store and got me a part-time job there on Saturdays. I could get an employee discount plus see all the new consignment clothing before it went on the rack.

My first day at the dealership was quite interesting. I was so naïve about life in general. Answering the phones, paging employees and transferring calls came easily to me. The supervisor thought my accent would differentiate his store from other dealers.

There I sat in the corner of the showroom at my little desk answering the phone and doing a pretty good job. The general manager, John, walked into the showroom and over to the sales office, cattycorner from my desk. To my surprise, he started yelling at a salesman. "Get your head out of your ass!"

I was petrified. I had never heard a supervisor talk to any employee like that. John was tall with salt-and-pepper hair. He had a presence about him that commanded respect... or fear, depending on your perspective and his current mood.

I sat in a state of shock. We had customers in the showroom. After the loud outburst, he walked out of the office very naturally as if he hadn't just ripped a new asshole for that salesperson. He looked around, then headed straight toward me.

"Good morning," I said shakily. In a completely calm and polite voice he replied, "Hey, the next time I am yelling at a salesman and we have customers in the showroom, would you mind just calling in the office and letting me know?" Concentrating to keep my mouth from gaping open in astonishment, I just nodded, and he thanked me then walked away.

In my mind, I thought *Is this a regular thing?* There was no fucking way I was going to call into that office and tell the general manager to quit yelling. Was he out of his mind? He could simply look at someone a certain way and they would just about shit their pants. It was quite the talent.

Everyone seemed to want to adopt me. There were five salesmen and two saleswomen along with a female finance manager in the shop, plus seven younger men in the used car department. The car business taught me a lot. They kind of became my family, looking out for me. I got a lot of advice around not marrying Todd. No one seemed to think it was a good idea. I got the "you're too young," "take your time," "there's no rush," "you need to be sure." Yada, yada, yada... all that advice fell on deaf teen ears.

I also got a lot... and I mean a lot... of attention. I thought all those mechanics who sat at my desk during their lunch breaks were just being nice. One of my most favorites sales guys was Jack. He was in his 50s and dressed to the nines—cuff links and perfectly matched suits and ties. Very fit for his age. He had a head full of silver hair combed perfectly. Initially I was frightened of him. He seemed stern, but then I got to know him. He had the bark but if he liked you, there wasn't any bite.

He was toughest on new salespeople. He had seen too many come and go. He also was quite adept at figuring out which ones were going to last, so he was slightly nicer to them. It usually took about six months for him to warm up to anyone.

Jack paid me the highest compliment I had ever been given. "You're an original, Reesy." That sounded like a pretty good label to me. It certainly made me feel special. He did this in a "fatherly" way. I didn't fully understand at the time, but he saw something in me that I certainly couldn't see in myself. I would learn later just how often he was looking out for me.

Todd's parents wanted to sell us their house as they were building a new home right behind it. Note... don't ever live right beside your in-laws. But their house was super nice. Way, way nicer and way, way bigger than anything I had ever lived in. It was a bi-level with three large bedrooms, two and a half bathrooms, and a large basement on a half-acre of land. They had built the house originally and kept it up perfectly.

Todd applied for the VA loan. The mortgage company said they needed my income to qualify, but it wouldn't count unless we were married. Of course I was excited. No marriage meant no house. And Todd really wanted that house. And I really wanted to get married. The sooner the better.

But I don't believe Todd had planned on getting married that soon. Still... qualifying for a loan and getting a new house were normal, good reasons to get married, right? Boy, did I have a lot to learn!

26 | Angels and Devils

We couldn't afford a big wedding and neither could my parents. Todd and I talked about getting married in Maryland because it would be an easier process, then we could hold some sort of reception at a later time. But my friends in the car business did not think any of this was a good idea.

Todd had changed drastically from when he was in the Marines. He started smoking and he quit taking care of himself. No more muscles. No more cool haircut. I also noticed that he didn't have any friends. This was foreign to me because I always had a lot of friends.

I learned that he was super shy in high school, and college wasn't for him. I guess my daddy was right. Meanwhile I was making tons of friends in the car business. I had also not given up on my education. I started taking paralegal courses at Penn State in Lancaster... on top of working full-time with a part-time job on Saturdays. I even met a friend in class.

I didn't have a wedding dress or the money to buy one as we were saving everything for the house. One day when I went to work, one of the women had organized a wedding shower. All the mechanics and salespeople bought me gifts and a cake. I was so surprised! The finance manager even gave me this white sundress I could wear to the wedding. It was so sweet for all those (mostly) men to do that for me.

The big day came and we drove down to Maryland. As I was crossing the street, I dropped Todd's wedding band. I paused a moment, staring at it rolling away as if in trance. *This is a sign, Reesy.* Perhaps it was some angel whispering to me, *"You really shouldn't be marrying this man. You can still turn back."* As usual, immaturity took over. I picked up the ring and we went into the little church and got married.

Afterward I didn't feel any different. I was now tied to this man forever and determined to have my fairytale life. All I had to do was be the perfect wife. The irony of that day was that I don't remember details of the drive to Maryland, the ceremony, or the person who married us. I couldn't tell you if it was a man or a woman. Hell, I don't even remember the exact date in May. Only that ring rolling across the street.

Then we applied for the mortgage and got approved to buy Todd's parents' house. Once we moved in, that's when things really got tough. Every dime went to pay the mortgage. I worked 8:00 A.M. to 5:30 P.M. at the dealership and all day Saturday at the consignment store, plus school. All work and no play.

We would occasionally do inexpensive things with his parents. I learned quickly that Todd did not like to spend money. We always ate at cheap restaurants and shopped at discount stores. Then one night at a fried chicken drive-thru, he told me I shouldn't order dessert as I could stand to lose a few pounds. What?

He wouldn't hold my hand in public. Yep, no public displays of affection. Heck, there weren't many private displays of affection unless he wanted to have sex. He also hardly said, "I love you." My self-esteem began to plummet. I tried to do anything and everything to prove I was the perfect wife. I made his lunches, cleaned his house, worked out to lose weight, did my makeup and hair every day to look nice for him... yet nothing seemed to move him. That just made me try harder.

I worked to remove the labels that Todd, his family and this place had put on me: "not good enough," "fat," and "dumb Southern girl." But I was working so hard that I didn't recognize the tremendous sadness growing inside of me. My confidence chipped away a little each day. I felt no love at all. My parents may not have been the best, but I always knew they loved me. I had never experienced loneliness before so I didn't recognize it until it was almost too late.

When Mama would call, on a good day I would tell her, "Todd was nice to me today." So many times she would ask, "Do you want me to come and get you?" while I cried to her on the phone. Of course I just said no and kept trying to win his love and affection.

We did everything Todd wanted. He hunted rabbits, squirrels, fox and deer. I never knew there were so many different hunting seasons—small game, bow and arrow, muzzle loading, doe season... and best of all, open deer season. For date night we drove around in his truck in the freezing cold with me holding a spotlight out the window so he could look for deer in the woods. What was I thinking?

I would come home from work and there would be dead animals lined up in the driveway. He even asked me to cook a rabbit. As the "perfect wife," I did... but only once. That was not part of my fairytale life. It was rather disgusting. Sorry to all you hunters out there. Okay, not really sorry.

Things were great at the dealership though. It was my happy place. People were actually nice to me there. Many of them thought of me as their adopted daughter. I was having fun, doing a great job and making friends. In fact, I was promoted to Cashier/Receptionist and got a raise. At least Todd was happy about that.

I also got lots of attention from the guys at work. One of the mechanics worked on my car so that I wouldn't have to pay dealership prices. Another thing Todd liked. I stayed late to talk with this mechanic while he changed my oil. It was nice to have someone be nice to me, so I wanted to prolong going home as long as I could. Over time, the mechanic and I began to confide that neither of us had a happy marriage. We found more and more ways to stay late and talk. This, of course started rumors. I think some of my closer co-workers actually wanted me to have an affair. They knew he was a nice guy. They also had seen a change in me that I refused to recognize.

I did my best to be the happy, bubbly person, but there was sadness behind my eyes. Todd and his family had slowly stolen all of my joy. I felt like a shell of my previous self. But I didn't really recognize it. I just knew I had to keep working. I could not fail. I certainly couldn't go back to North Carolina. Remember the whole quit college, broke up with high school boyfriend and let's not forget the money stuff with my parents? I had to keep trying. I had no other choice, right?

There was also a salesman who worked across the street in the used car department. His name was Eric and I was in awe of him. He would find reasons to walk over to the service department where I was sitting, or make up questions in order to call my phone extension. He was unlike anyone I had known. Larger than life. Broad shoulders, dark hair and striking blue eyes, with one of those business-in-the-front, party-in-the-back haircuts. Don't judge. It was 1989. You really had to be there to appreciate it.

Anyway, he wore double-breasted suits every day, and a black onyx ring that I found particularly attractive. I hadn't really known too many guys who wore jewelry. It fascinated me. Eric would walk into the service department like he owned the place, cocky with just the right amount of arrogance.

He exuded confidence and charisma. I thought, *Wow, this guy is like something out of a movie.* He epitomized my idea of the perfect bachelor. And because I answered the phone, I discovered that lots of girls called him too. He was clearly a ladies' man. The mechanic was nice and sweet, but Eric had the air of a "bad boy" and "super cool guy" which I liked. A lot. I didn't pay attention to the rumors that he had a bad temper. After all, I had been incorrectly labeled my whole life.

All of the people at the car business knew things at home were bad. Too many days I came to work with eyes red from crying. Being the friends that they were, some of my coworkers found a way to allow me and the mechanic to be alone at the finance manager's townhouse, under the guise of her teaching me her chili recipe. I think they all just wanted to see me happy and back to my old bubbly self.

So there I was, alone in the kitchen chatting away with the mechanic when boom, he kissed me—the sweetest kiss I felt since my high school sweetheart. Nothing else happened. But it reminded me of what I was missing at home. I finally began to seriously question my marriage. I also started to take a look in the mirror. It wasn't good. I looked the same, maybe even a little better. Yet, there was something missing. I started to see the glimpse of emptiness that was taking over and probably what all my friends were seeing.

I also started to get more and more curious about the used car guy. I mean, the mechanic was nice and sweet, but he was also married. I didn't want to be responsible for breaking up someone else's marriage, even as mine was falling apart. But the used car guy was single and available... and intriguing. He became increasingly creative in ways to come visit the service department to see me in person. Then I got another promotion— Service Secretary—and another nice raise. Something for Todd to love about me.

27 | Bat Shit Crazy

Todd's mother thought it was her job to tell me how to dress, what colors were best for me, and where she thought I should work instead of the dealership. She had her "colors read" and apparently she was a "winter," which meant she looked good in primary colors like black and red. She somehow decided I was a "fall" and should wear olive green and peach. If I wore one of "her colors" she would point it out and reprimand me. What a fucking psycho!

The dad seemed to get creepier and creepier. It was just that feeling you get when someone looks at you like they want to eat you for supper. I was leery of being alone with him. Every time he got near me, the mom would also seem to get uncomfortable and try her best to find a way to separate him from me.

About this time, Todd's sister Connie got married. She wore glasses over her deep-set, squinty green eyes. She had several moles that stuck out, round and bulbous and about the size of large peas. There was something just off and awkward about her.

I always try to find something pretty about everyone—maybe their hands, smile, personality, something—but this gal truly didn't have a thing. I was especially looking since she asked me to be in her wedding, and also to do her makeup and hair on her wedding day.

She was marrying a guy who was surprisingly attractive. It seemed an odd match to me. He may have been gay because he did act quite feminine, though not all gay men are feminine and not all feminine men are gay. I just couldn't figure out this match. If she was a 3 on a scale of 1 to 10, he was a solid 9, tall with nice eyes and a great smile. He also had a lot more personality than Connie and was much less socially awkward. I know I sound judgy. Maybe opposites really do attract.

I had only met Connie the previous summer and we hadn't spent time together. I awkwardly agreed to be her maid of honor because she didn't have many friends. To demonstrate how "special" I was to her and how important it was for me to be her maid of honor (insert sarcasm here) at the last minute, she changed her mind. She informed me her fiancé's best man's girlfriend was replacing me. Why? Because her fiancé's best man wanted to walk his girlfriend down the aisle, not me. More likely it was the girlfriend who didn't want him to walk me down the aisle. Whatever the case, clearly Connie had no idea what it meant to be a maid of honor.

Quite honestly it was so strange, I decided to just go with it. It really didn't break my heart. I was still expected to be in the wedding and do her hair and makeup, even though Todd wasn't in the wedding party. But if I would have said no, it would have given Todd's mother one more reason to dislike me.

So I focused on how the hell I was going to make this girl look beautiful on her wedding day. Not a job for the faint of heart. When she took those glasses off, I literally had to grind my teeth so my mouth wouldn't gape open. I mean, she didn't have eyelids unless she closed her eyes completely, so there wasn't anywhere to put eye shadow. And the giant mole was totally in the way of eyeliner. I was going to have to silently talk myself through this. Remember, I was barely 19 years old. In spite of all the challenges, I worked my magic. She looked as lovely as possible. Everyone said I did a good job.

The bridesmaid dresses were a light shade of pink in a Southern style with a big skirt that required a hoop underneath. It was as if the dress was made for me. The color, the style fit me perfectly. The other bridesmaids were as awkward and backwards as Connie. They didn't know how to do makeup. I'm also pretty sure none of them had ever seen a curling iron.

After the ceremony we walked through the receiving line. Todd's aunts and uncles all told me how beautiful I looked. I thanked them politely and kept moving. During the reception, Todd's mother came up to me and said in this accusatory voice, "What are you doing? Are you trying to steal the show from Connie?" What the fuck! I felt the lump in my throat. I held my breath and the tears back the best I could and walked away.

I was so confused. I had done everything I could to help Connie. When Todd walked over and saw me crying, he asked what was wrong. He at least had the balls to tell his mother how upset I was and that her behavior had been inappropriate. She came over and apologized, but the damage was done. I hadn't felt comfortable with her before and I sure as hell wasn't going to feel comfortable with her after that. I just wanted to avoid this bat shit crazy lady.

North Carolina kept calling my name.

After the wedding I was still sad and lonely. People would jokingly ask me as a southerner if I was still fighting the war. It took me a while to understand that they meant the Civil War. How fucking stupid! Once I told one of Todd's cousins as he was checking out at the dealership that we were "kin." He looked at me like I had three heads. "Kin... you know? Related." I truly thought I had moved to hell. God forbid you touch one of them or get physically close. In the South that's just how you talk and get to know someone. These people acted like I was diseased.

Finally I learned that Todd's "Dad" was not his biological father. Apparently, that person had left his mother when Todd was very young, and the new guy adopted Todd. The adoptive father and Todd's biological mother then had his sister. But Todd never spoke of any of this. These people weren't exactly "sharers."

One day I found myself at home before Todd returned from work. His father stopped by, though I don't recall the reason. Then out of nowhere, he reached out and grabbed my boob. Well, really it was more like honking my boob, if you know what I mean. We were standing in the living room and without warning he just honked away on my left breast.

I was so startled that I just stood there frozen. He was more than six feet tall and roughly 240 pounds. He could easily overpower me. My heart and brain raced a mile a minute to come up with all the kinds of things this man could potentially do to me. I also was in shock. Part of me wondered if I had imagined it.

Finally, after what seemed like an eternity, I straightened my back and attempted to stand a bit taller. In as stern of a voice as I could find, I said, "Don't you ever do that again! I mean it!" He shrugged as if to say, *"Oh well,"* and then left. Yep. No apology. He didn't even seem to feel embarrassed. He simply walked back home.

I stood in my living room shaking from head to toe, trying to process what had just happened. I knew I had to tell Todd, but I couldn't figure out how. Maybe this was why his mom had acted so weird. Perhaps he'd done this type of stuff before. Once the shock of it all started to wear off and the tears began to flow, I couldn't stop them. I was scared and shaking. What if he came back before Todd got home? How could he have done that to me?

When Todd walked in the door he found me on the couch bawling my eyes out. I knew I should tell him and yet I was afraid. After all, it would be his dad's word against mine. His mother already thought I was some sort of Southern slut who cornered her son into marriage. Todd kept asking me what was wrong. I had to tell him something. Before I could stop it, I just blurted it out. "Your dad grabbed my boob!"

"He did what?" Todd's voice quivered. So I had to tell him the whole story, explaining what happened in all of two seconds. "We were standing right here in the living room and he just reached out and grabbed my left boob." It was interesting how the event took only two seconds yet the incident felt like two hours. The memory has lasted a lifetime.

The good news was that Todd believed me and he was furious. He didn't even question it, so perhaps his dad had done things like this before. All I could hope was that it wouldn't make life any harder than it already was. I was sure his mom would pretend that she didn't believe it, and that his dad would deny it or say it was a misunderstanding. I was also pretty sure Todd would attempt a physical altercation with his father. But since his dad was so much larger than Todd, I wasn't sure who would win that battle.

Todd headed toward the door. I grabbed his arm and begged him not to go. "Please, please don't go over there." I explained how I had told his dad not to ever do that again and how he'd left without any further fondling. I told Todd that it would just make everything weird and awkward. Finally, he agreed he wouldn't say or do anything about the "incident"... but we definitely would not be going to family functions any time soon! Quite honestly, I was a bit surprised at Todd's anger. At this point, I didn't think he really cared enough to be that mad. Maybe...no, Todd was still Todd.

28 | The Straw that Broke the Camel's Back

Growing up, I thought it was super important to always get a kiss and an "I love you" before leaving the house. My parents may not have been the best, but at least I felt loved. At the end of every phone call, or when you came in the door, we told each other, "I love you." Mom and Dad always kissed and said, "I love you," when they parted. It was what I expected.

My life with Todd was not a fairytale romance. He told me I needed to lose weight. I weighed 125 pounds and wore a size 8, sometimes a 6; the men at work didn't seem to think I was fat. Todd rarely showed me affection. Definitely not in public. Only occasionally did he tell me he loved me and never complimented me.

I wasn't allowed to have decorative things on the counters of our home, the house I helped him buy. His idea of a date was going to the drive-up dairy palace, having a cheap chicken dinner, and for dessert we would go spotlighting for deer. His dad was obviously a pervert. Let's not forget his bitch of a mother. I truly felt I was living in hell.

My body was riddled with stress and anxiety. I wore an aura of sadness as my coat. I called my mother crying and could hear the worry in her voice. Again and again, she would ask if I wanted her to come get me. Of course I knew she didn't have the means to do so, since more than once she'd asked me to send her money, which I did. Plus, I didn't want to go back to that life and have to start all over.

The Reesy I had been was slowly disappearing. I was losing my spark, my essence... drowning in a life of sadness, disappointment and desperation. I didn't smile. I didn't stand as tall.

I did, however, keep hoping that Todd would start to love me more if I just kept trying. I would look better, do everything I could to please him. It was hard work and it took a huge toll on me. I didn't notice that I wasn't eating much.

Work was my safe haven. Everyone was nice to me there and I enjoyed my newfound friends. A new gal started working in the service department. She was a little older than me. We became fast friends as I transferred interest in the mechanic to the used car guy. The mechanic must've gotten the hint because he and the new gal became quite friendly. She was also in a bad marriage. When they finally got together, I was happy for them. They're still married today.

The used car guy continued to find ways to call my phone and stop by the service department. Every day after work, I had to walk across the street to my car. I would find out later, that once when I was walking across that street, he told his used car buddies that he was going to "marry that girl" one day. How was he going to do that? I was already married.

I hated going home. A group of my co-workers asked me to go out for drinks one night. I was only 20 so I wasn't sure how I would get served. They told me not to worry because I was with them. Also, one of the ladies lived near me and agreed to drive me home afterward. Finally, something social to do. Most importantly, something that didn't include Todd's family.

Continuing to be a good wife, I asked Todd if it was okay for me to go. He didn't seem to have a problem. I was so excited! I told him I would be home by 11:00. It was to be a few new car salesmen and couple of the office ladies. The used car guy would not be in attendance. It didn't matter. I was going out with friends for probably the first time since I had moved to Pennsylvania. I was ecstatic, to say the least!

We went to a fancy bar, or at least what I thought was fancy by my limited experience. I got served. They didn't even card me! I was having a great time when I realized it was almost 11:00.

There was no way I was going to make it home by the time I had told Todd.

I was raised that if you were going to be late, you needed to let the person know who was waiting for you. I wouldn't want him to worry. It was respectful. I asked the lady who lived near me if we could head out due to the hour. I used a pay phone... at that time it was a booth with a phone that you inserted a dime or two to make a call. Todd answered and I told him I would be home by 11:30. He sounded strangely irritated. What was new? A feeling of dread swelled the pit of my stomach. Something was off. The closer I got to home, the more nervous I felt. Hadn't I done the right thing? I wasn't drunk or acting crazy.

We arrived at my house and I thanked the lady who drove me home. I hesitantly walked inside. I had really hoped Todd was asleep. No such luck. There he was standing in the kitchen waiting. He looked angry in a way I had never seen before. His shoulders were all tensed up, a grimace on his face. I immediately began to apologize for being late. I explained how time had gotten away from me.

He started yelling. Apparently, my thoughtful phone call had woken him. He was pissed! I began my usual dance of how sorry I was for waking him. I just didn't want him to worry. He stormed off to our bedroom. I followed, dancing all the harder and begging him not to be mad at me. I also decided to be a little assertive. I boldly said that he had no right to be angry. Whoops, that was a bad idea.

He stomped into the bedroom. With rage in his eyes, he whirled around and threw me up against the door. His physical aggression took me off guard. Quite honestly, I would have never expected that. He pinned me against the door with one hand and wrapped the other around my throat. I was dangling like some sort of rag doll. Was this really happening?

I went into shock. Was he actually going to hit me? My heart started racing. I had never been hit by a man, and Todd was a trained Marine. He could do some real damage.

He gritted his teeth and his eyes seemed to glaze over. "You woke me and I have to get up at 5:00 A.M." He held me there for what seemed like an hour. I waited, holding my breath for the punch to come, or the choking. Then he just dropped me and stomped over to the bed.

After the initial shock wore off, I started to sob. So many thoughts went through my mind. I was confused. I had tried to do the right thing. Then he put his hands on me. Was this the beginning of more violence? I shook uncontrollably.

He must have felt badly because he later apologized. I was too shocked to really hear what he was saying. I think he tried to calm me down. It was a blur. My world was spinning out of control and I couldn't process what had just happened. I must have scared him because he did console me and calmed me down.

We talked and I apologized... What the fuck? That shit would not happen today! I would have kicked him in the groin, punched him, bit him, something. Not then. It was "my fault." I shouldn't have called. I shouldn't have been late. Maybe I shouldn't have gone at all. Afterward I barely slept that night. I lay sleepless trying to keep myself from shaking.

The next morning I got up at the same time as Todd. I hadn't slept anyway so why fight it? There was an eerie silence between us. I started to understand he should apologize for putting his hands on me. I should be mad, not him.

He knew how important it was for me that he tell me he loved me before he left each day. It was a small thing. That morning I was getting ready in the bathroom when I heard his truck start. What? No "Goodbye?" No "I love you?" Not even a "Kiss my ass." He just got in his truck and left without saying a word. I was more than hurt. I was devastated. Although I didn't know it at that time, it was the official moment I broke.

29 | The Off Switch

I cried while I got ready for work. I cried the whole thirty-minute commute. Then something interesting happened. Ever so slowly, the switch began to turn off. I wasn't sure at the time what was happening. All I knew was I dried my eyes in the parking lot, touched up my makeup, then got out of my car without a tear.

I walked across the lot in a zombie-like state. I really don't know how I made it to my desk, completely and utterly numb. There were no more tears left. Somehow, I completed my work duties. It was as if some higher power carried me through. God took me that day. All the pain, hurt and disappointment that man and his family had put me through had finally flipped my switch. All the labels of being too fat, not pretty enough, not good enough, not anything at all... left me an empty shell of who I once had been. Not an ounce of self-esteem remained.

The used car guy, Eric, checked on me several times. I gave him the shortened version of what happened the night before. Everyone else knew there was something wrong. There would be no change in my facial expression, but a single tear would roll down my cheek. Mechanically I dabbed it away as if it were an imperfection in my makeup. A sort of calm settled over me as I welcomed the numbness like a warm, safe blanket.

I couldn't be hurt in the world of numb. I didn't know or care how long I was going to be there. All I knew was feeling nothing was better than anything I had felt in a very long time. I don't think I ate that day. The world of numb feels no hunger. I didn't notice the day or the hour. I robotically did my work.

Mid-afternoon something began pulling me away from my safe new world... a nagging feeling of apprehension and dread. I realized that I didn't want to go home. I absolutely 100% did not want to go home. I couldn't go there. I just couldn't. I wanted the day to keep going. I wanted to stay in my world of numb. But time did what it does. It passed.

I usually got off work at 5:30. As other employees began to leave, I didn't know what to do. I called my mother. Bless her heart. (That's a real "bless her heart" versus the one Southern people say after having said something rude, as if that erases the shittiness of what you just said.) Here my poor mother was, 400 miles away without any means to get to me, and without knowing anyone she could call to help me, yet I was calling and telling her I didn't want to go home to Todd.

The minute I heard my mother's voice, the world of numb disappeared and I began to sob uncontrollably. I can't imagine how helpless she must have felt. The more upset I was, the more upset she became. As usual I had to be the parent and calm down, or she would have had a nervous breakdown. Never mind that I was pretty close to my own.

About that time, Eric showed up. I assured my mother that I would be fine. I would go home to Todd for the moment. I explained to her that I wasn't sure of the timing, but that I would call her when I got there. I told her I had a friend with me to ease her worry.

Like a knight in shining armor, Eric put his arm around me. He told me everything would be all right. I told him I didn't want to go home. He asked if I would like to take a drive. Wanting to delay the inevitable as long as possible, I agreed. I was willing to do just about anything to avoid going home and seeing Todd.

Because I was going to be late... and again because of those Southern roots in my soul, I called Todd to let him know I wasn't coming home right away. It was clear he was caught off guard by my calm voice. I am sure he thought he would be getting the same old let me dance-harder-and-be-nicer-so-he-will-love-me gal. What he got was the my-switch-is-completely-turned-off-and-I-don't-give-a-shit-if-you're-mad gal. Calm, cool and collected. I didn't give him much time to say anything except okay before I hung up the phone.

I picked up my purse and Eric led me right outside into his demo car, a pretty red Toyota Celica. I didn't know where he told his boss he was going. I didn't care. All I knew was I was in a car with a man who was being nice to me. Really nice. I felt safe and comforted. I didn't know where he was taking me, and I didn't care... as long as it wasn't back to my house of horrors.

As we drove, I told him all the horrible things Todd had done to me. I let go and cried. Eric told me I was beautiful and that Todd didn't deserve me. I let myself soak up every word. I let myself feel safe.

He drove up to a group of townhouses and said, "Mine's the one on the end. Do you want to come in for a while?" I knew I would have to go back home sometime, just not right that minute. I agreed to go in for a little.

Eric was from Johnstown, a town in western Pennsylvania, not exactly a thriving metropolis. He lived in this townhouse with one of his best friends, Tom—nicknamed Tuba. All those Johnstown boys seemed to have nicknames. Anyway, it was quite the bachelor pad, completely open space with a staircase that led to two bedrooms side by side, each with its own bathroom.

Since Tuba was home, Eric said, "Why don't we go up to my room?" I felt awkward meeting his friend with my bloodshot eyes and tear-stained face. Still living in the world of numb and not wanting to go home, I complied.

Being the late '80s and with Eric as the quintessential bachelor, there in the middle of his bedroom was a giant waterbed, neatly made with cool modern sheets and a comforter. He sat on the edge of that bed, took my hand and had me sit on his knee. I didn't fight any of it. He probably could've led me anywhere. It just felt good to have someone be nice to me and to give me attention. Let's pretend the "numb" led me right to his inviting lap. He was a big guy so I fit rather comfortably.

He continued to tell me how beautiful I was. I didn't even care whether he meant it. My self-esteem was so hungry for something positive, I breathed it all in. Gently he lifted my chin, as if in some romantic movie, and he kissed me. I shifted right into the world of fantasy. I kissed him right back. Okay, so I kissed him a couple of times.

Being a gentleman, he said we had to stop. In an instant, the world of numb came rushing back. I reluctantly said I did need to get home, but truth be told, I didn't want to leave. I would have stayed there forever just to keep from having to go home. I didn't even know this guy. He was kind of cute and he was being super sweet. Then I remembered I was married. "I gotta go," I said.

He took me back to the dealership. We seemed to get there much faster than when we left. That's the funny thing about time. One minute can feel like forever, or forever can feel like one minute.

I thanked him for being so nice to me. I wasn't crying anymore. I had calmed down a lot. I told him I would talk with him tomorrow. I got into my car and began the thirty-minute journey home. With each mile, more and more dread welled up inside of me. What was I going to do?

30 | I Gotta Go
or It's Gonna Kill Me

Todd was waiting for me when I got home. I wished he had been out somewhere. He tried to be nice but I couldn't even stand the sight of him. My whole body shook. He had the audacity to ask if I wanted to have sex. Are you fucking kidding me? What was worse was that he didn't even call it making love. He said, "Do you want to play?" Maybe he thought that if I agreed to have sex with him that I would be okay. Not.

He didn't know what to do with me. I wasn't crying or yelling. I had returned to the world of numb. I wouldn't eat. I had zero appetite. I didn't even know how I was going to sleep in the same bed with him. I asked him for a couple of cigarettes then locked myself in our extra bathroom, filled the tub with scalding hot water and got in. I lit a cigarette, closed my eyes and tried to steady my nerves.

I wanted to be alone. My hands trembled. The thought of crawling into bed with him made my stomach churn. So it went every night for many nights. I would go to work, come home, take a bath, smoke and find a way to sneak into bed.

I wanted to go back to North Carolina so badly. I wanted to escape that horrible place. Eric checked on me every day which was super sweet. He even said he would help me move out. But where could I go? I couldn't continue to live the way I was living.

There was an older lady who worked with me in the service department, divorced with two daughters of her own. Apparently, my mom called her and asked her to watch out for me. This woman asked if I wanted to move in with her and pay a small rent. She said she wasn't home very often so I could have the run of the place. I felt like I didn't have much choice. I had to get out of that house with Todd or I was going to have a nervous breakdown... if that wasn't already underway.

I told Eric it would be better if two of his friends helped me instead of him, since Eric was seriously angry at Todd and I didn't want a fight to break out. He rounded up two of his Johnstown buddies—Fudd, like the cartoon character Elmer Fudd (he liked to hunt), and Rick H.

I told Todd that I had to move out for a while. I was petrified he might be physically violent with me again, so I didn't tell him that I would never, ever be back. He didn't argue. He didn't even try to stop me. Perhaps he thought I would come running back. He didn't think I was capable. Little did he know that for my whole life I had taken care of business. At least my dysfunctional childhood paid off in this situation.

I am sure he saw me as weak since most of our time together I spent crying over his nonattention and his beating the shit out of my self-esteem. Boy, was he wrong. He didn't know me at all. In addition, he didn't know that I had the emotional support of Eric.

We set it up so one day after work, Fudd and Rick would follow me to the house and load my stuff into Fudd's truck. I didn't plan on taking much. The material things meant nothing to me. That house held nothing but bad memories. I had spent my young life learning how to start over every time we moved. Again, my dysfunctional upbringing actually benefited me.

I packed up my clothes and that same china. Todd said not one word and neither did I. I really couldn't believe I was doing it. My plan was to move out, save enough money for a divorce, then move back to North Carolina. It had to be better than this.

I drove away and didn't look back. The switch was flipped. Whatever feelings I had for Todd were gone. As I drove away I felt a sense of relief come over me like a ton of bricks had been lifted. I had lost the pureness of naivete. I no longer believed in fairytale lives. Or at least I no longer believed that I deserved one.

Todd and his family stole that from me. The labels coursed through my veins like a virus. I wasn't good enough, pretty enough, skinny enough. I had thoughts like, "If only I had been a better wife," "If only I had lost weight," "If only I was prettier."

A deep sadness went straight to my core. I had to survive. I could only take life day by day, hour by hour and sometimes minute by minute. I lived with the lady from work for a while then I moved in with Ann, Todd's friend's now ex-fiancée. They had broken up and she was living in a trailer and needed a roommate.

One day I got a call from Todd's mother... ugh! She used this fake, sweet sounding voice which I had never heard before. She shared with me how her and Vernon (Todd's dad) had their problems early on and she separated from him for a bit. But he'd made all these changes and everything was wonderful. I wanted to say, "Oh really, Darlene. Did you know your husband recently tried to feel me up and is quite the pervert?" That probably wouldn't have gone over too well. The gal I am today would have absolutely said that. Instead, the numb, beaten down girl I had become thanked her for calling and said that I would consider her advice. But no way in hell was I going back. Again, the switch was flipped.

While Todd never called me directly, he did make the infamous call to my mother. Once again, she had to explain to a boy that it was over. He had fucked up. She asked him, "How many times did Reesy talk with you?" He replied, "Lots." She told him, "I'm sorry, Todd, but it's over." He said, "I will never find anyone who loved me the way she did." Wow, really? What about loving me, asshole? Okay, sorry. Not sorry.

I don't believe he ever remarried. I saw his parents several years later. They shared that he had a girlfriend, and that she loved to go fishing and hunting with him. Oh, goody. All the while Todd's dad was eyeing me up and down. Once again, the gal I am today would have certainly said more. I would probably have made some ambiguous comment with enough question marks behind it to make good old Darlene ask a few uncomfortable questions to creepy daddy.

I now know that I never really loved Todd. Not the way you should anyway. I was in love with the idea of being in love. I was in love with being rescued from the hell I was living in with my parents. He really didn't stand a chance. He was no superhero and that was what I was looking for. That was what I needed. I used to sometimes wonder if I would still be with him if he had stayed in the military. He was so much better when he was away from his family and their craziness.

At the end, I knew my father had been right. Todd wasn't as smart as me. As much as I tried, we were never going to like the same things. More importantly, Todd had done a bang-up job of making me feel inferior. Perhaps he wanted me to be less... so he could be more.

31 | Nervous Breakdown and Visit Home

Since my separation was so new, Eric and I decided to keep whatever was happening between the two of us on the low-down. I still had plans to get divorced as soon as I saved enough money. Then I would move back to North Carolina. In the meantime, Eric was a great distraction. He was nice to me and made me feel pretty again.

Our first date was to Olive Garden in York. We didn't want anyone to see us in Lancaster. He held the door and pulled out the chair for me. It had been so long since someone was nice to me like that. Was this real life? Todd had started out pretty nice too.

Christmas was coming and I had luckily saved up vacation time so I could drive south and spend the holiday with my family. Eric was going back to his hometown as well, but asked if he could call me while I was home. I agreed that would be fine. I didn't believe he would actually call though. I really didn't believe anything any man said.

I set out for my long drive—400 miles over seven hours if traffic was good. It gave me a lot of time to think. I didn't realize how low I had gotten. I remember reaching down to scratch my tummy... *What the...?* My tummy was flat as a pancake. My whole life, no matter how low my weight was, I had never had a completely flat stomach. Yet, there it was, flat as could be. As I drove I surveyed the rest of my body and realized I had lost a lot of weight.

When I walked in the door at my parents' house, I saw the look of shock on my mother's face. I assured her that I was fine. I was so much better now that I was away from Todd. She said I looked gaunt and my eyes were almost glazed over. Her little girl had returned as some sort of skinny zombie.

I told her about Eric and my plan to move back home once I was divorced. In the meantime, there wasn't anything wrong with having a little fun. This new guy took me to nice restaurants, complimented me all the time and sent me flowers. I was going to soak it up until I moved. Plus, I didn't believe he meant any of it. I no longer believed in true romance. He was just a distraction.

Of course, there wasn't any money for Christmas presents but I didn't care. I was home where people truly loved me and I felt safe. I ran into Teddy at the mall. What a surprise. At least that was the look on his face. He invited me to come over and have dinner with him and his mother. I thought why not? I was a free woman after all. I had learned in one of my paralegal classes that Pennsylvania law said that once you were separated you could screw whoever you wanted to and nothing would impact your divorce. Not that I was planning on screwing Teddy. It was just nice to know I was free to choose.

I had a lovely time at dinner. Teddy said his mother had always thought of me as her favorite. He was as sweet as ever. When I got ready to leave, he stood by me at his front door. We started getting closer and closer and then, just like that, he kissed me in the nicest way. I soaked in the sweetness and familiarity. I began to remember what it was like to have someone want to kiss me. I felt a tinge of guilt because of Eric. But he wasn't my boyfriend. Oddly, I felt absolutely no guilt for Todd. So, I kissed Teddy back and then I left.

Surprisingly, when I got home, Eric called. He actually called me in North Carolina! I was happy about that. Not the way I would have once been happy. Nonetheless, it was super sweet of him. We had a lovely conversation—one where I definitely did not admit to my kissing encounter with Teddy.

32 | Divorce, Romance and Secrets

The holiday week came and went way too fast. It was time for me to head back to Pennsylvania. I promised my mother everything was going to be fine and that I would be home soon.

I found out later that she cried for days. My Aunt Jane claimed she had tear-stained eyes and devastation written all over her. My aunt was so concerned she finally had to say to my mother, "Gladys, she isn't dead." It's all about perspective. As a parent now, I can't imagine how hard it was to let me go. But she had no means to keep me there.

Back in Pennsylvania, I found Eric to be the most romantic man. Then again, I was comparing him to Todd so there was nowhere to go but up. He sent me flowers every week, sometimes twice. He took me to nice restaurants and the compliments never stopped.

I remember the first time he told me he loved me. We had been out to dinner. I wore a pretty green dress with black floral print. My hair and makeup were terrific and even I thought I looked nice. Playfully, he threw me down on the bed and looked me right in the eyes. "I love you."

Of course, I responded with "I love you too," even though I wasn't sure. I just knew it felt good. I drank in every drop of the romance. My self-esteem had taken such a beating. I wanted to believe I was lovable and not some horribly disfigured woman who deserved nothing.

Eric was like a warm, comfortable blanket that I couldn't get enough of. He was tall and big so I felt safe. But we still hadn't told anyone at work. I was more than aware of what waited for me back in North Carolina. Nothing had changed financially for my parents. It would be the same old story in the same old town.

So when things started going so well with Eric, I considered staying in Pennsylvania a little longer.

It was hard to keep the romance a secret from friends at work. I mean, when you get a dozen roses every week, people start to question. Poor Eric had to sit in the used car department and listen to all the perverted things the salesmen wanted to do to me, but not say a word.

Finally, one day he had enough of this talk. One of the guys said something crude, and Eric replied, "You better watch it. That's my girlfriend." Jaws dropped and then high fives started. All of his work buddies were happy for him. They couldn't believe he had settled down to one girl. To be honest, I didn't trust his loyalty, but I didn't trust anything at that point.

I decided to pawn my engagement ring to pay for the divorce from Todd. A lovely lady in one of my paralegal classes introduced me to the attorney she worked for who happened to specialize in divorces. I got $450 for the ring which would cover costs as long as there wasn't any fighting over assets.

Assets? The house contained nothing but bad memories for me. All I wanted was my car and my personal items. Mama used to say, "You can always get more stuff." She knew that all too well. My freedom and sanity were way more valuable than anything in that house. I was sure that Todd would not contest the divorce. I filed in April of 1990. I was 21 years old.

As word got around at work that I was dating Eric, some of my "father figures" were not happy. Eric had quite the reputation and they all thought I deserved better. But I believed he was just fighting the labels that had been put on him. One gentleman, John, assured me I could date whoever I wanted and that I shouldn't settle for Eric. "You just got out of a bad relationship. Why be in a hurry to get into another?" I know he meant well. I couldn't see it though. Eric had treated me better than anyone. He seemed perfect.

By the way, no one is perfect. I made the mistake of sharing this man's words with Eric. What happened next completely took me by surprise. John was the new car sales manager with a lot of clout, while Eric was merely a used car salesperson. Eric went after John like a bull headed for a red cape. I could hear yelling and see red faces. I was so upset. Why had I told him?

I had never seen someone so upset. *Wow, he must really like me.* I wasn't paying attention to the anger and rage Eric spewed at John. I was too busy with my heart melting over this manly gesture.

John stood his ground though. Something about "nice girl" and "you better treat her right," and then Eric with "I care about her" and "it's none of your business." In the end, they all calmed down and I privately apologized to John for Eric's outburst. John gave his fatherly speech again; I didn't pay attention to a word of it. All I knew was a man had just risked his job by defending how much he cared about me.

Maybe this was what love looked and felt like. I had done it wrong the last time. That's all. This time would be different. Right?

33 | Turning 21, a New Man and a New Family

I was in complete awe of Eric, and had zero thoughts of Todd. In fact, after the move-out day, I never saw or spoke to Todd again. Eric was the knight in shining armor of my dreams. Slowly I regained my self-esteem. I found my mojo.

Eric took me to meet his family the weekend of my 21st birthday, barely two months after I left Todd. Eric was the youngest of five, with two sisters and two brothers. His parents had recently separated after many years of struggles. Fun fact (or not really): each of Eric's siblings except for one had been divorced. *Hmmm... should I be worried?* But I was blinded by "love."

Eric's youngest sister and I hit it off right away. His older brother, the wife and their infant child were also visiting that same weekend. There was a first birthday party for the son of Eric's oldest sister. Eric's other brother lived with a wife and didn't have any children. I would be meeting the whole clan at the birthday party. No pressure. The good news was that his family was very accepting and didn't seem to judge me at all.

Eric told them he believed I was "the one" and so they treated me that way. Note to all women: if you want to know how a man is going to treat you, watch how he treats his mother.

Eric, his youngest sister and his friend Rick took me to a ski resort. Technically my birthday was on Sunday and this was Saturday, but luckily, no one at the resort cared that I was still hours away from legal drinking age. There was live music and dancing. Eric's sister really liked drinking Alabama slammers. By the end of the night, she and I were smoking cigarettes and saying how much we liked each other.

When we left the resort, none of us should have been driving. Eric took the wheel. It was after 2:00 A.M. and we were starving. Funny how alcohol does that. We ordered a large pizza and wings—the perfect after-drinking snack.

Eric's mom still lived in the large family home. We gathered in the basement and weren't exactly quiet. The next thing I know a loud female voice yelled, "What the fuck are you guys doing down there? You woke the baby!" *Oh shit!* We all froze. I was pretty sure from the sound of Eric's sister-in-law's voice, she was completely prepared to kill us all.

After she left, everyone started to giggle, but we attempted to be quiet. We thought we were doing a pretty good job. Apparently not. Here she came again, this time more pissed than the last. I decided to be the voice of reason and suggested that we go to bed. *How was I going to face that woman tomorrow?* Eric seemed completely unconcerned.

The next morning, I sheepishly got up for breakfast. Boy, did my head hurt. I was sure I would be vomiting at any moment but I was determined not to throw up. *Just breathe, Reesy,* I kept saying to myself.

I ate very little for breakfast. We still had to go to a one-year-old's birthday party. *Please don't let me throw up in front of Eric's whole family.*

Thanks goodness we only had to make a brief appearance. We cut the cake, sang happy birthday, and headed back to Lancaster. Eric considered the trip a success. But I wasn't so sure after the whole be-quiet-or-I-will-kill-you-incident.

34 | Work Is Great and a Whole New Kind of Romance

I got another promotion at work—Service Secretary—along with another raise. I was still taking paralegal classes at Penn State. When the finance and insurance position became available, I thought it would be a great fit, meeting each client to complete all the paperwork. It included working with banks to get loans approved, and offering customers extended warranties, loan insurance and various other products and services. The gal currently doing the job made it look quite glamorous. It would also mean a lot more money. I mean a lot more. Like double what I was currently making.

I was told that it was too soon after my last promotion. They probably thought I was young and inexperienced. That was okay because I still wanted to be a paralegal. My new friend from class told me there was an opening at the law firm where she worked. I applied for the job. With her recommendation and a great interview, I was offered the position. I was so excited! I had a great boyfriend and now a new job in the field I wanted to be in. Thoughts of going back to North Carolina faded.

I decided this time this relationship would be different. Rule #1: I would date someone at least two years before getting married. Rule #2: I would definitely live with the person before I married them... a painful lesson! Rule #3: I would never tell that person what to do. Todd and his mother had done that too much to me, and I was not about to do that to someone else. Rule #4: I would never let someone treat me the way Todd did.

Eric's romantic treatment continued. I stayed with him almost every night, only going back to my apartment to get fresh clothes. He had so many friends, and we had a great time. They visited every weekend. Eric did like to smoke weed regularly though. And by regularly, I mean almost daily. Okay, not a big deal. After all, it seemed like almost everyone smoked weed where I came from.

Keep in mind Rule #3. I was not going to tell him what to do. It was the fun life I had hoped for my 20s—romantic dinners, partying on the weekends and Eric right by my side adoring me all the while.

One weekend Eric and his roommate decided they were going to throw another party. He told me there would be booze, weed and cocaine. Wait, what? I had never done or been around cocaine. I was concerned, but... Rule #3. I was not going to tell him what to do. Or not to do.

I had no idea what cocaine even looked like. I knew it was a stimulant. I knew you snorted it. That was the extent of my knowledge. I presumed it would be similar to marijuana. Boy, was I naïve.

At a young age I'd decided never to do any hardcore drugs because of my Aunt Recie's death. Plus I didn't have the stomach for anything you had to put up your nose or shoot in your arms. Quite frankly it scared the shit out of me.

I was way more comfortable with marijuana. I had smoked plenty of it as a teenager and it was, after all, natural. In fact, Eric had a little saying that "Man made alcohol. God made weed. Who do you trust?" Eric and I agreed to respect each other's decisions. I would not be doing any cocaine and he would only do "a little."

There were thirty or more people in that townhouse. The keg was out in the garage. Some people were smoking weed, including me. But Eric and lots of his friends were doing it all. Once the cocaine came out, the atmosphere changed. I thought they'd snort some stuff and be done. Holy shit! Every twenty minutes these guys were snorting more. I know. I know. You are probably thinking, *Wow, you really didn't know anything about cocaine.* Clearly, I did not. They were all doing this weird jaw thing, grinding their teeth, moving their jaws side to side. I didn't understand how a person could drink beer and smoke weed—downers—then sniff cocaine—an intense upper. How could someone's body know what to do? It seemed to me with the uppers and the downers, they should have been sober.

Once they polished off the cocaine, there was another shift in atmosphere. One of the guys developed this crazed look on his face, and said he was going into the city to find some more. He was really determined. Thank goodness Eric stopped him. He was in no condition to be driving. I learned a new term. "That guy was really jonesing for some coke," the other guys said. Boy, was he.

I looked at the clock—3:00 A.M. I was exhausted, but these guys showed no signs of stopping. Again, I know what you're thinking. *That's what cocaine does, Reesy. It keeps you up all hours of the night.* I told Eric that I had to go to bed. He was perfectly fine with that. So up I went.

The next morning was horrible. Many of his friends had spent the night. As each one woke to an awful hangover, I noticed how incredibly grumpy they were. I mean really grumpy. I decided I didn't feel comfortable at all around people doing cocaine. I wasn't judging, but it was too much for me.

Rule #3 came back to mind. I told Eric I wouldn't tell him what to do, but if there was another party where cocaine was going to be happening, I'd just stay home. Eric did what I thought was the sweetest thing. He said, "If you're not comfortable with it, I won't do it anymore." Oh my God! This was true love.

My self-esteem was so low that him giving up cocaine for me was a romantic gesture. He was definitely "the one."

35 | Adult Toys, New Job, New Move and What a Temper

Eric loved boats and decided he wanted to buy one. But his bad driving record, all speeding tickets, meant he couldn't afford the insurance. Literally less than six months into this relationship, I agreed to having the boat put in my name. Eric insisted that he trusted me. Things were moving pretty quickly.

One night in May, Eric and his friend Heidi and another friend were out at the local bar while I was sleeping alone in Eric's waterbed. Around 1:00 A.M. Heidi busted in with Eric's guy friend in tow and jumped into bed with me. "Guess what?" Heidi asked, clearly intoxicated. I had cobwebs in my brain. Before I could even ask, "What?" Heidi said, "Eric's going to ask you to move in with him." Then she kissed me on the cheek and they left the room.

Having overheard the big reveal, Eric came in and asked, "So will you?"

Rule #2 answered for me. "Yes, I will definitely live with you." Lots of kisses ensued. Things were going just as planned. I was doing things differently this time. Well, except that we had only been seeing each other for five months. But Rule #1 only counted time before marriage, not living together (*see Rule #2*).

In May, I moved into the townhouse with Eric and his roommate, who would eventually be moving out. The townhouse was big enough for all of us.

Things were going really well. I started working at the law office. My friend who had helped me get the job also taught aerobics at an all-female gym. The gym was looking for someone to teach step-aerobics and body sculpting. Because of my bubbly personality and cheering experience, I got that job part-time. It was perfect. I started getting into the best shape of my life and was getting paid to do it. Timewise, it also worked out because Eric worked a lot of nights and Saturdays.

When you have a boat in Pennsylvania, you try to use it every single weekend because the season is shorter than in North Carolina. I was in great shape and had a killer tan that year.

As would be normal, when you live with someone, you do begin to see more of their flaws. I finally noticed Eric had quite the temper. Never at me, but I'd seen him use it on his friends. He often bragged how he'd gotten into a fight back in Johnstown with a guy in a parking lot of a pizza place. Apparently the fight was so awesome he got free pizza for a year. "Best fight I ever seen," the owner reportedly said. I have no idea how a fight could earn anyone free pizza, but Eric was super proud of this. Maybe he had earned some of those labels I'd heard about earlier.

When Eric got angry, his face would turn all red. Where normal people might grit their teeth, his tongue would sort of bend out. He'd get loud and curse a lot. If that didn't make the person back down, he'd move in close and puff out his chest, using his height and size to intimidate. But his friends from Johnstown would stand right back up to him. At least for a moment. Eventually, his bullying tactics won out. Otherwise he'd grab hold of the person by their clothes and sometimes by their throat, pushing them up against a wall. It was a terrifying thing to witness.

Despite this, he somehow managed to have lots of friends. A few never evoked his anger. I wasn't sure at first what made those select few immune. Later I figured out that they just didn't put up with his shit. They would have fought back.

The summer of 1990 was great. We spent lots of time on the boat with friends, had parties, and best of all Eric seemed totally in love with me. Flowers kept coming and so did the romantic dinners. Now that we lived together, he would cook delicious meals for us. He was really into photography and I was his favorite subject. I still don't know what it was, but that man took some amazing pictures of me. He would take me to parks and have me pose. He definitely knew all of my best angles. Once he had me crawl out onto these rocks in the middle of a stream and lay on my belly just to get the perfect shot.

It was strange going from feeling like one of the ugliest women to becoming the most beautiful in the world. It all seemed too good to be true. I had been so hurt and beaten down. Now this man comes along and I thought, *This is why God brought me here. I had to go through what I went through with Todd so that I could find Eric.*

As most relationships go, we didn't have any arguments in the beginning. I never complained about his friends coming over, nearly every night of the week. They thought I was awesome— kind of like one of the guys. I didn't complain about the daily pot smoking. As long as there weren't any other drugs, I was fine with it. Remember Rule #3.

Eric and I finally had our first argument. I don't remember what it was about, but it escalated from a conversation to a full-blown fight. I had grown up with two brothers and had a quick wit and smart mouth. My daddy was also a Marine and had no problem yelling. Because of this childhood training, I wasn't backing down. And I wasn't afraid of him.

There was a very innocent apple sitting on the counter. Once Eric realized his loud voice wasn't working on me, he slammed his fist down hard on that unsuspecting fruit. Apple and juice flew in all directions. The sound was like a shotgun going off. Holy shit! That shut me up.

Then there was silence for what seemed like a lifetime. I was in total shock and frozen in fear. So many thoughts ran through my head. Mostly I was thanking God he'd hit the apple and not me. Then I wondered if he wished the apple was me.

The tears came. I was shaking all over. Eric quickly came to my side and put his arms around me. "I'm sorry," he said. How could this be? He was the man of my dreams. I was not going to give up all of this romance over one little apple, was I? I melted into his arms, accepting his apologies, making up with kisses and hugs. That was the first time I faced the bully.

But once a bully knows how to push your buttons and how to make you back down, he will use those tactics again and again. Let's not forget, I am pretty stubborn. When I know I'm right about something, it's hard to change my mind. Most find it difficult to win a debate with me. At least that had been my experience, ergo why I thought I would be a good attorney.

I dismissed any fears for the future. I ached for the dream of true love and a happy ending. It was going to be just fine. Yeah, right.

36 | A Romantic Proposal

I awaited final paperwork on my divorce from Todd. In my immature mind that meant it was time to start thinking about getting married again. I mean, I had barely been married for a year the first time... that shouldn't really count as marriage, right? It was a complete mistake. This time it was different.

Eric and I planned a weekend visit to his family in Johnstown for Labor Day 1990. We had been together about ten months and living together for four. We were going to take the boat to a lake, and since Eric was off that Saturday we would have a three-day weekend.

We brought his friend Rick along so we could double date again with Eric's sister. I could tell something was up though. Eric was acting strange. His friends were also acting a little weird. Intuitively I knew he was going to propose. I started sniffing around, asking his friends some leading questions. I finally found one who basically told me it was going to happen. I never told Eric that I knew.

I was so excited. How would he propose? Where would he do it? Did his family know?

Friday came and miraculously, my boss said I could leave early. How convenient. I met Eric at home where my divorce papers had arrived. We packed and got ready to leave. Rick was going to drive a truck with a trailer to haul the boat while Eric and I would drive his demo from the dealership.

Eric was so edgy on the way there. He was bitching at Rick's driving and really kept his eyes on the boat. This was strange. I knew Eric trusted Rick, yet Eric would not take his eyes off of him and that boat. I thought we were going to wreck because Eric was paying more attention to Rick than to his own driving.

Thankfully we arrived safely at Eric's mom's house.

He asked if I would like to go to see the Inclined Plane. "Sure. But what's the Inclined Plane?" In 1889, Johnstown had a catastrophic flood—a wipe-out-the-town kind of flood. The land there is mountainous—at least to me. After that, the residents of Johnstown figured out a way to get people and things up the mountain out of harm if it ever happened again. They built a trolley-like cart that sits on rails, finished in 1891. It fulfilled its role for evacuation in 1936 and again during a massive flood 1977. Now it's a tourist site. There are view-finders at the top of the mountain so you can look down on the city. It was beautiful.

I wanted to take a shower and redo my makeup before we left as I was pretty sure this was it. He was going to propose. I felt as nervous as a cat on a hot tin roof. I started to question whether or not his friend had told me the truth. With adrenaline flowing and feeling all hyped up, I took the fastest shower ever. I am sure it broke some sort of record. Eric even mentioned how quickly I was ready.

Off we went by ourselves. It took longer to get there than I expected, probably because my heart was beating so fast in anticipation. Eric seemed cool and calm. Once again, doubtful questions filled my brain. I was really going to feel stupid if he didn't propose. I would have to act normal and not be disappointed. But if he did ask me, I was going to have to act surprised. My palms began to sweat. Damn it!

We finally arrived and I remember thinking it really wasn't much to look at. Eric asked if I would like to look in the view-finders. Oh shit! I decided we really were there just to see this thing. Okay, history and all that, but at that moment, I didn't care. I only wanted to know where the engagement ring was.

Eric put a quarter in the view-finder for me to look at the town. Then he started giving me directions. "Look down," he said. "Look at the top of that building over to the left. Keep looking." Like a beacon in the night, I saw it. On top of a roof stood Rick and his sister holding a gigantic sign across the building that read:

Reesy, will you marry me?

I gasped. I turned to face him. There he stood holding out the ring. Now that was a proposal! We went back to his mom's house to celebrate. I was absolutely elated! I guess I didn't let any grass grow under my feet after getting divorced the first time.

Working as a legal secretary was not exactly what I had imagined. First of all, the law firm would not actually give you the title of "paralegal" without a four-year degree of some type. It could have been in ditch digging. It just had to be a degree. However, they would allow you to do paralegal work, while paying you legal secretary rates, and... you guessed it... charging the client paralegal fees. I was beginning to learn why attorneys often got such bad reputations.

I also learned that a lot of duties depended on the attorney's specialty. I had the pleasure of working for a man whose father was the top dog in the law firm. He was a fourth-generation lawyer, also named after his father. His area of specialty was municipal law. Do you have any idea just how boring that is?

I spent my days answering the phone, greeting clients, and typing ordinances. It was the most tedious, uninteresting stuff ever invented. Using a good old-fashioned typewriter and a Dictaphone, I typed up what the attorney had dictated, usually a letter or document. There were foot pedals to go forward or rewind. I learned that attention to detail was not necessarily my thing.

This attorney was so stoic and pompous, no joking or kidding with him. In fact, at my first review he mentioned that I was basically too bubbly and that I needed to tone it down. How do you like that little box he put me in? He was asking me to not be myself. Little did I know that his father had locked him in his own little box.

My friend Denise, however, seemed to have an awesome relationship with the attorney she was assigned to. He was younger and way more fun. I liked him as well. He did his best to maintain professionalism without giving away the fact that he was totally checking out me and Denise all the time.

My attorney had two secretaries, but there was often not enough work for me. With attorneys it's all about billable hours. I had to keep a timesheet accounting for every minute, rounding up to six. If I had to leave a message and it only took one minute, I was supposed to bill six.

The good news was that because I didn't have enough billable hours, I got assigned to a new female attorney who specialized in divorce and criminal law, and also another attorney at the main office in Lancaster who was a Divorce Master. Sounds powerful. In Pennsylvania, a Divorce Master is assigned to divorce cases that, after two years of fighting, still can't make settlement. Basically, he was like a legal referee who came in and said, "Okay Mrs. So-and-So, you get this. And Mr. So-and-So, you get that." It was way more interesting work to me, because it was about people... and a lot more juicy. I was also actually pretty good at it.

I continued taking classes because other law firms would grant paralegal status, hence pay more money, if I received my certification. Legal work wasn't exactly as exciting or interesting as I had thought... and I definitely wasn't making near the amount of money that I thought I was worth.

37 | New Career, Temper Tantrums, and Counseling

Around two years into my career as a legal secretary, the finance position at the dealership became available again. I learned from our friend Frank that I could earn $50k a year—way better than the $20k I was making at the law firm. Next thing I knew, I had an interview with John, the general manager. Remember the man who had scared the shit out of me the first day I sat in that dealership answering the phones? After I got to know him, he really wasn't that scary. Unless he was yelling. Anyway, he already knew I had the personality for the job, and that I'd learned the detail stuff from working with attorneys. He offered me the job on the spot.

I mentioned that I was enrolled in class. He agreed to reimburse my tuition because he needed me to start as soon as possible. I was scared to make the move because I had always planned to go back to school. However, that $50k was calling my name... and I wouldn't have to work two jobs anymore. The final decision came when I started talking to the more fun attorney and found out that he barely made $50k a year. What?

I was still apprehensive, but I gave my two weeks' notice and started back at the dealership. A lot of training was devoted to me since I had zero experience at the new job. But I was really good at it. I got to work with people. More importantly, I could be my bubbly, joking self.

When I got that first commission check, I almost shit my pants. Frank admitted he had been conservative in his estimate. It was more like $70k. I couldn't believe a poor Southern gal without a formal education from Chocowinity could make that kind of money. It was awesome.

Frank worked the same position, and he and I would switch back and forth every other week from used cars to new cars. The only negative was the hours— 9:00 A.M. to 9:00 P.M. with just one day off a week, one Saturday a month, and all Sundays. But I wanted a house and we needed the money.

Everything was going as planned with Eric. We hadn't set a date yet, since it takes money to get married, and my parents surely didn't have any. Eric still lavished me with gifts and flowers. From the outside, he looked like a great fiancé. But he smoked pot almost every day and wanted to buy boy toys like a BMW. Our fights escalated as I was just not the type to back down. It was not uncommon for him to call me a bitch, or when it was really bad, he would pull out the old Cee-U-Next-Tuesday word.

With all this fighting, what do you think I did? I did what every girl with low self-esteem, yearning for true love and security would do... I asked him to go to counseling.

I found a lovely lady in her late fifties who had just completed school. She saw clients in her brightly colored sunroom. Eric reluctantly agreed. We went to one session together, which did not go well.

Note: There are a couple of rules you need to know about me and my Southern upbringing in regards to marriage:

1. Never argue in front of people. Arguments are for behind closed doors.
2. Sex is part of your responsibility as a wife.
3. Never go to sleep angry.
4. Be respectful to your spouse.

The counselor suggested that before we work on the relationship, we should work on ourselves. This made sense to me. I signed up for once-a-week sessions. Eric continued to not want to participate. And by not participate, I mean he didn't go to more than a couple of sessions. But that was okay. I could fix us both, right?

While I really liked my therapist, not much changed, except that I learned some communication skills that helped disarm Eric's anger. Sometimes.

38 | Second Time's the Charm?

Eric's roommate asked me to model some Victoria's Secret purchase I made. As you can imagine, that went over like a fart in church. We moved out of the townhouse into a cute one-bedroom apartment above a garage and behind our landlord, who had a wife and three daughters plus one on the way. We were allowed to have pets. We also didn't have to sign a lease.

I became fast friends with the wife and I adored her daughters. We hung out several nights a week when Eric was working. She was a great confidante. I vented to her all the time about Eric.

Even with all the red flags, Eric and I set a wedding date—Saturday, February 15, 1992. We chose the 15th instead of Valentine's Day, because lots of our friends were in the car business and had to work on Friday nights.

Since we had to pay for the wedding and didn't have a lot of money—and because we only had a one-bedroom apartment—I couldn't pay for my parents to come to Pennsylvania. Their hotel cost would have been yet another expense they couldn't afford. I couldn't either. To relieve the pressure from all of us, I decided to tell them we were having a very small wedding and it was okay for them not to be there. I was sad not to have my daddy walk me down the aisle though.

I bought party invitations and handwrote them to save money. We chose to get married at a hotel with a beautiful room with a waterfall, hosting the reception there, and then staying in one of their luxury townhomes that night. I asked a friend to take the pictures and another to cater the food. The only "professional" thing we did was buy a beautiful wedding cake—a three-tiered heart shape with white icing and red roses all around the edges, white cake with raspberry filling. Amazing!

Eric's brother would walk me down the aisle. The landlord's three little girls would be my flower girls. One of my best friends from North Carolina would come up and be my maid of honor. I asked only that she buy a red dress. I didn't care what it looked like. She did a beautiful job, very much validated by all the single guys at the wedding who wanted to get to know her better.

February 15th came. It was a gray day with some snow, some sleet and some rain. I only felt a little apprehension. Not like I felt the day I married Todd. I was just naturally nervous. I couldn't believe the weather.

I arrived at the resort. The room was set up beautifully. The fountain was flowing and there were flowers all around. The Mayor of Mount Joy was there to marry us. Neither of us attended church and someone had told us that he performed weddings for fifty dollars. Perfect.

When it was time for the wedding to start, we learned there had been an accident on the main highway. Several guests were stuck in that mess. Not knowing how long they would be held up, we went forward with the ceremony since the wedding party and Eric's family had all arrived. It was short and sweet and finished about the time the rest of the guests got there. Not a problem. We would celebrate at the reception.

When it came time to cut the cake, I had envisioned us neatly placing small bites in each other's mouth. Eric, who loved to show off, decided to smash the cake right in my face. I smashed back. He was a foot taller than me and had a much longer reach. I had cake everywhere including my dress. Everyone seemed to enjoy the moment, so I tried not to be upset and ruin the "fun."

Eric and I spent the night in the same hotel's luxury townhouse. We had decided to do our honeymoon later as we didn't have money left over for anything else at the moment. Each time I went to counseling thinking that I was not going to go through what I had gone through with Todd. I was sure I was making the right decision this time. That's what I kept telling myself. This time was different.

39 | Gifts of Love and Abuse

I was doing great at my new job as finance manager. Soon Eric had a disagreement with the used car manager and went to work at another dealership. Selling cars was in Eric's blood—his father and both his brothers were in the car business, too. Eric had some talent with selling, however, now he had me to fall back on financially. That made it a lot easier for him not to put in the extra hours or work up to his potential.

Every time we had an argument it was the same story. Eric would raise his voice. I would raise my voice. He would get louder. I would get louder. After his yelling didn't back me down he would start with the name calling.

During one argument we were standing in the kitchen. In his rage, he took the sprayer from the sink and sprayed me right in the face. It was not the haha-this-is-funny spray in the face... it was an I'm-going-to-humiliate-and-shut-you-up spray in the face. I stomped out of the apartment and down the driveway. I was so mad I didn't know what to do. The tears came. How could he do that to me? For me, he might as well have physically hit me. It was so degrading. Instead, the bruises were all on the inside where I couldn't see them. No one else could either.

Of course he would make up with me and then the gifts would come. Things would be good for a while. For Eric, it was all about appearances. From afar, he was a doting, romantic, sweet husband. Only our closest friends knew the truth.

He loved showboating how wonderful he was. For our first anniversary, we went to dinner at this restaurant that accepted limited reservations for their private wine cellar. When it came time for dessert, they brought out a heart-shaped cake (like our wedding cake) with a tiny gold bow in the middle. Eric asked me to pull on the bow and out popped a small box. Every girl knows those little boxes mean jewelry. I opened it up and there inside was what most women receive as a ten-year or more gift. There were five marquis-shaped diamonds across the ring. It was gorgeous and unexpected. It was also financed. So really, I bought it for myself because, like most of the other bills in our life, I paid for it.

Statistics say most divorces happen due to money issues, or how to raise children, or sex. Money was definitely our issue. I would much rather have someone want to spend time with me than buy me stuff we couldn't afford. I wanted to save for a house. I wanted to have children. How would any of that happen? I started to feel like I was married to a child.

Eric had an amazing ability to somehow turn everything into an argument. And I would often find myself apologizing. We would start arguing about something he had done or said to me, and masterfully he would change the subject to something I had done. Counseling helped teach me how to turn the conversation back to what I was upset about. When he would do his magic trick, I would say, "We can talk about that later. Right now, we're talking about you." This would only enrage him more.

Eric also knew how to insult me. As per my Southern upbringing, he knew I would not fight in front of other people. It didn't take him long to figure out that I would not argue back if we had company. He had free rein to say whatever he wanted and know that I would only turn red in the face and not do a thing about it.

Despite all of this, I soldiered on with the marriage. I loved Eric, or thought I did. How could I get another divorce? I was only in my twenties. Who would want a woman who had been married twice? That would not be a fun label.

Was I that big of a failure? I knew I had to try harder. I had to prove that I was good enough for Eric to change his ways and love me. Once again, I found myself dancing as hard as I could to be the perfect wife.

40 | New House and He Loses His Job

I wanted a house so badly. Because I had moved so many times growing up, I longed for the security of having a place to call home. Eric and I found one pretty quickly in a small neighborhood where all the streets were named after seasons. It was a two-bedroom, bi-level with flowered wallpaper—that would have to go—on Autumn Drive. It had a partially finished basement, one-car garage and an unfinished addition on a half-acre lot full of trees. When I say full of trees, I mean it was hidden in the middle of a forest.

We walked around to the backyard and, much to our surprise, found a beautiful in-ground pool. I was sold. There was a nice deck and stairs. The owners also had lined that area with more trees which made it very private. Never mind that the house needed a shit-ton of updates. We could fix the cosmetic things. Did I mention it had a pool?

Eric sold his BMW to lower our debt and help us qualify for a bigger mortgage. We settled in October, early in the day. When we were done, we both went back to work. A few hours later I got a phone call from Eric. He had lost his job! Immediate panic ensued. He said he had been fired for under-performing... aka he hadn't sold enough cars. In addition, they didn't like his bad attitude.

What would we do? We had just bought a house. How would we pay for it? Memories of my childhood came flooding back. How many times had I heard my father say he got fired? This couldn't be happening. I held it together until I hung up the phone.

The used car sales manager in my office wasn't the most sensitive person in the world, but he walked by and saw me crying. He was not surprised when I told him what happened to Eric. Remember Eric had once worked for him. Surprisingly, he was kind. He started to remind me of the positives. At least Eric's boss had waited until after we settled on the house, since they ask you at closing if you are still employed. We would've had to start all over in getting approved for a mortgage. The sales manager also reminded me how much money I was making and that financially, I could make the house payments all by myself if needed. He really calmed me down and made me feel so much better about the situation. It was a much unexpected gift the sales manager gave me that day.

Our dealership was located on Manheim Pike, along with many others, such that it was known as car dealer alley. If you were half decent at selling cars, you could just walk across the street and get a different job. It was like a little community. Everyone knew everyone and your reputation would follow you. It also was not uncommon to be hired back if management changed or you had connections. Luckily Eric's reputation and labels weren't widely known. He easily got another job at the dealership right next to mine.

We moved into the house and began peeling wallpaper and repainting. We also removed thirteen trees, but there were so many it didn't even seem noticeable. Many of Eric's friends had trade jobs and knew how to lay tile, or build a deck, and they were always willing to lend a hand in exchange for food, beer, and weed. By the time we were done renovating, we had a three-tiered deck, a tiled bathroom, new carpet, new furniture, and had torn down a wall between the kitchen and living room to give the space a modern look.

Eric had no problem spending money. Especially mine. We decided I would pay the mortgage and groceries and he would pay the utilities and car payment. Yeah, that's fair... not! Eric didn't seem to give our debt a second thought.

As a side note, money represents power. We never had a joint checking account. I had mine and he had his. Of course, the tiny savings account we opened was in both names. But I had no way of knowing what he was spending. I could see the bills when they came in, however any "extras" he purchased I would never know completely. At the time, I didn't think there was anything wrong with having separate accounts, though I feel differently about that now. If money equals power, shouldn't that power be shared in a marriage? Food for thought.

41 | Eric's New Toy

We decided to sell the boat. Maintenance was expensive. Gas was expensive. And there was also the aggravation of Eric needing to request a truck as a demo every time we wanted to tow the boat somewhere.

Eric had named the boat "Wake and Bake." This moniker attracted other boaters with the same marijuana-friendly mindset. We became friends with a couple about our same age who had a slightly smaller boat. When we were ready to sell, they quickly jumped on the opportunity.

Since Eric had sold his BMW and now we were selling the boat, it meant that Eric didn't have a toy. This always signified trouble. Or at least that was how I saw it. I wanted to have children and Eric wanted a snowmobile. As usual there was yelling and name calling. Somehow things were my fault and the snowmobile won.

With our debt load I would always need to work. I don't mind working, but I would have to keep making that kind of money since clearly he found it easy to lean on me. How would we every afford a baby unless he was the one having it? If things were going to be financially taken care of, it would have to be me. Same story, different man.

Apparently you don't just buy a snowmobile. You need all the protective clothing and helmet, and a trailer to tow it, along with travel to get to someplace that has enough snow to be able to use it. Eric was never satisfied with average, so he needed the fastest, fanciest snowmobile available. He wanted all the extras. Only the best for Eric.

He also had this amazing talent of being able to talk his friends into things, so two or three followed his lead and purchased snowmobiles. After all, what fun would it be to snowmobile alone? I certainly wasn't going snowmobiling; I was too busy working. I also really dislike being cold. Since none of his snowmobile buddies were married, they didn't have to discuss purchases with anyone else. He would have his toy and his friends to play with him.

In the meantime, Eric didn't do well at the next dealership. Same old story. He'd get pissed off at management, arguments would ensue, and he would either quit or get fired. Later he worked for a small used car dealership run by one older man, Dick. They hit it off and decided that Eric would run the whole show as the owner was getting older and needed the help.

Dick allowed Eric to do whatever he wanted with the cars. Eric was actually pretty good at staging them in the lot. He also seemed to do better working alone, pretty much his own boss. He would periodically argue with Dick. Nothing major. But working for a small company meant no benefits. I had to add Eric to my insurance which raised the cost automatically deducted from my paycheck.

Fortunately, Eric did increase Dick's business quite a bit. So much so that Eric hired another salesperson, Jeremy, since someone needed to be there every day from 9:00 A.M. to 8:00 P.M. Barely over 21, Jeremy was a sweetheart of a guy. He lived with his parents, but became a regular visitor to our house. And by regular, I mean pretty much every night. Jeremy would enable Eric to still get his play time in. And of course, it didn't take long for Jeremy to have a snowmobile as well.

Eric also rationalized that this new job would allow him to borrow a truck from work anytime he wanted to tow the snowmobile... we wouldn't have to buy a second vehicle. Eric was very talented at justifying his toy purchases. None of them included a positive for me.

42 | Fun and Games for Eric but Not Reesy

Our house quickly became a hangout. Almost every night after working a twelve-hour shift, or more, I would come home to Eric and his friends smoking dope. For his birthday in July we had to have a big party to celebrate him. One time he actually rented an RV and used it as a combination dunking booth and karaoke machine. Again, always the best for Eric.

That winter Eric tried to teach me how to ski. In North Carolina, when it snows, everything shuts down. I really hate being cold; it physically hurts me. So skiing did not have a lot in its favor. We rented all the stuff and headed to Ski Roundtop in Harrisburg. After a short lesson where I learned that you should put the points of the skis together to stop, Eric popped me onto the ski lift. Not the bunny hill... which is where I now know I actually belonged. But no. Eric had grown up skiing and was excellent. He had taught several of his friends how to ski, but apparently had much more patience with them than me.

We reached the top and somehow I managed to successfully get off of the lift. I stared down that big white mountain and almost had a heart attack. I looked back at Eric and said, "Get me back on that lift thing! Then get me off this mountain now!"

Well, he was having none of that. "Just relax, Reesy. I'm going to help you." My real ski lesson began. Over and over I fell. He became frustrated, yelling at me, saying I wasn't listening. Finally, he decided to come up behind me and put his arms under my armpits, attempting to take me down the hill with him. What a fucking disaster! He let go and I couldn't stop! I fell and I fell hard. So hard the ski patrol came to make sure I was okay.

Somehow, I struggled and finally made it down the hill. "You go right ahead and ski as long as you want," I told him. "I'm going into that ski lodge over there for some hot chocolate." Off I went and off he went. I was so relieved to get those skis off of me. I didn't give two shits how long Eric stayed away. I sat with my hot chocolate and a video game called Galactica.

As I started playing, sipping on my hot chocolate now and then, a loud noise caught my attention. A teenage boy dropped a pizza. I turned to look at him, and his little face went bright red. I went back to playing my game. I was finally warming up when pizza boy stood beside me watching me play. He starts with, "Hey, are you from that middle school?"

That's right. I was being hit on by a teenager. I mean, I didn't have on any makeup, but still I was 22 years old. Perhaps I should have taken it as a compliment. All I could think was that I'd almost died on the mountain and now I was being hit on by a child. I never ever went skiing again.

Eric also really wanted me to like snowmobiling. My first ride was at his mom's house in Johnstown. Just a "little ride around the yard." What do you think happened? As he sped around a corner, he threw me off of the thing. Luckily, I landed in a big pile of soft snow. Eric said it was my fault. I hadn't been hanging on correctly. He could've asked, "Are you okay?" but no. He just bitched at me for not leaning right.

Usually he had to travel to find enough snow to ride in, but one time we got a huge snowstorm. Everyone came to our house. I decided to try it again, ever the optimist. I still wanted to be a "good wife" and make Eric happy.

He dressed me in lots of warm clothing and put his extra helmet on me which seemed way too big. I climbed on the back and wrapped my arms around his waist. A considerate husband would've taken me for a nice, slow and gentle ride. Not Eric. I should've remembered that he always bought the fastest of everything. We took off. And when I say took off, I mean he went from zero to 60. For double fun, the helmet raised up and blocked my view. I couldn't see a thing. All I could do was hang on and scream. I thought I was going to die.

When would it stop? It felt like forever. *Hang on, hang on,* I kept saying in my head. *Don't fall off!* I was so cold and absolutely terrified. Finally, my ride of torture stopped. I didn't even know I was crying. There was no apology. Just a "Calm the fuck down. You're fine."

Guess what? I never did that shit again either.

43 | Married Life Is So Lonely

Life at age 25 saw me working 50-60 hours a week, and cleaning house on my one day off while Eric spent his evenings hanging out with friends, getting high, and most weekends leaving me to go somewhere snowmobiling.

I didn't have many girlfriends at the time. I worked so much, plus it was a male-dominated business. Many of the wives didn't care for a young Southern gal working with their husbands. So we got a dog—a golden retriever named Cooper—who kept me company when Eric was away. Mostly, I would sit and do jigsaw puzzles, cross stitch, or shop. By now you know I am a people person. I do not do well alone.

When Eric was home, we spent a lot of time fighting. I couldn't seem to do anything the way he wanted. Once when I was making a dessert, he literally yelled at me in front of our guests, *"You have to fold that in, not stir it!"* He would also complain that I didn't cut the vegetables small enough for the salad. My god, I couldn't seem to do anything right.

One year my parents and aunt were coming for Thanksgiving. Our kitchen wasn't very big, so in the middle of cooking all the various foods for a feast, he walked in and started yelling at me about what a mess the kitchen was. I was so embarrassed and hurt. He knew I wouldn't fight back in front of company—especially my family. A few tears may have escaped into the mashed potatoes. After that, I gave up cooking. He was good at it and I didn't get criticized or yelled at. So here you go, Eric. Have at it!

I worked hard to anticipate his next move so I wouldn't aggravate him and cause an argument. I tried to keep the peace. I hated the name calling the most. Sometimes when the fights were really bad... mostly when I wouldn't back down... he would shove me around. He never actually "hit" me. He would just push me down on the bed or shove me against the wall. He was a foot taller than me and 100 pounds heavier. As much as I tried to hide it, I was intimidated.

Most of all, I was so lonely. No more romantic dinners. It was actually safer that way. If I could avoid his attention and let him focus on his friends, I was less likely to be yelled at or embarrassed. I was constantly walking on eggshells. I would attempt to anticipate anything that would upset him and do my best to avoid those things. It's not easy being a mind reader.

Eric always wanted to keep up appearances though. He continued to send me flowers at work. He would buy me cards and jewelry, and bring me dinner to work, making sure that everyone saw. He kept a picture of me on his desk. Lots of people thought, *What a great husband!* Only a few knew the truth—my family and our friend Jeremy. Inside, my self-esteem was taking another beating. You can never know what goes on behind closed doors and between two people. Don't be too quick to judge.

I craved attention. Being an unhealthy emotional girl, I did what many do. I wore short skirts and low-cut blouses, getting the wrong kind of attention. I started taking "supplements" to lose weight. I was a size 6. We didn't own a scale so I don't know how much I weighed but I was small. One day Eric said, "You're getting a belly. You should run around the house a few times." What the fuck? Meanwhile, he was gaining weight by the minute. He so wanted me to be less so he could be more. Where had I heard that before?

The presents he bought, the flowers he sent, the love notes he wrote... none of them were for me. They were all for show. Maybe he thought that's all a good husband was... an appearance. He did have a very dysfunctional upbringing. Whatever it was, I found myself lonely and still craving attention. So many weekends spent by myself in that house. Loneliness consumed me.

44 | Before You Know It Happened

We decided, or rather Eric decided, to host another party—one we couldn't afford. We invited a lot of people including some from the car business. One sales guy brought his wife Lori who was a little younger than me. After several drinks we became quick friends. Little did I know she would save my life one day.

When her marriage didn't work out, we stayed friends. Lori liked to dance and so did I. We started going out on the weekends to local clubs. Sometimes Eric and his friends would tag along, but mostly we went alone. One divorced woman plus one unhappily married woman out on the town together is not necessarily a great recipe.

This next part is not easy for me to tell, so don't judge. I already feel badly about it. Or go ahead and judge me, but it won't do you any good. I've already done penance for my actions of October 1994. Try to understand where my mindset was. I was so very lonely. No matter how much attention I received from the guys at the club, my self-esteem had not improved from weekends spent doing jigsaw puzzles and watching movies by myself. The men at work flirted with me. It was in my nature to flirt back.

Once I was training a new gal in the dealership when a salesman came in. He needed something but I needed it to be done differently. I must've stood pretty close to him, being my usual flirty self. I eventually got my way. When he left, the trainee asked, "How do you do that?" I didn't understand what she meant. "You know... get them to do whatever you want. I can't do that." I was taken aback. The look on her face when she said it wasn't exactly a positive one. I didn't even realize what I had done. Let's call it being "charming." I prefer that label. To me, it was harmless and meant nothing. I have come to understand that flirting in the North and flirting in the South are two very different things.

Anyway, at work I still alternated weeks between working in the new car department and used cars. The latter had all male salespeople, most under age 35, plus one female title clerk. The general manager would usually leave by 5:00 every day unless it was the end of the month (the end of the month is usually the busiest since all salespeople are trying to close those last few deals to get to a next level of commission), and on Wednesday and Thursday nights, the sales manager was also off. That's when the wholesale buyer, who was also a previous salesperson and son-in-law of the owner, "managed"... or rather he just appraised cars and hung out.

Certain times of the month are always slow, sitting around waiting for the next customer. Not too many are disciplined enough to do follow-up phone calls or send letters to previous clients. So if the salesmen didn't have customers, neither did I. I needed them to sell cars in order for me to do what I did. When I worked in the new car department, I spent a lot of time in my office reading magazines or doing puzzles, but in used cars, I hung out with the guys. They were just more fun... probably because the general manager's office was not in their building and he was unlikely to just show up at any given moment.

One Thursday night when the used car manager was off, a bunch of us ordered dinner. This was a common thing to do. It was late, so rather than order from a restaurant, we went next door to Burger King. I ordered a chicken sandwich... you know, because that's healthy.

So we were all sitting in the sales office eating together. I went to the restroom, located back in the shop. It was dark except for one light shining from the showroom window. When I came out, there stood Jacob—the wholesaler/previous-used-car-guy/son-in-law of the owner—standing right outside the door. I almost ran him over. Before I knew what happened, he kissed me. Not just a peck on the cheek. Full-on, tongue in my mouth, long wet kiss.

I was in shock! My mind started racing. The first thing I thought to say was that I had chicken stuck in my teeth. He ignored that and kissed me again. I must admit, I felt the passion in his kiss and I kissed back. I somehow came to realize he'd been wanting to do this for a long time. All I could keep saying between kisses was, "I have chicken in my teeth." I said that about three times. He didn't seem to care one bit.

The next time I said, "We have to get back to the showroom," in what sounded like my voice. But I really didn't want to go back. I wanted to replay what had just happened. I was trying to process whether or not it had really happened or maybe somehow I had imagined it. Maybe the chicken was bad. More pressing in my mind was that I wanted to try it again without the chicken thing going on. The surprise of it all had me reeling.

We walked back into the showroom like nothing at all had occurred. No one was the wiser. I couldn't believe the others couldn't read it across my face. On the inside, it was a very different story. I couldn't believe how much I had enjoyed it. It had been a long, long time since I felt passion like that. I truly didn't understand why Eric was still with me. He certainly didn't seem to like me anymore. I put the thoughts of those kisses away, sure it wouldn't happen again. I was positive it was a fluke and Jacob was just being Jacob. He could be a little outrageous. Wait... I hadn't noticed when high school sweetheart Greg liked me either.

45 | I Did Plan on This

Jacob was not the kind of guy I would have expected to be attracted to. He wasn't ugly by any means. He had dark hair and eyes, but he wasn't tall or big in stature. I usually liked bigger guys. I had a rule: *Never date a man with longer hair or a smaller waist.* Jacob wasn't that small. He just didn't fit my previous "type."

He was also loud, high strung, obnoxious and rumored to use cocaine. I heard he had gotten pretty heavy into it and his family, including his in-laws, stepped in to help him get off of the stuff. He couldn't possibly be doing that anymore.

He was also kind of rude, chauvinistic and a sexist. He nicknamed me "little P," which embarrassingly meant I was someone he and the guys wanted to lick where I pee. *I know. You don't have to say it.* He called the other finance manager "big P," since she was taller. *Again, I know.*

Other than all of that, he was quite charming.

Okay, I know what you're thinking. You're screaming that I did not just describe someone who is Reesy's version of charming.

But when he sold cars, he was the top guy every single month, by a lot. In more formal social situations, he could be charming and likable. Still I didn't think I liked him. Not to the extent of tongue kissing.

As a finance manager you spend a lot of time with the sales manager, or in this case whoever is covering when the sales manager is off or on vacation. You actually spend more time with the sales manager than the sales guys.

While this man didn't exactly act married, I knew his wife was the owner's daughter, and his career was in that man's hands. I never thought he was unhappy in his marriage, though there were rumors that they both had their issues.

Jacob's flirting with me intensified. More surprise kisses. More coordinated I-will-meet-you-in-the-back kisses. During the encounters, I felt zero guilt. I was so lonely and it felt good to have someone give me such special attention. When he was on the road, he would call just to say hi. We would eat dinner together when I worked in used cars. He was so nice to me.

Meanwhile at home, Eric continued to treat me like shit, constantly criticizing me, yelling and calling me names. I kept doing the "trying to figure out his next move" dance so I would not cause him to be angry.

I also kept thinking, *Reesy, what in the hell are you doing? This is the owner's son-in-law.* If Eric found out, he would kill Jacob, me, or both of us. All the while it was like a drug I couldn't get enough of. The sweetness, the attention, the kisses. Slowly and without really knowing it, I began to develop romantic feelings for this man.

We started staying late on the nights we both worked in used cars. After all, I always had to wait until the last customer left and so did he. We would turn off all the lights and go to my office and make out. Things started getting more intimate than just kisses. Rumors began to fly. People aren't stupid.

One night we were in my office and had just started making out when, thank God, we saw the general manager pull up on my side of the building. Oh shit! Luckily, Jacob was quick on his feet and said, "Let's just go out the other door and act like nothing's happening." That is exactly what we did. We walked out the other side, said good night and got in our cars and left. I was still trying to calm my pulse as I drove home. I hoped he hadn't seen anything.

I knew exactly why I was doing what I was doing. I was so unhappy at home. I was petrified of Eric. Maybe deep down I was petrified to be alone. The same old thoughts were there. I had left everything in North Carolina. How could I go back now? I was a successful finance manager making plenty of money. But school was far out of reach. Nothing had changed with my parents. I still sent them money quite often. I just wanted to enjoy the moments I had with Jacob. I had no idea why he was doing this to risk his whole way of life though. And I had no idea I would fall in love with him.

As we became closer, I learned he was also very unhappy with his marriage. They had many issues. He made them seem quite extreme. He claimed to be as unhappy as I was. He also felt stuck. He stayed because they had a son together, and Jacob adored him. I could understand that.

46 | Does Size Really Matter

As adults, there's only so much kissing you can do before things start to get more intimate. But Jacob seemed to have an issue with his, um, you know. Even I was quite surprised the first time I saw it. I had not seen very many, and his was definitely below average.

Note: For any men out there who suffer from this same "problem," I can't speak for all women, but me and my friends really don't care about that if we love you. Especially not if you make up for it in other ways. Quite frankly, if things are too large, that's not much fun either. Show affection, kiss someone, love them. These are the things that truly matter.

In addition to his "package" complex, Jacob would not get completely "excited." Now this does bother a woman. Was he not attracted to me? Why not? After all, he was the one who came on to me first. Yet there it was. Or rather was not.

I started to question him. Jacob said it was because he felt inadequate. Since Eric was such a tall, big guy, he figured Eric was huge all over. Jacob was concerned he wouldn't satisfy me.

Let's set the record straight. From the experiences of me and my friends (yes, women do discuss all this), big hands and big feet don't mean a thing. You won't know until you see it.

As for what you see in porn (not that I've watched a lot of it), that doesn't represent an ordinary sexual encounter. *No!* Men, you should explain this to your sons because if something they've seen on the internet or in a magazine is their first experience regarding sex, they're going to think that's how it is in reality. Boy, will they not only be disappointed, they will be disappointing. Get my drift? It's so easy for them to get their hands on it... pardon the pun. Everything is online. If you don't think your teenage boy is doing a little porn surfing on the net... well, all I have to say is denial is not a river in Egypt.

Next, there are certainly extremes in both directions. We already passed the point of TMI, so I'll just keep going. Extremes are usually not good either way you find them. I'm a petite girl and not interested in anything giant that could potentially hurt my lady parts. Bigger is not always better. Unless of course we're talking about shoe collections.

Regardless of size, it should be about the experience, the romance, the connection. When you're loving and attentive, nothing else matters. Don't lose your confidence. No one needs yet another label.

I found that I did love Jacob. I told him that. And I told him that he was wonderful to me and I loved being with him. I was completely satisfied. But it seemed no matter how much or often I encouraged him, he would still occasionally have this problem. I noticed a bit of a pattern. It occurred on Fridays, the day he went to the auto auction. What did that mean?

47 | Punished for My Transgressions?

About six weeks into these make-out sessions, I received a phone call from my daddy. He never called. I always talked to my mom. When I heard his voice, I instantly sat up straight, senses fully alert.

He said, "She left, Reesy."

What?

"I went to work and came home like I usually do, and she was gone." Then he said, "And I can't find her."

He had called all the places and people he knew. No one knew where my mom was... not my brothers, not Aunt Jane, not me. Mom had just disappeared. She left a note and said she couldn't live like she'd been living with him anymore, told him she was safe and not to contact her.

My heart was beating like a drum in my chest. I could hear it. And boy, could I feel it. Panic set in.

I called my aunt and some friends. They all said they didn't know where she was, only that she was safe. I was devastated. I also felt powerless. Why hadn't she called me? Was I being punished for what I had been doing with Jacob?

A week passed and still no word. I had to just keep working and hoping to hear from her. I went from fear to anger. How could she not at least contact me?

Two of my best friends from high school were coming to visit, Becky and Dayna. I tried to stay focused on that. About three weeks into Mom's disappearance, they arrived. We were sitting in my living room talking when the phone rang. I picked up. It was her! She said, "Hello," and I fell silent. I didn't know what to say. I didn't know whether to yell at her, cry or just hang up.

Finally, I asked her where she'd been and why she hadn't called. She explained how she just couldn't take it anymore with Dad. He had been abusing prescription drugs, taking valium and pain meds to the point where he was nodding out. Then he would drive to work. She would ask him to call when he got there so she knew he hadn't killed himself or anyone else. She told me she'd sat him down to talk about his behavior, told him she would leave if he didn't straighten up. Of course he made promises. But then he would get his prescriptions refilled, and the very same night he did the same exact thing he had promised not to repeat.

She was done. She knew if she didn't stay away, he would talk her into going back. She packed all of her stuff in trash bags and left. She still wouldn't tell me where she was. Only that she was safe.

I got an "I love you" before she hung up. I was angry, upset, a hot mess. I continued to question myself: What if I hadn't left home? Could I have kept the peace? What if I had been there to help financially? What if I hadn't been fooling around with a married man? Was I being punished for all the bad things I had done?

Becky and Dayna comforted me. We decided there was nothing left for me to do so we should just have a good time. That's exactly what we did. That's exactly the medicine I needed.

Over several weeks I spent many hours on the phone with my daddy talking about their marriage. He began to accept that she was not coming back. He had begun working regularly and had benefits. We talked more than since I'd moved out. Then he started telling me bad things about their marriage. I really didn't need to hear that stuff. However, I felt I had to be there for him. He confessed that they should have divorced years ago and that they stayed together for me and my little brother. *Don't do us any favors*, I thought. I would have much rather seen them be happy over the years.

The story was the same with Mom. She said she stayed too long. Unexpectedly, she confessed she had met another man. *What?* That's right, at the age of 57 she met a man who absolutely took her breath away. She was living with him in Pinetown—about thirty miles away, the same town where my high school sweetheart Greg was from.

How could I judge her? After all, I was not exactly being loyal. I knew how unhappy she had been. I'd seen alcoholism consume her. I'd seen my father quit a job just as my family was about to dig out of a financial hole from his previous unemployment. Now the prescription drug thing. It was the straw that broke the camel's back. She found a man who took her breath away... a man with a job, a home, and who said he loved her.

My father was quick to get back on the market. He never was good at being alone. Back then there were these dating phone numbers you could call and meet women. So he met himself a lady. He claimed he was really happy with her.

Here I was seeing a married man. Mama was living with a man other than my father. Daddy was dating some woman. I bet the small town I was from was just abuzz with gossip. Much like the dealership where Jacob and I worked. I'm sure labels were flying up North and down South. I did my best to push the guilt away. After all, my parents seemed happier. Jacob said he was happier, and I felt happier. Wouldn't everything be okay eventually? One could hope.

48 | Gotta Face This Mess

I decided I needed to go to North Carolina and visit my parents. I found a great deal on a flight for $120. I got no argument from Eric, and Jacob was super supportive. But there was nothing anyone else could do. I had to face this situation alone.

I planned to stay at my dad's house—aka the last house I had lived in before moving to Pennsylvania. Ironically, it was the house my parents lived in the longest. Mom wanted me to meet her new beau, Nelson, and his two sons. Really only one of them was his biological son. The other two were nephews whose mother couldn't take care of them. I wasn't sure if that sounded nice, or completely sketchy.

Dad picked me up from the Greenville airport, about thirty minutes away. I must admit, he looked great. I guess I was expecting him to be barely able to function. He did have a sadness behind his eyes, but there was also a determination I hadn't seen before. I believe he had decided he was going to survive.

Over the years, most of the contact with my father was when I would come home to visit, which was not very often. We arrived at the house. Daddy's credit had recovered after all those years of financial trouble, and now he had a brand new television with surround sound. I put my stuff in my old room, which seemed so much smaller than in my memory.

I was going to visit Mom in Pinetown. Even though I didn't want to meet her "new family," I pulled up my big girl panties. It was really far out in the country. I was sure at any moment the guys from *Deliverance* were going to jump out of the woods and attack me. There was no such thing as GPS then, so I had to follow directions like "Turn this way by that house" and "Go about five miles where you won't see anything but farmland or swamp" and

"It's the blue one behind the half burnt down house that Nelson's alcoholic brother squatted in."

I nervously got out of the car. I felt like I was on display as the boys and a few of their friends came out of the woodwork to see Gladys's pretty daughter. Their eyes were all over me. They were definitely checking me out. They weren't so bad either—polite and welcoming. I was pretty sure they were considering whether it would be incest to have me for lunch.

Then Mom came out and I gave her a big hug. I was still kind of pissed though. However, knowing she was safe overrode my anger. I'd missed her. We hugged several times and I worked hard not to cry.

As we stood there, out came Nelson. Keep in mind that I thought my daddy was rather handsome, and so did other people. Even with all of his health issues he was still a cutie. So when I saw Nelson, I was shocked. My jaw hung open. Youth had certainly left him, and working outside had not done any favors to his skin. He did have striking blue eyes and a head full of gray wavy hair that was combed nicely. He was clean. He wore jeans and a flannel shirt with a t-shirt underneath—the usual uniform for men in the South who lived in the woods and worked hard for a living. Then I noticed his arms and hands did not match the wrinkles in his face. They looked like they belonged to a much younger man. What was most shocking was that he only had three teeth.

I guess I was expecting... well, it's hard to explain. I had been looking for a big step up from my dad. My mother, on the other hand, was looking fabulous. She had lost weight. She looked relaxed and comfortable in her new home. My mind flooded with thoughts and emotions. First and foremost, she had a roof over her head and from what I could tell was being taken care of.

As I reflect on this relationship, Nelson was a good ole Southern boy, more the type of man my mother was used to. Daddy was a northerner. Even though he didn't have any money, he still had an air of sophistication. He was intelligent and well-spoken.

But that didn't seem to matter to my mom. She looked happier than I had seen her in a very, very long time. Deep down I knew she'd had enough of my dad's habits and his seeming inability to keep a job or take care of her. Nelson was different. And he seemed just as smitten as she was.

After seeing both my parents, I needed a night out with friends. I had to escape for a little while. Becky and I went to some small bar in Greenville and commenced to getting really intoxicated. So much so that I decided it was a good idea to make out with some college guy... no sex... just kissing.

Afterward I was in no shape to drive home and neither was Becky. I got a taxi. When I drink, as you can tell from the above-mentioned make-out session, I get super friendly. I decided to ride in the front seat with the driver. I'm sure he was just glad to get this drunk girl home and be rid of me.

I got to my dad's house and went straight to bed. I had to fly home the next day. I awoke to a severe hangover. Oh my, did my head hurt! I was pretty sure I was going to throw up at any minute.

Luckily, my parents decided to keep things civil for me and my brother. We had breakfast together at the airport, where again I fought the urge to vomit. My plane was a little puddle jumper and the flight home was rough. I felt so bad, I didn't even care if we crashed. It might have felt better than what I was feeling at that moment.

49 | Heartbreak Overload

Some good things came out of all of this. My dad and I got closer. We talked almost every day on the phone. He and my brother even made a trip up to Pennsylvania to visit me. Daddy found a girlfriend, and Mom had Nelson, and everyone seemed to be getting along just fine.

Then things continued to heat up with Jacob. Subconsciously I didn't trust any man, but Jacob said and did all the right things. He was amazing. But so were all the others. I ended up putting him through every possible psychological test of faith ever invented. Not consciously, mind you. It was just my fear and mistrust.

A year after my parents split, things started to go downhill with my dad's new girlfriend. I was working in the used car department and Jacob ordered us both dinner—chicken parmesan. The phone rang. It was Mom and she sounded weird. "Are you okay?" She kept assuring me that she was fine. I told her I was eating and that we would talk later. I wanted to get back to Jacob.

No sooner did I walk away from my desk when I got another phone call. This time it was my younger brother, Jerry. "What's wrong?" I asked. I could hear him start to cry. He asked, "Have you seen Eric yet?"

Mom took the phone from him. I begged her to please tell me what was wrong. Her voice trembled. She said, "Your dad had a heart attack." My heart started to beat out of my chest, faster and faster. I was afraid to ask the next question. I finally found my voice. "Well, is he all right?"

The pause seemed to last forever. She finally whispered, holding her own tears back, "No honey, he is not all right."

Silence. The kind of silence that leaves the air thick. So thick it felt like all the air in my body had been sucked out.

About that time, one of the used car salesmen walked by. I called his name through my tears. He came in and I somehow told him what had happened. He put his arms around me just in time to make sure I didn't fall over.

I don't remember hanging up the phone. About that time Jacob came into my office. Mom knew all about Jacob. She had apparently called him first that night. But neither of the men in front of me knew what to do. They just stood there and tried to be consoling.

With my office door open, I had a direct line of sight to the showroom entrance. I saw Eric come bursting in at an almost run. Apparently Mom had called him, too.

I was in a fog, a state of disbelief. Shock and pain drilled into my chest. Somehow, with Eric's help, I gathered my stuff and got into the car with him to go home. I don't know what happened to that chicken parmesan.

Eric and I were going to leave immediately the next morning for North Carolina. Before I could pack though, I needed to do laundry, because Eric changed often and I wore at least two outfits a day—one for work and something comfy when I got home. So as usual, there was a shit-ton of dirty clothes. That night I did load after load of laundry through continuous tears.

I would lay down between loads. Eric would come in and hold me. I sobbed and sobbed. The sound of this crying was different, foreign to my ears. I didn't recognize it even though it was coming out of my own mouth. I know now it was the sound of a breaking heart. There was physical pain in my chest—my heart being ripped apart. I never knew you could actually feel your heart breaking. But I did. Nothing I'd experienced in my life was so painful as that day... December 5th, 1995, a little more than a month before Daddy's 50th birthday.

Eric and I left early the next morning. I did my best to not cry the whole drive. I was so shaky and unstable, exhausted. I couldn't sleep or rest. I kept thinking there had to be some mistake. Maybe when I got to North Carolina, my daddy would actually be okay. And of course those small little thoughts in the back of my head that somehow this was my fault... maybe it would not have happened if I hadn't left.

I didn't want to stay with Mom at Nelson's house, and I couldn't handle staying at Daddy's house either. We decided to rent a hotel room nearby in Washington, NC. I met Mom at Dad's house. We walked in and I went straight to his room. I picked up one of his t-shirts and clutched it to my face. It smelled just like him. I brought it out to the living room, sobbing the whole way. Mom sort of freaked out. "I just can't take this," she said and started out the door.

Once again, I was going to have to be the parent. I found the strength to quit crying and followed her out the door. I told her that I was fine when I truly was not. Memories of childhood came flooding back... all the times I had to step in and talk to Daddy for her, pouring liquor down the drain to keep her sober, telling the ER doctors about Daddy's issues the time he had aspirin poisoning... and always the money. Always the money.

I knew I had to hold it together since Mom seemed incapable. She didn't allow me to have the meltdown that my heart longed to have. Maybe that was good. Or maybe it would have been nice for her to let me be a child for once. But that wasn't going to happen.

We went back inside. We discovered my dad had just refilled his prescription for valium. Mom said, "Why don't you take one so you can sleep?" That seemed like a good idea. I was a hot mess. We decided to all meet at the funeral home the next day.

By the time Eric and I got to the hotel room, the medicine kicked in. "I don't think I can get undressed." He must've thought I was just expressing my exhaustion. "No, you don't understand. I don't think I can take my clothes off or put on pajamas." That valium packed a punch.

Mom had a phrase for that feeling that valium gives. She would've said it "knocked my dick in the dirt." Of course I didn't have a penis, but if I did, I know just where it would've been—in the dirt, next to me where I'd be sound asleep.

At the funeral home, I knew Daddy would want to be buried in his Marine dress blues. We set the ceremony for the next day. He had been going to church with his ex-girlfriend so we asked that minister to perform the service. I wrote something about my father and asked this man to read it since I wouldn't be able to.

I learned my father had gone to the grocery store and just collapsed. His grandfather had suffered from heart disease and Daddy always said that when he went he hoped it was a massive heart attack and done. He must've said that a hundred times. Be careful what you wish for.

I also learned that an ambulance had been called by this ex-girlfriend. It had been payday so he'd picked up his prescription and headed to the store. At the hospital he had been listed under her last name. Again, odd. But there was nothing left in his wallet. No money. A ring had gone missing and some other miscellaneous items. I truly believe that woman, that bitch, stole his stuff. I had zero desire to see her at the funeral. Hopefully, I would be able to hold back my urge to punch her in the face.

The funeral home gave the family the opportunity to see Daddy before anybody else that night of the viewing. I was so nervous. I had never seen a dead person before. I trembled as I walked into the room. Eric held my hand. He was being very supportive. I made the slow walk to the casket. I could see Daddy's military hat.

The closer I got, the more I thought I couldn't do this. With sweating palms I walked forward. There he was. The funeral home did a great job with his uniform, as Daddy had put on weight over the years. It looked just like he was sleeping. I touched his hand. It was so cold. I hadn't expected that. He'd always had really warm hands, yet these were cold and hard. I wanted the warm hand of my daddy. I had to settle for closing my eyes and remembering what it used to feel like.

The rest of the night did not improve. Not that I expected it to be a party. I had hoped the initial shock and trauma of seeing him in his casket would be the hardest thing to face. Boy, was I wrong. Apparently the ex-girlfriend thought it was a good idea to bring her six-year-old granddaughter who had adored my dad. This poor child was sobbing and screaming. The girlfriend kept saying, "It's my fault. I broke his heart." The little girl was making the same sound that I'd made. I heard the hurt in her cries and I couldn't console her. I couldn't go near her grandmother, aka *that woman*. But I did want to help the child. I just did not have it in me emotionally to go over there.

Instead I walked outside with my mom, Eric and Aunt Jane to smoke and try to erase that child's cries from my mind. A man was leaving that I didn't recognize. Out of nowhere, he looked at my mother and pointed his finger. "This is your fault! If you hadn't left him, he wouldn't be here." This man said nothing else. He just walked away. My mouth was agape. Mom was devastated. I thought Eric was going to lose it and beat the shit out of this stranger.

Luckily we got through the rest of the night without incident. Next was the funeral. The preacher did a lovely job. He read what I wrote. I wished I'd had the emotional stability to read it myself.

We left through the processional line. Three large black men were dressed in gorgeous suits. The first one explained how they worked with my daddy at Walmart and how much they liked him. "You know, you were always the apple of your daddy's eye. He was so proud of you." I felt some lightness in my heart over that statement. It was nice to know that he told his co-workers about me and that he was proud of me. In the moment I was too much of a hot mess to thank that co-worker properly. I hope he knows that what he said made a difference.

At the cemetery they played "Taps" and "Amazing Grace." The Marines folded the flag and handed it to me. That was really special.

Eric's family sent the biggest peace lily I have ever seen. Later I found out they couldn't believe how inexpensive flowers were in North Carolina. It was beautiful. I still have it, over twenty years later. It has been near death a few times and I have brought it back to life. It is a sweet reminder of my daddy.

But I knew I was going to have to get back to work soon. Eric called and told them I would be out for a week. I made one last trip to Daddy's house where I took a few mementoes. He was so proud of being a Marine. I selected several t-shirts with all kinds of crazy Marine sayings, along with two of those valiums. I was emotionally and mentally exhausted. I had nothing left. I needed to rest.

When I reflect on that time, I can't imagine anyone not believing in God. I know it was God who carried me through. I was a walking zombie. I am pretty sure there were times He held my hand and times when He carried me. I know it.

Death is a strange thing to handle. I questioned myself so many times. Was I being punished because of Jacob? Would Daddy have lived if I hadn't moved away? I believe God knew that my father had suffered enough. He had been abused by his mother. He had been through Vietnam. He lost his wife. He chased his demons with prescription drugs. I like to believe God knew he needed the rest.

There are a few pieces of advice I would share with anyone who has lost someone. The pain never goes away, but it does get better. At first you think about it every day, almost every hour, and it hurts. Then it starts to be a few days before you think about it again. And it hurts. Days turn into weeks, weeks into months. And it hurts. Now it is those special days that still hurt. For me it's Father's Day.

Another bit of advice came from a man I worked with who had lost his son. He recommended talking about the person you've lost. He would say, "Let me tell you about my son," and he would talk about the good things and the fun times. Talking about good memories of my dad helped me too.

If you have a friend who loses a loved one, know that there is no need to say anything. Just be there. Sit with them. Hold their hand if they want. Let them cry. Maybe you cry with them. One of the greatest gifts I received when my daddy passed was my dear friend Tammy who came to my daddy's house and stayed there with me all day. She just sat and talked with me and was present. I will never forget that great gift. I was comforted by her presence. I know not everyone is the same. I can only say what helped me. I hope that if you lose someone maybe one of these things can help you.

I returned to work a week later. I would still break down. It was hard. What was worse was there was a rumor that the general manager wasn't going to allow me to have vacation because I had taken a week off. I was furious about that. I could not comprehend someone, anyone, being that cruel.

I learned that Jacob had been worried sick. He had no way to contact me. I certainly couldn't have called him even though I really wanted to. There was just no way. Eric was always around.

50 | Moving On in All Kinds of Ways

Our love affair picked up right where we left off. We discussed leaving our partners… but what about our jobs? Rumors at work were already flying. I'm pretty sure everyone knew. Everyone except Eric. We had to make a move soon.

Luckily our reputations in the car world were good. I was known as one of the best finance managers in the business and Jacob was one of the best car guys. He set up a meeting with the general manager of the dealership right next door. They sold Mitsubishi, Subaru, and Mercedes Benz. Their used car department wasn't doing too well, and that was somewhere Jacob could shine. It also just happened that they had an opening for a finance manager.

The GM and sales manager both knew me through work reputation, and because Eric had worked there for a short time before getting fired. They didn't hold that against me. I got an interview and was offered a job on the spot. While I would still be a finance manager, the overall position was better. I would have every other Saturday off as opposed to only one per month. Best of all? My salary would double and my commission would be better.

Jacob was the kind of guy to make a big exit. He was not going to just leave by himself. He decided he would take as many people as he could, so along with me he brought two salesmen and the recon guy to start his team.

When I went into the general manager's office to resign, I was surprised that he tried to convince me to stay. Apparently not everyone knew about me and Jacob. I was still angry about losing a week's vacation because of my father's death, and since I was pissed and feeling brave, I told him that was one of the reasons. Just to add salt to the wound I said I didn't think it would've gone the same if he or another sales manager had a death in the family. He wriggled in his seat over that comment. I could see he was holding back his normal pissed-off reaction, but I didn't care.

Just like that, five of us walked out. It was quite the scandal in the car world. Word gets around pretty quickly. But it would have been more scandalous if they knew the true motivation to get out of there.

One of the first days on the new job, the salesman asked me to "spot" a car for him. That's when a customer decides to buy on the spot. I took great care of the customer and sold them an extended warranty. The salesman gets a bonus if I do that, and this salesman was so thankful and pleased. He actually thanked me. I was never appreciated like that at the other place. It was also a relief to be away from the nasty talk and sales managers grabbing me.

With the addition of Jacob and his sales team, the used car department started booming. I was doing paperwork for over 150 cars a month by myself. This was unheard of in the car world. I worked my ass off, but I was also making over $80,000 a year. Here I was, a poor white girl without a formal education making more money than most of my friends. I had done it all by working hard and not letting those labels tell me I couldn't be successful.

The work soon got overwhelming. I would go in at 7:00 A.M. just to get started on all the deals I was going to have to deliver that day. The owner was a hands-off guy who only visited now and then. One day he came into my office to tell me what a great job I was doing, then made the mistake of asking if there was anything I needed. I couldn't help myself. Exhausted and delivering a record number of deals, I replied to this multi-millionaire, "I really need some help here or you're going to find me dead in this chair."

He actually responded nicely and got me an assistant. The first gal was bat shit crazy. I can't even begin to explain her. It was quite apparent she had been hired for her looks—petite with short skirts. From my perspective though, she was lazy and dumb as a rock. They had not involved me at all in the hiring process. Would have been a good idea as I could spot that dumbass a mile away. So that didn't last long.

The next time they included me. This woman was in her mid-twenties, tall, blonde, and a local Lancaster gal. She was much smarter than the last one. We also became friends. Or at least I thought we did. The gal from the parts department, Lisa, also became a friend, but she didn't live locally. Lancaster County is pretty conservative so most of my really close friends were not from the area. Work life was good. I got to see Jacob every day, I had a new friend, and now I had help. My new job was working out great, even though home life with Eric was still the same.

In the car industry, salesmen turn over quickly. If they aren't making it at one place, they move on to another. Or they leave because there are definitely better places to work. Most are charismatic, talkative, likable and often attractive. That's what makes them good.

One day, Lisa came to my office. "Hey, did you see the new man candy?" I asked who she was talking about. "The new sales guy, Brent." I knew he had three kids and was only 23 years old. I thought he must be stupid. (Funny how no matter how many times life tried to teach me not to judge a book by its cover, I was still doing it.)

Car salesmen don't have the best reputation. However, some customers really treat them like shit. Sometimes they give false names. Sometimes they put black tape over the check engine lights on their trade-ins, in hopes of getting more money. And most days they try to beat up the salesmen on price.

But the car business taught me many life lessons. It showed me I was not someone who should be sitting behind a desk away from people. It made me tougher and gave me confidence. It showed me I could make money no matter what label or box I had been put in as a young person. So I will be forever grateful for my time there.

51 | How Could He Do That to Me

Jacob had followed through on getting us out of the dealership with his father-in-law. The next step was going to be separation from our spouses. He seemed completely in love with me and willing to do anything for us to be together. He even asked if he should go ahead and buy the ring before I'd left Eric. He would definitely take a big financial hit—child support and probably alimony since his wife didn't work outside of the home. He would also be giving up a huge future inheritance.

On the other hand, I was the reluctant one. I realize now that I was testing Jacob. Every man I'd ever known had let me down— my dad leaving so many jobs, the high school boyfriend taking me for granted, and then there was Todd and of course Eric. Subconsciously I was seeing just how much Jacob could take.

I didn't tell Eric I was leaving, in part because I was scared of him. I would get sick, and make excuses. But there was something else in my gut making me wonder about Jacob and his possible recreational use of cocaine. He did have the whole erection problem. He would also often have white stuff around his nose. Then a friend told me he never knew another person who could hide his drug use better than Jacob. And he had personal experience with the stuff. I was rather taken aback since I knew the extent of this man's experience with drugs and people who did them.

Nonetheless, the rendezvous continued. Jacob bought a beautiful townhouse. He let me give approval before he bought it. After all, it was supposed to be my home too. But then some of Jacob's friends began to say things like, "She's never going to leave Eric," and "There are plenty of other women out there." Finally, the very frustrated Jacob was convinced to go out on a date with a girl one of them knew.

I mean, who could blame him? I had been stringing him along for about three years. He had left his wife, bought a house and was ready to marry me any day. Yet, I was devastated! Apparently, I could add him to the list of men I couldn't count on. Yes, I realize now I was totally wrong. For me at the time, he hadn't passed all the tests. He didn't wait forever. And I could barely hold myself together. I immediately scheduled a visit back home to North Carolina where I could just break down.

I decided to take the train as I wouldn't be able to drive, and flying was too costly at the time. Eric would take me to the station. Unfortunately, one of the biggest hurricanes in history hit and my train got canceled. Some track had been washed out, and there was only a chance that it would be fixed by the next day. Boy, did I need that to be fixed. I was an emotional mess. I had to work hard to not show Eric just what a hot mess I was. I'm sure he thought it was just the delay in seeing my mom.

I didn't understand my reaction. I had never been so devastated. We made the trip back to the train station in Philadelphia the next day and God was smiling down on me. I got on a train to Virginia and then a bus to Rocky Mount where my mom was waiting to pick me up.

I saw her and immediately I broke. Tears and tears and more tears. My heart hurt. I couldn't believe Jacob had done this. I thought he really loved me. I thought he would wait forever. Again, I know, I know. I hadn't left Eric. It was truly my fault. However, that didn't matter. Mom was so understanding and supportive. I spent the week crying and trying not to cry. I even cleaned her whole house just to keep my mind busy while I cried.

The week came and went and it was time to go back. In Pennsylvania, nothing had changed. Eric was still an asshole and Jacob was seeing this girl. Worse than anything, the company Christmas party was coming and... you guessed it... Jacob would be taking her.

I mentally prepared as best I could. I also took extra time to look my very best. I had now reached the anger stage. Driving to the party, I remember listening to Alanis Morissette's "You Oughta Know." Her music was pretty angry back then, like me. I made Eric play that song over and over on the way to the party, about a guy going out with another girl and the original girl asking if she does things in very explicit ways and how the second girl definitely doesn't measure up. I'm sure Eric didn't understand what the deal was with this song. I just kept having him play it over and over and louder and louder.

We arrived at the party with those lyrics echoing in my brain. I had gotten myself all wound up from the song, truly mad and ready to face Jacob and his new girlfriend. We found a table and sat with Lisa and her date. There Jacob was sitting with his buddies, the same ones I suspected had talked him into going out with the new girl. She wasn't exactly hideous. However, I felt I outshined her in many ways.

I wondered if she knew about me and Jacob. I wondered if she knew I wanted nothing more than to punch her right in the face, even though it wasn't her fault. She was just an innocent victim. But I hated her. And I hated him. I wanted him back so badly. The only man I ever believed would not disappoint me... had done just that.

Okay, a final *I know*. It was totally fucked up thinking. It was my fault. I had not left Eric. Jacob had done everything he said he would. And yes, okay, maybe I deserved this. I'm quite sure his friends thought I did. Nonetheless, the ache in my heart continued.

52 | Is My Switch On or Off?

Work was hard. I had to be close to Jacob every day. It didn't take long, maybe a week or two, until he wanted me back. He begged and pleaded and said I was the only woman for him. He would be patient and wait as long as it would take for me to leave Eric.

I was ecstatic! For a second. I felt the biggest relief of my life. He really did love me. He knew he had made a mistake and after all, I hadn't done anything I said I would do. He wanted to pick up right where we had left off. But something was wrong.

It was gone. The big "it." My heart had been broken. My switch had been flipped. I'd "lost that lovin' feeling." I tried to get it back. Romantic dinners with him professing his undying love for me didn't work. I searched everywhere but still couldn't find "it." How could it be gone? How could I get it back?

You know the "it," right? That kind of love that lasts a lifetime. I thought I had found it with Jacob. My soulmate. My knight in shining armor.

Wait... remember me? I'm the gal who doesn't go back and forth. I'd already lost all trust in men before Jacob. Now he'd failed as well (even though it was my fault). He didn't pass the test and after my heart had broken into a million pieces, he was not going to put the pieces back together again no matter how much I wanted "it" back.

Jacob still wanted to marry me. He begged me daily. He cried. His friends talked to me. Again, the offer of the ring before I would even leave Eric. I can imagine the labels: "cheater," "she's never going to leave him," and no doubt more.

Life with Eric wasn't any better. My friends still never saw the monster he was behind closed doors. What was the truth? Who was I and what did I want? I didn't know. I just wasn't happy.

Eric was a terrible husband who wouldn't go to counseling. Jacob was, most likely and unfortunately, a cocaine addict with many other issues. And I was totally fucked up.

The best thing to do when you're a mess is to plan a beach trip with your best friends. Lori and three of my high school friends—Dayna, Becky and Connie—planned a weeklong vacation to Nags Head, NC. Afterward, I planned to bring my mother back to Pennsylvania to visit for three weeks and then I was going to leave Eric. I would not immediately go live with Jacob, since I wasn't sure I would ever live with him. But I was, however, going to leave Eric. I would stay with my friend Lori. This was the plan.

I was 28, I'd grown my hair long and dyed it blonde. Thanks to some diet pills, I was down to size 6, sometimes a 4. It was the only time I'd felt like a hottie, which of course completely had to do with my weight. Feeling pretty on the outside definitely doesn't mean you feel or are pretty on the inside. All that mattered to me was I was ready to let off some steam.

In my opinion, my friends were also hotties, so this trip was going to be epic. Eric had no problem with me going away since he had done so many of his own trips. We selected a week in August, which is usually hot as hades in North Carolina. Especially at the beach. Becky found a large beach house that was semi-oceanfront. I shared a room with Lori and everyone else had their own.

Our days went like this. We'd get up and be on the beach by 10:00 A.M. We'd lay out all day. It was so hot, we had to put our beach chairs in the water. But we were experienced sun worshipers so it was not a problem. Around 3:00 we'd go in and take a nap, eat and then head out to a nightclub called Kelly's.

Alcohol was not a problem for five attractive women at the beach. Drinks were free. Well, they were free for us. There was one little thing missing that we all wanted... weed. Don't judge. Connie decided she was going to find some for us. While we all wanted it, the rest of us were nervous about asking strangers. Connie had no fear.

That first night, drinks were flowing. Dancing was happening and fun was everywhere. Connie told us she had found a "local" who could get us some weed and that she was going to leave with him. This would violate Girls' Rule #1: We come together, we leave together. But she was determined and before you know it, we couldn't find her. These were the days before cell phones. We had no choice but to eventually leave and head back to the house.

The next morning, she still hadn't returned. We were all nervous. The mind tends to wander in these types of situations. Had she been kidnapped and killed? Or was she just sleeping off the drinks?

As we were contemplating whether to file a missing person's report, she showed up with a giant bag of very potent weed. In addition, she'd made a new friend who wanted to cook us all dinner. He was a shrimper by trade. Connie had hit the jackpot! No pun intended. He had plenty of weed, caught fresh seafood for a living as a nice local, and he wanted to make us dinner. Let me tell you, there's nothing like fresh-caught seafood from North Carolina.

53 | Is the Universe Telling Me Something?

The next day, we continued our routine, and the shrimper guy invited us for dinner. We dressed up and went to his house. What a spread this guy had for us! Amazing shrimp and all the fixin's. In the middle of dinner, one of his friends stopped by. You should have seen the look on that guy's face. He walks in to see his friend making dinner for five lovely ladies. Shrimper guy was beaming with pride.

After dinner we went back to Kelly's. As we were walking in, a group of handsome young gentlemen were walking out. I spotted one with dark hair and dark eyes, maybe 5'10", so not quite my usual tall. But super handsome. He took a quick look at me and I seized the moment. I gave him my "hello there, handsome" smile. Needless to say, they all turned around to come back.

It was lip sync night. Connie, Dayna and Becky decided they were drunk enough to get on stage and perform Salt-N-Pepa's "Push it." Oh my! Connie did know all the words but Dayna and Becky pretty much just danced. Meanwhile, Lori and I tried to be supportive by hiding under the table and periodically giving them a shout out.

After that performance, we all needed a drink. At the bar waited the group of handsome young men who had followed us back inside. The cutest of the group asked to buy me a drink. That's right. He picked me. I couldn't believe it! Historically I'd never felt like I was the prettiest of the group. I was overjoyed and a bit shocked. This super cute guy asked if he could buy me a drink. His name was Michael Jacob. Yet another Michael.

But here's the thing. Jacob's middle name was Eric... and Eric's middle name was Michael. This guy's name? Michael Jacob.

He was from Princeton, New Jersey, which was way closer to Pennsylvania than North Carolina. Being a believer in fate, I was totally interested. It also didn't hurt that he was a super hottie.

The rest of that night was spent dancing and having drinks bought for us by the Jersey hotties while still paying attention to shrimper guy. After all, he had made us dinner and bought us drinks and he was really nice. Becky said he was interested in me, but I didn't see it. And unfortunately, I was not attracted to him. Of course, I couldn't see it. He was too nice.

The New Jersey boys had rented a house in the northern part of Outer Banks. They invited us over for a Thursday night party, so once again we repeated our sun worshipping, napping, and getting all decked out. I chose carefully what I wore that night— a super short skirt that showed off my tan legs and a black bodysuit that showed off everything else. A little extra time was spent on my hair and makeup. I was feeling pretty good about myself. Yet, I was still nervous. After all, what was I doing? Jacob was back in Pennsylvania patiently waiting for me to leave Eric. And Eric? Well, Eric was intentionally blinding himself to our ever failing marriage.

Nonetheless, I soldiered on to go see the Jersey boy. I was too intrigued and he was way too cute. We arrived around 7:30. Michael was attentive. Comments were made that we looked like Barbie and Ken together. Cute, right? He was digging me and I was really digging him.

54 | Good Beginning, Bad Middle, Back Home

The New Jersey boys had to buy a blender so we could have frozen daiquiris. One started playing his guitar and another did some grilling. Michael though, only had eyes on me.

I'm not sure exactly how it happened. Drinks were flowing and Michael and I made our way to a room. We did not have sex, but there was lots of making out. Suddenly, we heard Becky and Connie yelling. Apparently, one of them overheard a Jersey boy say, "This is just like a whorehouse." Chaos ensued. The girls started yelling that they wanted to leave. The other Jersey boys acted confused and denied what may or may not have been said. I just wanted to go back to making out with Michael.

There they were again. The labels. Just because we were five lovely ladies dressed to go out dancing, and we came to your rented house and drank lots of frozen drinks, it doesn't mean we're whores or even going to consider sleeping with any of you. But we were the ones labeled naughty. How's that fair?

What about them? They'd certainly gone out of their way to make us feel welcomed. At what point had we turned into sluts? No one had taken any clothes off. It was just a group of gals and guys drinking and having fun at a beach house.

The ladies were determined to leave. I was determined to stay. So once more we broke Girls' Rule#1. They left. I stayed. I mean, I hadn't heard the rude comment and Eric was being a complete gentleman. Plus it was like the universe was telling me I didn't have to be with Jacob Eric or Eric Michael. I could be with Michael Jacob. Right?

The next morning, I woke up beside Michael. No, we did not have sex. I really didn't know what was happening between us. I just knew he was cute. He drove me back to our beach house. I gave him the house phone number, not sure if I would ever hear from him again.

But the next morning, the day before we were going to leave, the phone rang. It was Michael asking if I wanted to get together. I said we could go shopping and hang out for a little. It was a lovely afternoon. We walked around, held hands and caught lots of kisses. When I left, I gave him my work number, explaining that I spent more time there than at home. In reality, I was still living with Eric and certainly wouldn't want the fallout from that phone call!

I went back to the beach house and unfortunately Eric had left a message. I called him back. "What were you doing?" he asked. I told him I went shopping. "By yourself?" I told him the girls didn't want to go. He hesitated but then it was all fine. "I'll see you tomorrow," I said reluctantly and with much sadness in my heart.

We continued our tradition going out to Kelly's that last night, even though we were all pretty much partied out. Surprisingly, the doorman said, "I got you girls tonight," and let us in for free. It was a much more calm evening. None of us wanted to overdrink as we were driving home the next day.

The next morning, five very tan, partied out gals left the beach. I was sad. I was also thankful that Lori was riding with me, and more thankful still that I wouldn't have to deal with Eric alone. Two and a half hours later we picked up my mother and began the seven-hour drive home.

It was nerve wracking for many reasons. First, I didn't want to go back to Eric. Second, my mom was a horrible backseat driver. Really, she was just nervous, but when she's nervous, she talks and talks. Which was fine until we ran into a bad thunderstorm. It was pouring. I could hardly see out of the window. I needed every ounce of concentration, but she seemed determined to distract me. In addition, she was popping valium like it was candy. Meanwhile, it was raining cats and dogs, giant trucks were flying by, and all the other cars weren't happy with how slow I was going. I was on the verge of screaming.

Down South you're taught at a young age not to sass or talk back to your elders, particularly your parents. That being said, I was about to lose my mind and possibly wreck. I finally said, "Mama, will you please be quiet?" Later she reported that I'd told her to shut up, but I would never say that to my mother.

Finally, we arrived. Lori left and my mom—after downing I don't know how many valiums—went straight to the couch and fell asleep. I was also exhausted. It was great having her at my house. While Eric did not change his behavior much, he did react less often and without as much meanness when she was there.

On Monday I went back to work, wondering if I would ever hear from New Jersey boy. Either way, meeting Michael Jacob pretty much solidified that I didn't have to be with Jacob, and that those feelings I once had for him were gone no matter how hard I tried to put it back together.

That week I would work my twelve-hour shift then go home and play Yahtzee with Mom. I've shared with you how often she listened to my ex-boyfriends pour out their hearts. She had this very special way about her that naturally invited people to open up and talk. She was always willing to lend an ear to a troubled heart. And there were plenty who wanted to talk with her. While I worked, a male friend who was going through a divorce would come and visit my mom and talk with her. There was another guy who came to visit her as well. Mom certainly was not lonely while I was working those three weeks. She was giving out therapy. She was so good at it. There was something about the way she would tell you that everything was going to be all right. You would just believe her. She was amazing that way.

55 | Holy Shit, He Actually Called

About three days back, a call came for me at work. "Hello." It was him! It was Michael! I couldn't believe it. He called and he wanted to see me. I explained that my mother was in town but after she left I would come see him. How the hell was I going to do that?

Mom's visit came and went. I was sad to see her go. However, I had to follow my plan and leave Eric. And I had to go see Michael. It's amazing how motivated I can be when it comes to what I want and a cute boy.

I was a nervous wreck, afraid of what Eric might do. I came home from work and told him I needed to separate. He, of course, acted completely surprised, even though I hadn't had sex with him and wouldn't say I love you, along with so many other things I had attempted to do to let him know I was unhappy. He begged me to stay.

I packed some clothes and makeup and got into my car. He came out, crying and begging me to stay. I cried too. Was I doing the right thing? This was the second marriage I was going to walk away from. Was it really that bad? Remember all the romantic things Eric did? Remember all the nice gifts and cards? Wait... remember the name calling? Remember the pushing and walking around on eggshells trying not to set him off? I had to go. I had to... and this was the only way.

I arrived at Lori's and immediately drank a glass of wine and smoked a cigarette. Lori had a one-bedroom apartment with a kitchenette, one bathroom and a living room. My new bed was a brown, plaid couch with a flat pillow. It wasn't great, however, Lori wasn't going to yell at me or call me names or push me around. And besides, I was scheduled to go see New Jersey Michael the following weekend.

Eric called me every day, and every day I told him I wasn't coming home and that I needed time. I gave the same message to Jacob. He was happy I had left Eric. But he was not happy that I didn't want to spend time with him.

Friday came and I got into my car for the three-hour trek to Princeton. Most of the drive was on the turnpike which wasn't so bad, but the closer I got to New Jersey, the worse the traffic. I am not an aggressive driver. I don't speed and I am very cautious. These are not good attributes for getting off an exit during 5:00 traffic in Jersey. The cars were so close they were almost touching. Yet I knew if I didn't make a move, I would be left sitting on that exit, passed by everything in sight. My palms were sweaty, my whole body tense. Finally, I slipped into the blur of cars and left that deathtrap exit.

I arrived at Michael's apartment complex. And there he was, just as cute as he had been at the beach. If not cuter. He gave me a hug and helped with my luggage. It was a little awkward. After all, it had been over a month since we had seen each other. Did I mention he still looked super cute?

I took a shower and got ready for dinner. We went to a quaint bistro where we sat outside. Very light conversation. I hadn't decided if I was going to sleep with him or not. I had been a very good girl at the beach. What must he be thinking? I did, however, pack some nice lingerie in case it went that way.

Back at his apartment, I decided the first night was not the night to sleep together. I bunked on the couch. Should that have been a sign? He let *me* sleep on the couch instead of *him*?

Michael had planned Saturday for us to visit Princeton University's museum. Cool, right? He held my hand and was super polite. He paid for everything. It was going really well. At least in my mind.

We got back to his place and I thought, *I have to close this deal.* I mean the universe had brought this man into my life, right? Out came the lingerie.

It was not a great experience, to say the least. In fact, he didn't even "finish," if you know what I mean. That had never happened to me before. What was the problem? He was certainly aroused. I was beginning to question my decision.

We went to sleep. The next morning he was as sweet as he could be, holding my hand, giving me little kisses. I thought, *Well okay, maybe it was just performance anxiety.* We went to lunch to finish our weekend. I left with another kiss and his promise to call, and saying we would see each other again real soon. Yahtzee!

56 | I Don't Think I Got the Message Right

I went back to Lori's apartment to my new bed, aka her old worn-out couch. I was positive I would hear from Michael any day.

Back at work, the first call I got was from Eric. "Where were you?" he said in his most quiet but bullying voice. "I tried to call and no one knew where you were." I told him I had to get away and had driven out of town and stayed at a hotel. I needed time. He was not happy. I did not care at all. I said goodbye.

By midweek, no call from Michael. He was probably busy, right? I thought he had a good time. It ended with a kiss and "see you soon." Didn't he mean that?

Women, or at least the ones I know, analyze everything a man does or says. For example, when a man says he doesn't want a serious relationship, but sleeps with you anyway, we interpret that to mean we can change his mind. We are positive we can charm our way in. Also, we tend to accept any lame excuse for a missed call, a stand-up, or pretty much anything to keep him interested. Perhaps not all women are like this, but the ones I hung around with definitely were.

I used to want to host a TV show I'd call "What Does He Really Mean?" There would be a panel of guys, maybe celebrities, maybe not. There would be either female guests or a hotline where women could ask this panel of men what exactly a guy meant when he did or said "X." Because, let me tell you, there is a ton of miscommunication out there.

During this time, "Sex and the City" was a popular show about single women in New York and their romances and troubles. It was one of the closest things I had ever seen to real life with women in their mid to late twenties looking for a serious relationship.

I saw Lori do this all the time. She currently liked a guy, and when he was in town he did come to see/sleep with her. She did everything kinky he asked. She had me take photographs of her in lingerie to send to him, and she dragged me to an adult video store and politely asked where the "black man/white woman anal" section was, because that's what he wanted to watch and do. In the end, he was never serious about Lori. But how could he give her up? She was a good time and did absolutely everything he asked.

So here's how it usually goes. Girl meets boy and is immediately attracted. He seems to feel the same. At least, he acts that way. After a drink or two, he becomes nice so she goes home with him. She sleeps with him and, of course, he doesn't say no. Why would he? The girl can't understand when he doesn't call her back in a day or two, or a week or three, or won't take her calls. What is it? *"What's wrong with me?"* Truth be told, at some point, I'm sure the guy mentioned his commitment issues, but they were ignored because how could he sleep with someone and not be truly interested?

Here's what I have learned. It's both parties' fault in these scenarios. The man can't help himself, truly. As mama always said, "A hard dick has no conscience." When guys get excited, all the brain cells flood to the second head... at least guys in their twenties. The woman may have heard the man say he doesn't want anything serious; she just doesn't want to hear it. She is sure she can change his mind. Most women will not just sleep with a guy without some emotional attachment. Often we create the emotion after we have sex, based on the guilt we feel about it. I'm not saying this is every woman. I'm just saying it was that way for me and the ladies I knew.

Why couldn't I call Michael? I mean it was 1998 and women could call guys. But it was generally my rule not to exhibit such behavior. However, my sweet friend Lori saw my desperation and, as usual, convinced me he was busy and that it would be perfectly acceptable for me to call.

I dialed with my hands slightly shaking. He answered. He sounded happy to hear from me. Or was I wanting to hear that? He said he had been busy, and was in fact still busy, and that he would call me back. Yeah, right!

No call for a week. I tried to phone him again. No answer. I left a message. What had happened? My mind was reeling with questions. Did I miss something? He was so nice to me. We had a great time. Let's not forget the universe. Wasn't he the one? My heart hurt. Not because I thought I loved him. It was more a feeling of sadness, disappointment and why-oh-why did I sleep with him?

I finally decided to write him a letter. Those of you who have never experienced life without social media probably find it hard to believe. Back then I had no choice. He wasn't taking my calls and I needed answers.

Note to men: I would have been much better off had Michael said, "I'm just not that into you." Here's why, plus an apology. It would be so much easier to move on, without stalking some poor guy and looking desperate. If you are a guy exhibiting "ghosting" behaviors toward women and then end up feeling like you have to hide behind every corner, please consider just telling us the truth. Not in a mean way. It can be done kindly and truthfully. Only then will you truly be free. Or at least you will feel less guilt... presuming you felt guilty to begin with.

I hoped Michael felt guilty. Really guilty. I deserved his formal rejection... not some I'm gonna invite you for the weekend, be super attentive, sleep with you and say I'll call just to never hear anything from ever again. Not right, New Jersey boy. Not right at all.

57 | Eric Wants a Second Chance

Lori was divorced and on the prowl, and I was separated and on the prowl. My serious co-dependent behaviors were urging me to find a new man. I had never been alone.

I spent the weeks working. Starting Thursday nights and all weekend, Lori and I would go out for drinks. If there was a good band playing, we would go see them. Lori had a thing for a drummer in a band called Johnny O and the Classic Dogs of Love. Fun music and Lori could shake her ass at the drummer stage front.

Lori had this amazing talent to not only get a guy to buy her a drink, but to talk him into buying drinks for all of her friends. I guess it didn't hurt that her clothes left nothing to the imagination, along with lots of giggles, slight hand touches, smiles and sexual innuendo. It worked every time. But I was often the designated driver. I couldn't count on her for that role.

Meanwhile, Eric kept calling and begging. He said he would change. With Jacob, the feeling was gone and I started to see all the flaws I had overlooked before.

Lori mentioned that she liked a guy that I worked with, so I told him about it. He met us out one night and the two seemed to hit it off. I warned Lori that he had a reputation and I was sure he didn't want a relationship. It made no difference to her. She could change any man, right?

One night after work, he came over. There I was sleeping on the old plaid couch while listening to the moanings of Lori and car guy. I tried to cover my head with the pillow. I began to have uncomfortable thoughts about whether car guy would try to mess with me. Frequently Lori's "friends" thought I would be just like her, having no problem with one-night stands, sex in parking lots of bars, doing pretty much anything a man would ask.

As these thoughts swirled through my mind, my stomach started to ache. I felt a lump in my throat. I quietly cried on that brown plaid couch with the flat pillow to the sounds of Lori and car guy doing the dark and sticky. I missed a comfortable bed and bedroom and feeling secure. What was I going to do?

Eric and I met for lunch. He promised he would spend more time with me and that we would do things together. He even cried. I kept thinking about that itchy, brown plaid couch with the flat pillow, along with Lori now inviting different men over. I told Eric I would think about it.

A day or two later after work, I went "home" to Lori's. I took some medicine I hadn't taken before and suddenly my palms and feet started to itch. I was hot and my heart was racing. I was having some sort of reaction. Eric called at just the right moment. He said, "Come home." I was crying and itching, wanting only to sleep in a comfortable bed. I left Lori's saying I may or may not be back.

Of course Eric took care of me. I arrived at my real home to his open arms, with Benadryl at the ready. I was a mess. Tired of partying. Tired of bars. Tired of being hit on by men who only had one thing in mind. And I was tired of sleeping on that ugly fucking couch.

The Benadryl kicked in and the itching eased up. I crawled into bed and felt that old familiar feeling of security and warmth. No thinking. Just sleep.

That's all it took. The next night I went back. I had such a stigma about myself. How would any guy every want me after two failed marriages? Other than Jacob, of course.

Things were good, sort of. Eric did as promised, spending more time with me. He was super attentive. Here's the thing. I do believe people can change. But it takes work. Maybe counseling, which I had begged Eric to do. He just wouldn't. Old behaviors slowly crept back in.

Snowmobiling was the thing. And his machine wasn't fast enough or good enough. He had to have a more expensive one. So there were the trips. We had talked about having children. I said I would not attempt to get pregnant unless he quit smoking pot for at least thirty days. I hadn't read any direct correlation between birth defects and pot smoking, but we had two friends with children who both had issues. And you guessed it. They were both daily pot smokers.

Life continued as it had always been. I worked my ass off, making more money than Eric while he went snowmobiling and played with his friends. I found myself, once again, extremely unhappy. Was this to be my life? I couldn't go back to that itchy plaid couch, even though Lori was a great friend and said I could stay over anytime that I wanted. I just couldn't go back to that. I wanted Eric to be the man I needed him to be.

But he was who he was.

58 | Different Kind of Therapy

I met this lady who got me involved in a multi-level marketing business. She introduced me to another gal named Sue who became a good friend. Sue lived in York and was amazing. She was my first lesbian friend. We had lots of laughs. I confided in her about my unhappiness and that I wanted to go to therapy. I said I had been before, for five years, but nothing seemed to change.

We both knew I was really emotionally fucked up. Truly unhappy. I would still go out with Lori, not wearing my wedding ring, dressed like I was looking for a hookup. In reality, I was looking for a replacement. I couldn't be alone. I wouldn't say that out loud, but it was the truth. Maybe being alone is what I really needed to do.

Sue said she had been seeing a different kind of counselor. She explained how it was changing her life. "What kind of counselor?" I asked. She was super vague. She basically said it was hard to explain and that I should just go. It was not traditional counseling so insurance wouldn't cover it, but she kept assuring me that it would make a difference. "Go one time and see," she said.

Sue was my good friend and I trusted her, and I was so unhappy. Something had to change. I had moments of wondering why I was even alive. How could I have children when I was still raising Eric?

I made the appointment.

This counselor was about a 30-minute drive from my work. I had no idea what to expect. I was greeted by a lovely lady in her early forties with long hair who didn't wear a lot of makeup. She was pleasant. There was something different about the way she spoke to me. It was very intentional.

Her office was unlike any therapist's office I had been in before. There were at least three different large pictures on the wall with what looked to be angels. Bookshelves were filled with manuals and spray bottles with labels. There was a sense of calm and serenity.

I was still nervous. With a traditional therapist, you usually walk into an office with comfortable chairs, but not a lot of decorations. The counselor will ask probing questions designed to make you think and feel your emotions. Usually you are doing most of the talking while the therapist nods and takes some notes. When you hit a "hot spot" they will ask more probing questions. Before you leave, you may be asked to set some sort of personal goal for follow-up at the next session. And if they are good, you may be given some "tools" for how to deal with your emotions/situations as "nothing changes if nothing changes." That's one of my mantras and it's also the hard part.

Traditional therapy sessions had brought some relief for me. Mostly because I dumped all my shit on the therapist. Quite frankly, I have no idea how those people do it... client after client, all day every day, unloading their bullshit. That's got to be exhausting and energetically suck the life out of you. It takes a special person to become a good therapist and an even more special one to survive it.

I was truly desperate, hating myself on so many levels. I was unhappy and lonely. My marriage was a nightmare, and yet again I was on the prowl for another man to rescue me. I knew I was fucked up. If I had not walked into that office that day, I'm not sure I would have survived. I might have hurt myself... or Eric might have finally gone over the edge and hurt me. The sadness and desperation ran deep in my soul.

59 | This Could Actually Work

She didn't do a lot of explaining or ask any probing questions. She simply told me we would use kinesiology, the study of body movement, to help. I would hold my arm out like a chicken wing. She would first push on it as I held it strong. She would have me say, "Yes," and then push firmly down on my arm. My arm would stay in the chicken position for "Yes." She would then have me say, "No," and when she pushed on my arm, it amazingly went down—chicken arm stays up on yes and goes down on no.

Was this real? I didn't hold my arm any differently for the yes or the no, yet each time I said yes it stayed up, and each time I said no it went down. I also didn't do a ton of talking.

She asked me to touch different points on my body, and then she would test my arm. When it would go down, as in a "no" response, she might either have a question or she would pull out a spray bottle and spray all around me.

Next she said I had a goal. This goal would be something I could listen for and hear what it would be. I didn't understand. She then taught me something amazing. She explained that we all have a small quiet voice inside of us. Some call it intuition. Some call it a higher power, perhaps God. At the time, I wasn't sure what I was going to call it. But I quieted my mind and listened. Then I listened harder and waited. There it was. I could hear the small quiet voice. A full sentence came out. I really didn't know what was happening. I just knew that I had not made up that sentence myself. I had "heard" it.

She reminded me that I had to "listen" to find the "action" goal. That's right. Not a traditional goal, a movement. *What?* There were many steps to it. Basically, it started with me sitting on the ground and sort of growing up like a flower. Amidst all of this, I started to cry. I hadn't meant to. I didn't even expect it. I mean,

I wasn't talking about anything. I was just doing these actions that "came" to me. My tears flowed. I was overwhelmed with sadness. We moved through the actions as they came to me, and I went from crying to becoming this beautiful flower and feeling joy that I hadn't felt in a long time.

And then the session was over.

At $80 in 1998, it wasn't cheap, and it wasn't covered by insurance. All I knew was that I felt better. I didn't exactly know what it was all about, but I knew I wanted more. I scheduled the next session for two weeks out. I couldn't really afford to go more often.

I left the office that day with a feeling of hope. I didn't even know what had just happened. I just knew that I was somehow so much better. It was a spiritual experience. At the time, the best way I could explain it was that going to see her once was the equivalent of seeing a traditional therapist ten times. More importantly, it seemed the issues were fixed right then and there.

As with any type of therapy or counseling, or whatever you want to call it, when solving your issues, it's like peeling back an onion. Or rather lots of onions. Once you start to peel back one issue from the top layer, it can lead you deeper, back to another core issue. This was going to take time, and even though the sessions were ten times more effective, I was still really fucked up. How many layers would it take to clean up 28 years of dysfunction?

60 | Still Trying to Find Happiness Wherever and However I Can

Eric resumed his old behaviors. Now instead of snowmobiles, he wanted four-wheelers. Nothing could stop that boy and his want for toys. Then he coaxed all of his snowmobile buddies to do the same. How would we ever afford to have a child?

Work was okay. Jacob still begged me to come back, although that was getting less and less. They hired a new gal, Jackie, to be my assistant. She was a bit younger than me, with white-blonde hair and big blue eyes. While she wasn't fat, she was a bigger girl. Single and living with her parents, she had a toughness about her which you really need in the car business. We became fast friends.

In addition to Jackie, a familiar face returned. Do you remember "man candy"? The guy who worked with me a few years ago with the three kids had come back. This time however, he was a sales manager. He seemed more grown up.

Jackie had quite the social life. She'd gone to college near Philadelphia so that was her favorite place for her and her friends to go out. She invited me along for one of these girl trips. I asked if I could bring Lori, and of course she agreed.

We asked to borrow a van from the used car department and Jacob, eager to please, said yes. Five ladies piled in after work on Saturday and headed to a hotel in Philadelphia. Lots of personality and lots of laughs. There was a sense of immaturity, or maybe it was innocence. I had clearly experienced more of life, but still, it was nice to be hanging out with girlfriends and having fun.

We checked into the hotel and had a few drinks there, since apparently booze was super expensive at the clubs. Then we got dressed in our best clubbing clothes. Me, of course, went without my wedding ring.

Philadelphia clubs are a far cry from the ones in Lancaster and York. We went to one called Egypt. It was ginormous! There were five different rooms playing five different types of music— contemporary, techno, '70's... and quite honestly, I never made it to the other rooms. We had a blast, drinking, dancing and laughing.

Jackie, being the assertive gal that she was, made some rules. The first, I already knew: We come together, we leave together. If anyone wanted to bring a guy back to the room, that was on them. However, no one would go home with a guy. That's the safe way to club in Philly. Well, really any club. Another rule was that when we leave, we were to make sure to keep our heads down, stay together, and don't let anyone talk to us. What in the world? Did all the guys turn into pumpkins? Oh, you'll see!

Jackie told us that after Egypt closed, a club right around the corner was open for one more hour. All the other ladies wanted to go, so who was I to disagree? Closing time came at 2:00 A.M. so we began our journey through the ocean of people, headed around the corner to spend the next hour dancing.

It was unbelievable. As I was walking out, I made the mistake of making slight eye contact with a guy. *Boom!* He was beside me before I could even look away, totally trying to pick me up. "Where were you all night?" No, dude. Not interested. I started the walk again and whoops, I looked up. Yep, *boom*. Another guy was all about picking me up. Was there blood in the water? The sharks were out and looking for prey. So this is what she was talking about. Apparently 2:00 A.M. meant time to get someone to go home with.

It seemed like it took forever to make our way outside. Coupons were being handed out for the other club since both venues had the same owner. It was going to be $15.00 for just one hour. Holy shit! I hoped it would be worth it.

I was feeling no pain, except for a little sick in my belly. I really couldn't handle my liquor. We made it to the one-hour club which was a let-down from Egypt. Only one room and the music was okay. Just a space full of really intoxicated people looking for one last chance to hook up. I only wanted to dance.

We taxied our way back to the hotel where we all shared beds. I knew what would happen to me. I don't get sick the night of drinking, but when I wake up? Look out! On cue, I vomited the next morning. We had a two-hour drive back home and our first stop was McDonald's—the best cure for a hangover... grease.

I could only handle a few fries and a Sprite. I also threw up behind the van before we left. The soda helped me through the ride home. We got back to our cars and home I went, exhausted. Eric never gave me a hard time about going out. How could he? He smoked weed every day. His friends were at our house every night, and let's not forget all the snowmobile and four-wheeler trips.

I had a great time though and met some new friends. This became a monthly event.

61 | Another Beach, Another Boy

I continued to see my spiritual counselor and was feeling better, but I was still unhappy with Eric. Lori and I decided we needed a beach trip.

I had another female friend at work, Eileen. *Bless her heart.* She was super sweet... and that's where it stops. Eileen was divorced with two children. Her ex-husband was a deadbeat and left her with very little. She worked in the service department for not much money. She'd recently gone on a diet and lost a significant amount of weight, but her shape was sort of plain. Italian with olive skin, her nose was enormous... with a mole on the side. Thick, black-rimmed glasses did nothing for her dark bug eyes and small mouth. Again, bless her heart.

Eileen was originally from New York, and other than her children, she had no one else locally. She would come into my office and we would talk. She had lots of financial challenges. I thought it would be nice to invite her to the beach with me and Lori. Lori and I would pay for the gas and the hotel. Eileen would only need money for food. She was ecstatic!

We decided to go to Wildwood, New Jersey. *I know, I know.* I hadn't had much luck with Jersey boys, but it was time to give it another shot. We got in Lori's car after work on a beautiful Friday and headed out for the three-hour ride. I didn't know what to expect. I'm used to beautiful, clean, North Carolina beaches.

We rented an inexpensive hotel room about a block from the beach. It wasn't super fancy—just two beds and a bathroom. But how much time would we be spending in the room anyway?

The diet pills I had been taking from the multi-level marketing company had really worked. I had long blonde hair and wasn't afraid to show off my body. I wore a size 6 and sometimes a 4. A four! I never would have dreamed it. I was the thinnest I had ever been, other than the emaciated nervous breakdown gal I was when I left Todd. That doesn't really count.

First thing on the agenda was to go dancing. I wore this light blue and pink skort that showed off my legs with a white t-shirt and chunky white sandals which were totally "in." I curled my hair, put on makeup, off with the wedding band and I was ready. Lori dressed similarly and I let Eileen borrow a cute, short brown, sleeveless dress. I also did her makeup. I wanted her to have a good time and feel good about herself. She seemed pleased with her overall appearance. That made me happy.

Out we went! We walked to avoid needing a designated driver. Our first stop was this bar right on the boardwalk. It was swimming with men and women ready to party. The air was electric and smelled of the beach, various perfumes and colognes, and pheromones from all the guys and gals looking to have a good time.

It was $1.00 well-drink night, so all mixed drinks made from the lowest liquor shelf were just a buck. We immediately began taking advantage. I should have known better.

This attractive man approached me and handed me his card. He was a doctor. Or at least that's what the card said. Don't all attractive doctors out on the prowl hand out their business cards? I didn't care. He was cute. I was drunk and he wanted to dance with me.

Closing time came and, of course, the handsome doctor offered to walk us back to our hotel. I had developed blisters on my feet from the cute chunky shoes, which the alcohol had numbed, but I was going to feel it tomorrow. When we arrived back at our hotel, there were seats outside of our room and the doctor offered, since he was a doctor after all, to take me to the bathroom and examine my blisters. Thank goodness Lori was sober enough to refuse him for me. He had a "I'm gonna take advantage of the drunk girl" look. Lori told him it was time to get

Reesy to bed and that he could go. After a kiss or two or three, he left.

On par, I went to sleep just fine and woke before the other ladies. This time I was sure I was going to be able to lay in that hot, hot sun and be just fine. I stumbled my way to the bathroom. I even shakily showered and shaved my legs. Then it began. Yep. I started vomiting and vomiting. My stomach churned. I tried Sprite. Threw that up. Lori brought me a breakfast sandwich. Threw that up. I think I broke a blood vessel in my eye from vomiting so hard.

Lori and Eileen tried to be patient and kind until I finally came to the conclusion that there was no way I would be able to lay in the beating sun without vomiting on the beach. No one wanted to see that display, so with some "I'll be okay," the ladies headed out without me.

Sometime that afternoon, I hadn't thrown up for about an hour. The blisters from those very cool shoes started talking to me, along with my churning head and throbbing gut. It seemed I wasn't going to die after all.

A knock came at the door. I thought maybe Lori and Eileen had forgotten their keys. Somehow I managed to pull my ever-so-sore body out of bed, make the long trek to the door and open it. Stupid! I didn't look out the window to check to see who was there. I had expected to see Lori and Eileen.

There I stood in a pair of shorts and t-shirt, looking slightly green. Staring back at me with a big smile was the doctor boy. He was not nearly as cute as he had been the night before. He walked right in and asked how I was. I explained how sick I had been. Then without warning he tried to kiss me. "Oh my gosh, dude! I've been throwing up for hours." You would think that would've turned the guy off. Doctor boy was beginning to make me nervous.

He tried again. My heart started to race. I was so weak from vomiting, and he was a pretty big guy. I told him he should leave.

He reminded me of his credentials and said he could help me. Oh really? He said he could massage my diaphragm to relax it.

I was feeling so poorly. Would that really work? He sat on the bed and said, "Come here and sit between my legs and lay back. I'll massage your diaphragm. I promise it will make you feel better." He explained that my stomach was probably spasming and massaging it would help. It sounded legitimate. I was also desperate to feel better. We had another night of fun planned and I wasn't going to be able to enjoy it under the current circumstances.

He sat on the bed with his back against the headboard while I sat between his legs and laid back. He started to rub my diaphragm ever so gently. It did feel better. What the fuck? Then he put his hand on my boobs. I somehow found the energy to sit straight up. "Stop it!" Did he really just do that? He apologized and promised not to try anything else in his "I'm a doctor and really want to help you" voice.

I hesitantly sat back down. "Where are your friends?" he asked. I told him they were at the beach, and then the hair on the back of my neck started to stand up. "When will they be back?" My heart started racing. In my best trying-to-stay-calm voice I said they should be back any minute. I needed this guy to leave. I was shaking. He seemed perfectly content to stay. What was he going to try next? This is the shit you read about in the news.

"I have to see you again," he said. "Will you be out later?" I was ready to say anything he wanted, just to get him to leave. "I'm not leaving until you promise you'll come out tonight at that same bar so I can see you again." I was hesitant. But he wasn't leaving. I looked him in the eye and said, "I promise," even though I had no intention of seeing this doctor-pervert ever again. I just wanted him to leave.

I thought of all the police dramas where the girl gets raped because she let some guy she just met in the door. "I promise," I repeated. "I just need some rest and my stomach needs to feel better."

God was looking out for me. Right at that moment, the door opened and there were Lori and Eileen. I let out a breath of relief. He once again repeated his request and I echoed my promise while Lori and Eileen gave him their very best stink-eyes. He reluctantly kissed me on the cheek and left.

My whole body was shaking. I was still nauseous, but the ladies wanted to go out to dinner. The mere thought of food made my stomach turn. Luckily, Eileen had some weed. I smoked just a little and it calmed my stomach. I was able to get dressed. But there would be no alcohol for me that night!

62 | The Adonis Saves My Life

Dinner was nice, though I only ate soup. Lori wanted to go back out, but Eileen, on the other hand, had no desire. Unfortunately, not one guy had hit on her the night before. She was lonely... and there just wasn't a physically redeeming quality about the gal. Most guys couldn't get past her looks to find the sweet girl I knew. At least guys at a bar. So Eileen went back to the hotel while Lori and I went out.

I refused to return to the same bar where doctor boy would be waiting to pounce. She agreed that we would try a different place. It was like a graveyard—no good music, small crowd, definitely not a fun scene. Lori had one drink and I continued with Sprite. Then the begging began. She pleaded with me to go back to the Friday night bar. She assured me that she would protect me. "And if doctor boy is there, we'll leave." I hesitantly agreed. Turns out that after three or four drinks and a few shots, Lori couldn't protect me from anything.

In her best slightly-drunk, flirty, on the prowl move, Lori spotted her prey. She struck up a conversation with a cute guy who had with him a 6'4" man with dark hair and eyes, strong jawline and the biggest muscles I'd seen in real life. I'm not sure if he was Italian, but his olive skin made him look like an Adonis.

As Lori was talking with Adonis's friend, Adonis moved in toward me, smiling with perfectly straight, white teeth. He was named Greg, from East Brunswick. *Oh no, another Jersey boy!* I wasn't going to fall for that type again. And wait, another one named Greg. It seems I've always had someone named Greg in my life. There was my sweet cousin Greg, my longtime friend from school Greg, then my high school sweetheart Greg. Oh no, Universe! I'm not falling for that shit either! Be quiet, Adonis boy! I have no interest in you!

Then I found out he was a wholesaler in the car business. That's someone who goes around finding used cars, either from individuals or the trade-ins from new car dealers, then resells them or takes them to auction. So we had the car business in common. Turns out he came to the Manheim Auto Auction, just down the road from my dealership, a couple of times a month.

Lori wanted to go out on the beach with Greg's friend—just to talk... *yeah, right!* Before she was able to leave, I spotted doctor boy. My heart started to race again. I wanted to disappear, but Lori wasn't having it. She was pretty drunk and really into this guy so I did my best to play it cool.

I decided I needed a defender. Greg didn't seem to be drinking, so I asked if he would do me a favor. I explained the night before and he gladly agreed to sit with me while Lori went off with his friend. Apparently, we were supporting both of our friends getting laid. We sat at the bar. He ordered a beer and I ordered another Sprite. Out of the corner of my eye, I saw doctor boy staring at me like a bear fishing for salmon.

Greg and I talked a lot about the car business. He was super nice though there was no sign of interest from him at all. A perfect gentleman. I guess I just wasn't his type. But he was big and handsome and I needed the protection. And truly after the night before, I wasn't interested either. He was very cute though. *Stop it, Reesy!* Every now and then I would take a quick glance to keep tabs on doctor boy's moves. Where did he go? Maybe he left. Oh no. He was making his move. I warned Greg. "Just relax. I'm right here," he said.

The next thing I knew, doctor boy was literally standing right beside me. I could feel his energy and eyes all over me. My gaze remained fixed on Greg's face, making sure to keep my back toward doctor boy. Would he start something? I couldn't imagine. While doctor boy wasn't small, Greg was huge. Greg just kept talking. He had his eyes on the situation. He wasn't going to let that guy touch me.

We kept talking and talking and finally doctor boy must've gotten the hint. He left. I relaxed my shoulders and could actually breathe again. I thanked Greg, while Lori and his friend came back in, looking no worse for the wear and the sand. It was closing time so Greg, being the gentleman that he was, offered to walk us back to our hotel. We stopped and got pizza along the way.

About an hour later we arrived back at the hotel. Lori and I put our purses in the room and we were greeted by a more than usual bug-eyed Eileen. Turned out doctor boy had paid a visit! He had knocked but Eileen didn't answer. So he'd started banging on the door. Eileen said she whipped open the drapes and yelled, "She's not here!" I'm sure that was quite a sight!

Lori wanted to go back to the beach again with Greg's friend. My original plan had been to say goodnight to Greg, as he clearly had no interest, and go to bed too. But I was scared that doctor boy would come back. Without asking, Greg offered to stay. Lori left for fun in the sand while Greg and I sat on plastic chairs outside of our room.

We talked and talked. No doctor boy, thank goodness. Finally the sun began to peek out. This man had spent the whole evening and night protecting me. He had bought me a Sprite and a slice of pizza, and not one move. Did he not find me attractive? It had seemed like he was interested in everything I was saying. Neither of us was drunk. What was his deal?

So I did something I usually don't do, knowing fully that it could get me in trouble. However, being the gal that I was, I decided to take a chance. In my most innocent yet flirty Southern voice I said, "Are you going to kiss me?" His eyes popped open and just like that he leaned over and kissed me. And then he kissed me again. It was really nice!

We decided to make our own trip to the beach. Not for sex, but we would enjoy many kisses and hugs. The bugs were horrible. I thought they were going to eat us alive. We both decided it was time to get some sleep back in our separate hotels so he walked me back to the room with one more kiss goodnight. Or rather, good morning.

Lori was asleep when I got back, but Eileen was awake and pissed. Doctor boy had not only knocked on our door at 2:00 A.M., but he also started calling. That guy could just not take a hint. Out of guilt and even though I was absolutely exhausted, I went for a walk with Eileen to help calm her down.

It was Sunday. We had planned to lay on the beach for a little and then head home. At the room we got our suits on and then Greg pulled up. He wanted my number. He had actually been one of the calls to the room, but Eileen had presumed it was all doctor boy. I really don't think she had much fun at all.

I gave Greg my work number with the same I'm-getting-divorced-but-still-living-with-the-ex story. He kissed me and off he went.

Lori, Eileen and I walked onto the beach. It was the first time I saw it in the light of day. Ugh! Not a Carolina beach. The sand had dark spots and it was really far to get to the water which was dark and muggy. No way was I going to get in. Then a syringe rolled up on shore. How disgusting! We laid out briefly then decided it was too hot and we weren't getting in that water to cool off so we left.

I arrived home without an ounce of sleep, but with possibilities of a new love on my mind. Did I mention what an Adonis he was?

63 | Once You Do Something It's So Easy to Do It Again

Here is what I found. It was so easy to cheat on Eric again. At first I thought it was because I had done it before and not gotten caught. I came to realize the truth was that I was afraid. Afraid of being alone. Afraid of Eric. Afraid no one would ever love me after all the shitty things I'd done.

I wanted someone to love me with their whole heart. I wanted someone to put me first. It was so easy to agree to see Greg when he called. He wanted to see me. I wanted to see him. He was going to be at the auction on Friday so we agreed to meet at Lori's apartment.

I got there first and waited. The knock came at the door. There he was, as cute as he had been at the beach. His muscles were just as big and his smile just as handsome. One thing led to another and we did what we had not done at the beach on that brown, plaid itchy couch. I didn't feel right about making out on Lori's bed.

Greg was a pretty good kisser. That being said, there wasn't a lot of foreplay involved. At least on his part, if you get what I mean. At that point in my life, I had an imbalanced view of sex. I mostly felt that it was for the man. *I know, right?* Let's just say since then, I've figured out a lot more about sex. More on that later.

Needless to say, it was anticlimactic. Again, at least for me. I thought this was perhaps normal for the first time though he seemed to enjoy himself. After, I told him about our little trips to Philly, and asked if he and some of his friends would like to meet me and some of my friends there for a night of drinking and dancing.

I told Jackie all about Greg. She already knew about Jacob. She knew about Eric. She didn't seem to judge me. I had told her about my unhappiness with Eric and the things he had done to me. She worked with Jacob and could clearly see his flaws.

Saturday after work, we loaded the van with ladies and headed to Philly. We checked into the hotel and were getting ready when the knock came at the door. There Greg was again looking super handsome. And there were his three friends. Not as handsome but still pretty cute.

Jackie and one of the other ladies were in awe at how handsome Greg was. The minute he wasn't looking, I got the "he's so hot" smile and nod.

Off we went. Greg and I had a great time dancing, but none of the guys paid any attention to Jackie because one of her friends, Gina, snagged it all. Lori's conquest from the beach hadn't come. I guess he didn't want any more sand in his underwear.

Greg had gotten us our own hotel room next door. There would be no other hook ups that night. Hey, I brought them together. The rest was up to them. But even after a few drinks, there just wasn't any chemistry with any of them.

Greg and I spent the night together. Same sort of sex. Not a lot of foreplay on his part. What I'm trying to say is that he did not venture "downtown" at all. I was confused by this. Any man I had been involved with was more than eager to take the trip, but did he just not do that? I didn't think it was me. I hadn't had any complaints before. Maybe he didn't feel close enough to me yet. See, there I go justifying his behavior.

The next morning, much to my chagrin, I had to vomit. Luckily, it was not long lasting. I took a shower and fixed myself up in super cute jeans and a plain white t-shirt. We were standing at the door to say our goodbyes. Greg stood back and did a complete once over from top to bottom like he could have me for lunch. I'll never forget what he said. "Yeah, you look good." Well thanks, big guy. I think. He gave me a kiss and we parted.

On the drive back from Philly, Jackie said, "Don't you have enough men?" At the time, I thought she was joking. I must have needed a giant red flag flying in my face to realize things were not okay with her and my complex relationships.

64 | My Spiritual Search for Happiness

I knew seeing Greg was not the right thing. I wanted so badly to be in love. I wanted a soulmate. I really wanted it to be him. Or was I trying to fit his square peg into my circle? I knew I was still a mess. I wanted to be needed and respected. I wanted to be the most important person in someone's life. I wanted to come first. Was that too much to ask? One of my best friends once asked me if I should be married at all. Was that true? I didn't know how to be alone. I couldn't even fathom the thought of being by myself. One thing I knew for sure was I needed to continue with my counselor.

I told her about Greg. There seemed to be no judgment in her eyes as we began. She asked, "Whose reality are you in when you are with Greg?" What? She was saying I wasn't myself when I was with him. Kinesiology arm check... no, I wasn't in my own reality. She asked, "Whose reality are you in?" I stopped and listened to that small still voice and... oh my gosh, I was in my mother's reality! "Okay what percentage of the time are you in your mother's reality when you are with him?" I listened. Oh no—100% of the time I was in my mother's reality when I was with him. Greg was dating my mother. Not me.

Let me explain a little more about this type of counseling. This counseling came from the study of the body's memories that have been embedded as early as childhood. Memories can be good and they can be bad. They can also be subconscious and self-sabotaging, which can block you from being your true authentic self. If you think of your body like a computer, as information goes in, we process it. Sometimes we take ownership as if it belongs to us, when in reality it could belong to the person who helped to put that information in our "computer."

This work through geometrical input helps clear negative information out of your system. It erases it and fixes it forever...

unless of course, you keep going back to the same person and/or behavior. In either case, it definitely helps you become more equipped to handle situations differently. It was also, to me, a study of the way energy is exchanged between individuals. I once saw an exhibit where ice crystals had been formed, and as individuals would stare at them, thinking certain thoughts such as joy, happiness, sadness and anger, it was amazing how these crystals reacted to positive thoughts versus negative ones. The positive crystals were bright and beautiful and clear, while the negative ones looked dirty and distorted.

I once had a test performed at a chiropractor's office who practiced this work as well where I put my hand on a machine and it spit out an image showing a sort of glow around my hand. At the time, I had broken part of my glow. After an adjustment and some clearings, he took another image and it was much better. I believe we all have this field around our body, where disease... dis-ease... starts to imprint and eventually reaches our bodies, causing sickness and other maladies, both physically and emotionally.

After sessions I would find myself thinking more clearly and feeling better. I didn't completely understand how it all worked. I just knew it did. I was hooked. I had discovered a way to feel better.

I found that I had a lot of self-sabotaging thoughts about myself, mostly from childhood. I felt responsible for everything. My grandmother had told me that it was my fault that Daddy had his nervous breakdown. Was that true? Would my parents have stayed together if I wouldn't have moved away? What was wrong with me that Eric wouldn't be a good husband?

Up north I had found my outside beauty. Growing up, I always felt like the ugly duckling, the "chubby girl with the pretty face." I had developed much earlier than most of my friends. In fourth grade I weighed 104 pounds while they were more like 75 pounds. I was one of the first to get my period. At 12 I looked 16, and at 16 I looked 18. I guess that's why mostly older guys had liked me.

What I needed was to discover my inner beauty and with all of this counseling, I was beginning to see my true authentic self. I was starting to like who I was. Through my sessions and self-awareness, self-reflection and movies, I decided I was a sort of Elle Woods from *Legally Blonde*. Most saw me as this bubbly blonde, not so smart, who survives on her looks. I had learned to use that to my advantage in a negative way. I was also a bit of Van Wilder, meaning that I just did things my own way and not necessarily the conventional way. Through this spiritual work, I discovered I could be all of those things and still be amazing. I could embrace my true authentic self without shame and without trying to be someone I thought others wanted me to be.

Another discovery I made was a relationship with God. Because my father had been forced to go to Catholic church and had not had a good experience, we did not attend very often. I could count the number of times on two hands, usually with a friend who invited me. Coming from the Bible Belt, this would be viewed as embarrassing... or perhaps shameful. My friends would sometimes share Bible stories and I had no idea what they were talking about. I did my best to hide it.

These sessions allowed me to develop a relationship with God and I began to learn a lot of the things I had missed out on as a child. There were also "homework" assignments. The first movie I was asked to watch was *Clueless* with Alicia Silverstone. I had no idea why it had been assigned. I just did as I was asked because this stuff was working. Sure enough, there was a message. I was walking around clueless and it was time to get clued in and become aware of the world.

One of the great things about the work I was doing was that I could attend classes about how to work on myself and work with others. I was ready. My friend Sue, who had told me about my counselor in the first place, also wanted to attend a class. The first one would be held in Boulder, Colorado, in February. I prayed for the money to go. Eric certainly wouldn't complain after all he spent on snowmobiling. But it was rather costly. First, you had to fly there. The class was $400, and there were products to buy like sprays and drops that had been integrated to help with clearings. There were also food costs. None of that mattered. The money came and I went.

I signed up and Sue and I flew together. It was amazing. I met the lady who discovered and developed this work. I was a bit intimidated being around all of these enlightened people. We worked in groups. Of course, you just didn't pick any group. You would listen to your higher power and find the appropriate one. Luckily, it worked out. I left Boulder more interested than ever, and on the way to becoming my true authentic self.

65 | It Doesn't Matter How Cute They Are

The girls wanted another weekend away because it was one of their birthdays, and when it's your birthday, you get to choose where we go. She wanted Atlantic City. I invited Greg.

As per the norm, the gals loaded up a van on Saturday after work. I had spoken to Greg earlier and he said he and some of his friends would meet us at the bar. But he wasn't there. What? I tried to call as Eric and I had gotten cell phones, because of course Eric had to have one. No answer. I left a message. More time passed. Was Greg standing me up? The night went on without him. I was truly upset but didn't want to ruin everyone's fun over my rejection.

As men do, Greg called and gave some lame excuse. As women do, I accepted it and agreed to see him the next Friday at Lori's.

The ladies scheduled another trip pretty quickly to a club in New Jersey on the beach. I decided I would show Greg. I would look my absolute best and pretend not to care what he thought. That works, right? Reindeer games.

It didn't matter. I bought this super tight, sexy dress. I straightened my now below-my-bra long blonde hair and put on chunky silver shoes that matched the dress perfectly. I was looking good. When Greg saw me, he seemed to agree. I got a big hug and kiss hello.

He was going to ride with his friends to the bar and meet me there. We all walked in and were greeted by a topless, muscular barman serving shots. Not only was he serving shots, but he wanted to pick me up and pour the shot down my throat. I've never been so brazen in my life. I jumped up and wrapped my legs around his hips in that dress that barely covered my underwear. I was going to prove to Greg that I didn't need him... thereby making him want me. Isn't that how it works? He certainly was super attentive the rest of the evening.

The next spiritual class was in Lancaster over Easter weekend, so at least there wouldn't be any travel costs. It was amazing as always. I still continued my sessions, introduced to essential oils by Young Living. I had a knack and knew instinctively what to do with them. My counselor called me "the oil lady." Young Living offered a class called raindrop therapy, a layering of oils on the back and feet to improve overall health. I signed up.

At work I was becoming good friends with Brent. He was a practicing Mormon and knew a lot about the Bible. I would often ask him questions and he would spend lots of his down time in my office. He made me laugh. I was glad he was back.

Greg and I continued our relationship, if you can call it that. The more I remained in my own reality, the more I questioned my feelings for him. There was no depth. No deepening of emotions. I started to question whether I even liked him. It didn't matter how cute he was. And I mean he was cute. The kind of cute that stops a girl in her tracks. But cuteness couldn't overrule my emotions.

66 | A New Friend and This Isn't Working

Pretty much every moment that Brent and I didn't have a customer or weren't working on a deal, we spent it together. Either in his office or mine. When we weren't talking about the Bible, we were usually laughing. I trusted him. There was something about him that made me feel comfortable. Pure friendship.

Brent would get irritated when Greg stopped by the dealership on his way home from the auction. I thought perhaps it was because Brent thought Greg wasn't good for me. When you spend twelve-hour days with someone, you really get to know them. Brent wasn't exactly an open book, but he was super funny and kind. He was actually one of the only straight men I knew who didn't hit on me or try to have sex with me.

I finally realized things with Greg were never going to go anywhere. I decided to work on my marriage. Perhaps through this spiritual work, I would be able to fix my relationship with Eric and maybe have a baby. That was really my big dream.

I started to not take Greg's calls. One day when I was working in the used car department, a call was transferred to me without letting me know who it was. I hated when they did that! It was him. I said, "This isn't going anywhere. We both know that. We're not in love and you certainly don't seem to want it to go any further." He seemed shocked, I guess because I was saying all of this very matter of factly. No tears or sadness. He said he understood. And that was that. I had shed enough tears the night he stood me up. It was over and I didn't have one sad second about it.

Despite all the time we spent together, Brent never once mentioned that he was having problems of his own at home. He never once said a single bad word about his wife.

Once a year, Brent and his best friend Sean, who lived in Arizona, would make a trip to Mexico. They would go to bars and strip joints and just let off steam. He would tell me about their escapades when he returned. After one trip he brought me back a beautiful Mexican blanket. I took it home and showed it to Eric as this great present from my friend at work.

Brent tried to get me to be friends with his wife. He said she could use a friend like me. He saw my intelligence, my humor and strong opinions. To him I was more than a short skirt. I invited his wife to go with me to an oil class. She agreed but then backed out at the last minute. She'd had a fourth child in January and was very busy.

Brent would tease me and say how all the guys at work were in love with me. I didn't really believe him. Then I was invited to lunch by the Mitsubishi sales manager. I thought he was my friend too. We went to Olive Garden.

My hands were on the table when he reached across and said in his most serious tone, "I have feelings for you." I was in shock! Was Brent right? Couldn't I just have some guys friends? As my cluelessness cleared, I was speechless.

I had to take a breath and answer carefully since I still had to work with this man. I explained to Mitsubishi boy that I liked him very much as a friend, however, I was working diligently to repair my marriage. He seemed to take it well. As soon as I could get Brent alone in my office, I told him about the encounter. He was not surprised. "It will pass," Brent assured me.

Because he was my friend, Brent offered to come and have raindrop therapy at my house after work on a Saturday afternoon. I had done several sessions for other friends and they had all gone well. He arrived while Eric was mowing the grass. I had the massage table set up in the back sunroom/dining room. It was tranquil there.

In order to do raindrop therapy, the client would need to take off their shirt, socks and shoes. Before we began, I would utilize some of the work I had learned at my spiritual class to help the person be clear and to receive all the goodness from the oils. This usually went really well.

I had some struggles with Brent. It seemed I couldn't get him completely clear. I was a bit confused by this. I mean we were close friends. Maybe that was it. I did the best I could and then felt it was better just to begin with the therapy.

Mind you at this time, Brent had been taking martial arts lessons and was very, very in shape. I had never seen him without his shirt. Why would I? I noticed he looked quite good. *Stop that thinking!* I also noticed he had the nicest chest hair I had ever seen. It wasn't too much and it wasn't too little. It also looked kind of soft. *Stop looking.*

He climbed up on the table. You start with a massage oil to create a base for the other oils as some cannot be applied directly to the skin without being diluted. As I began to rub this massage oil on his back, a brief thought flashed through my mind. *Wow, this is kind of nice.* What? I shook my head as if to erase the thought. *Stop that, Reesy. You can't be thinking that about a client, let alone your friend.* I shook my head again and continued with the oils.

Then his back began to turn really red. That hadn't happened before. He said, "I'm feeling a little warm back there." Oh no! I had to do something. I was afraid. Luckily, I knew that lavender cools. And boy, did I lavender up his back. Thank goodness, it helped and he said it felt better. About an hour later, we were done. As far as I was concerned, it was a success. No back fire and he left seeming happy.

Monday came and back to work. Something was off. Brent seemed to be avoiding me. I hoped I hadn't hurt him physically.

I mean I did almost set his back on fire. Was he weirded out? Finally, he came into my office under the guise of having to fax something. He stood there with his back toward me, then looked over his shoulder and said sort of sheepishly, "I felt something. Did you feel something?"

Like what? A spark? A connection? I had felt something. I remembered the thought I had shaken away as quickly as I could. Brent was my friend and apparently a happily married man with four children. Or was he?

Our conversation was interrupted by a salesperson. Brent left my office. My mind started spinning and suddenly I realized that I liked this man. I mean really liked him. I liked him as a person. I loved his humor. I loved spending time with him. I thought he was one of the kindest, smartest men I had ever known. And we were friends. Could there be more?

Then all I could think about was kissing him. Wouldn't a kiss tell me if there truly was a spark? But he had never said anything about his marriage being in trouble, even though he knew mine was a mess.

Once at a picnic, he and his family came. As opposed to them all walking together, he walked ahead with her trailing. I would never allow that sort of thing. I believe you walk beside your partner, not with one or the other leading. Come to think of it, he hadn't ever mentioned anything at all about his marriage. I did a lot of talking about Eric and how terrible it was for me at home. Not a word from him about his home life. What was this "Did you feel something" stuff? I had to know more. I had to have just one kiss.

It was Saturday and our day ended at 4:00. The two of us stayed behind to talk. He was sitting in my office looking all cute. And after all of the sharing I had done, he finally decided to tell me more about his home life.

Things were not as they appeared. He and his wife had many problems over the years. They just kept having babies. He had wanted to leave before and even went to his parents to talk about it on more than one occasion. They sent him back every time. He didn't know what to do. He had such responsibility—four children. He did not want them to suffer. He loved them very much.

I suggested that we should try at least one kiss to see what it would feel like. He was so strong. He wouldn't do it. He admitted to having feelings for me. However, Brent was a loyal man, so we parted and went to our separate homes... me still completely intrigued at the thought of kissing him and the potential answers it would bring.

67 | What Exactly Is Happening Here?

Work was way more interesting after that day. Brent still wouldn't kiss me. However, he did still spend a lot of time in my office. So much so, that his boss mentioned it to him and asked him to back down. He tried. It didn't really work.

In May, Brent left his wife and moved in with his parents. I was going to get that kiss one way or another. And then one day he gave in and it happened. It was in my office after work on a Saturday afternoon. The sun was shining through the glass windows so very brightly. It was just like the movies in slow motion. At least that's the way I remember it. He moved in a little closer and then I moved in a little closer. He put his hand on my neck and he put his perfectly shaped lips against mine. Were there doves flying over us? There was definitely a spark. More like Fourth of July fireworks! One kiss was not enough for either of us. One more. One more. *Okay, we have to leave or I'm going to attack him.* Once again, we parted. Only this time I went home to my house and he went home to his parents.

Over the next few weeks, I learned that the picture you see on the wall of a young handsome married couple with four adorable children may have looked perfect... but it was not. Brent and his wife had gotten pregnant during senior week at the beach. They hadn't even been dating for a year. Being a good Mormon boy, Brent always did the right thing, so he married her. They had already planned to marry anyway. He was headstrong and wanted to "save" her and have a nice big Mormon family.

Brent would, of course, not allow his children to attend daycare. His wife would be a stay-at-home mom, taking care of the kids and the house. Once one child reached a more independent age, she wanted another. Brent wanted to keep his wife happy even though all the financial pressure was on him. At the end of the day, they were just not well matched. I think more than one of us has tried to fit that square peg in a round hole.

We decided that we would go out away from work. I was still living with Eric, and Brent was still staying with his parents. When Eric went out of town on a four-wheeling trip one weekend in June, we decided Brent would pick me up. So many cars came and went at my house, no one would ever notice another.

Brent picked me up in a nice Mercedes he had borrowed as a demo. We went to a nearby town so we wouldn't run into anyone that either of us knew. We laughed the whole drive in the car, so much so that I embarrassingly spewed Sprite out of my nose. He found that even funnier. I was so comfortable with him and was able to laugh at myself as well. He reached out and held my hand which made my heart beat faster. At least my palms weren't sweaty. Okay, maybe a little. I was nervous about these new feelings.

We went to a little pizzeria in Shillington. After dinner we played pool then headed back to my house. Would I get another kiss?

He was not feeling too comfortable about coming inside. After all, he was separated. I was not. Even though my marriage had surely been over a long time ago, he dropped me off and parked down the street. When we finally sat down inside together, I kissed him. Whew! He had the best lips ever. It was Fourth of July all over again.

Somehow, before things could get out of control, or before I pounced on him, he pulled away and said we had to discuss our situation. He felt terribly guilty. He also missed his children and was constantly worried about them and the care they were receiving. It was quite the downer after the fireworks kisses. But Brent was my friend first and foremost. No matter how hot I was under my skirt, I respected what he wanted. Or at least I was going to try.

It was June 16th at around midnight when I said, "I guess we'll have to see where we are this time next year." With that, he gave me a kiss goodnight and went back to his parents' house.

68 | He's In, He's Out, and I'm Confused

Monday came and Brent was acting strange, kind of avoiding me. That was hard to do since we worked on every deal together. Finally at closing he came into my office and sat down. "I've decided to go back home." *What?*

He said his wife had brought the kids to his parents' house with pictures and cards in hand, begging daddy to come home. *Are you fucking kidding me?* Please understand... I was not angry about him going back home... (okay, well maybe a little)... but I was pissed that anyone would use children in that manner.

Because of my upbringing, I'm a firm believer that people should not stay in a loveless marriage for the sake of the kids. Hear me out. Where do you think you learn how to be in a relationship? I'll never forget both my parents saying to me how they wished they had separated years before. They had stayed for us. What did that teach me? It taught me how to be dysfunctional, how to cheat on my spouse and generally be unhappy in marriage. When unhappy people stay together, the children know. They know way more than the adults give them credit for. Why not teach children how to be happy and be with someone they truly love? Find a way to separate as cordially as possible and keep the kids out of it. Yes, children want their parents to be together. However, they also want their parents to be happy. More importantly, don't parents want their children to find a spouse that is a great match for them? Someone they can grow old with and be truly happy?

It's easy to say those things when you are not faced with four children looking at you and begging you to come home. The look on Brent's face when he told me this was not one of happiness. It was one of fear and sadness. His eyes looked ever so worried. His shoulders were slumped even though he attempted to stand tall in his decision.

He also broke the news that he would try to stay away from me other than work-related conversations. There was too much... just too much. There would be no more secret meetings in the accounting department after hours for a quick kiss. He had to go back.

I felt the lump in my throat. I did my best not to cry. Once again, we parted. This time there were no kisses. Only one man believing he was doing the right thing, and one woman completely let down but trying to be understanding for her best friend.

I thought a lot about what Brent had said. He was the first man I was friends with before having romantic feelings. I guess that's why it felt so different. It was hitting my heart hard.

He had been the voice of reason, right? Perhaps I should just work on my marriage as had been my plan before the "raindrop therapy" session. Perhaps there was such a thing as a soulmate. No. I had to get that out of my mind. I had to find a way to make it work with Eric. I wanted children and my biological clock was ticking. I was 31 years old.

On Monday, things were awkward. Brent completely avoided me. I found a way to tell him that I understood and that I, too, was going to work on my marriage. I said I had been thinking of all the nice non-materialistic things Eric did for me. "Oh yeah, what's that?" The only thing I could think of was that he would bring me coffee every Sunday morning from the local convenience store. At the time, it didn't seem lame. But it was. It was just the only thing I could think of.

Over the next few weeks, work continued to be awkward. We didn't even have our usual friendship. Brent spent most of his time avoiding me and I spent most of my time trying to respect that while not feeling hurt. Make no mistake. I was hurt.

There were no more calls, no more time spent laughing. It sucked! One night when he was off and I was working, the phone rang. It was Brent. He asked the weirdest question. "What kind of gaming system should I buy the kids?" He explained the options and the cost and together we decided. He was super friendly and actually sounded like his old self. I hung up very confused.

The next week there was a "bring your daughter to work day." He brought his oldest who was around 9 years old. She spent most of her time in my office. I loved kids and she was adorable. We had lots of fun together that day. Brent and I were back to being friends, trying to bury any romantic feelings as deeply as possible. At least that's what he was doing.

Brent was set to go on vacation with his wife and kids and his wife's parents to the beach in, of all places, North Carolina. Each day when he took the boys to the local arcade he called me while they played games. Those romantic feelings were bubbling up no matter how hard he tried to fight it.

When he returned from vacation, once again, Brent moved back to his parents' house.

69 | So Help Me, I'll Rape You; So Rape Me, I'll Help You

Lori and I decided to go out dancing on a Saturday night. She promised to be the designated driver since I was always the one not drinking. I should've known better. Lori not drinking lasted for about two seconds. "I'll only have two." And then came the guy... you know, the one she gets to buy her and her friends a drink.

Once she had enough to drink, she got horny and wanted to go home with this guy. There was no Jackie there to talk her down and remind of her of Girls' Rule #1. I was freaking out and in no shape to drive. I also feared for her safety. She had just met this person. He could be a serial killer for all we knew.

Then I remembered we were in the same town where Brent lived. He certainly would not let a drunk friend drive home, would he? I came up with a proposal for Lori. First, I would check her guy's driver's license and collect his phone number. Next, I would call Brent to come pick me up. If he would do that and take me back to Lori's house, only then would I stand for her going home with this perfect stranger.

I went to the payphone so there would be no cell phone tracking for Eric. Brent answered, thank goodness, and I explained the situation. He agreed to take me back to Lori's apartment where I planned to call Eric and say I was too drunk to drive home. My little plan to get Brent alone was working.

He arrived at the club in a red Corvette. It was a demo, however, it was still a red Corvette. He had on grey sweatpants and a grey sweatshirt and no shoes or socks. I had never seen Brent's feet before. I found it odd and slightly cool all at the same time.

The drive was about thirty minutes. I spent most of that time thanking him and trying to feel him up. It was challenging in a stick shift. We arrived at Lori's way faster than I hoped. I asked him... more like begged him... to come in. He did his very best to be a strong man. I was not making it easy. And it was going to get harder. A lot harder.

He agreed to come in for just a minute. Okay, a minute. Sure, just for a minute. The first thing I did was call Eric. I couldn't very well have him show up at Lori's with Brent there. He offered to come get me and I said that wasn't necessary. "I'll be home first thing in the morning." This really didn't help Brent's mental state. He was once again separated and I was still not.

He looked so cute in those bare feet and all that sweetness coming to pick me up so I wouldn't have to drive home. This was so different for me. I knew this man and I actually liked him as a person. He was literally the very first man I had gotten to know before wanting to jump his bones.

Under the circumstances, or rather under the influence of alcohol, I had no problem making the first move. I wanted another of those magical, fireworks kisses. It did not disappoint. Being the gentleman that he is, Brent suggested that he should leave. I decided to show him my red silk underwear in order to change his mind.

Here's the thing. Men are visual. Show them a little red silk underwear and they'll follow you anywhere. He was trying very hard to keep his head on straight. And it was hard and straight. Before things got out of hand, he stood up to leave. I blocked the door, trapping this 6'2", 220-pound man. I wasn't making it easy for him. He stayed a few minutes more and a few more kisses. In the end he was much stronger than me. I would have totally slept with him. He left with one last kiss.

There I was once again facing the brown, plaid, itchy couch for a bed. Brent was my friend, my very best friend. If I was ever going to sleep with my best friend, I should at least make sure it wasn't on a brown, plaid, itchy couch.

Brent suffered from tremendous guilt over his children. He was not confident in his wife's ability to care for them. Once again came the "I'm going to try and stay away from you" talk and "I'm going back." He told me that he was a mess. But I hadn't left Eric either. That being said, I was finally coming to terms with the fact that I wasn't in love with Eric any longer and that I really needed to leave him whether or not there would be a Brent in my life.

Once more Brent went back to his unhappy marriage to be with his children. The same thing happened. He once again realized how unhappy he was. She would behave in some passive-aggressive way by writing letters and leaving them in his sock drawer.

One fine day, he went for a jog with a friend. Panting and tired from a five-mile run, what do you think he saw on his front porch when he got back, in front of all of his neighbors and his friend? Garbage bags of his stuff.

His friend was shocked but Brent just laughed. It had finally been enough and she kicked him out. Once again, he went to live with his parents. It was getting close to that year from our first "friend" date.

70 | The Universe Speaks. Again.

A spiritual class was coming up and I was excited. Brent was so off-again on-again. Eric was still an asshole. I needed strength to do something, anything. I couldn't keep living like that. Even if living meant living alone. On the last day of class, the facilitator did an exercise like nothing I had experienced before. She asked us to close our eyes and imagine we only had forty-eight hours to live. "What will you do with that time? Who will you spend it with? Now imagine you are dancing with your soulmate."

Tears cascaded down my cheeks. I started to imagine myself dancing with my soulmate. As I looked up to see the face of this person, it was him! Brent! Not Eric. Much like the time I had done raindrop therapy and tried to shake my romantic wondering, I tried to shake this image away. *Just relax, Reesy. Stay with the exercise.* But there he was again. It was definitely Brent. Brent was my soulmate?

I felt sure. Brent was the one! He was my soulmate. Now what would I do?

Brent told me on more than one occasion that he was fucked up and probably shouldn't be involved with anyone. However, I had seen his face as clear as could be in the soulmate exercise. How could I stay away? He sure couldn't, despite trying.

Meanwhile, Eric wanted another four-wheeler. A more expensive toy. Another reason I wasn't ever going to be able to have children with that man. He wouldn't quit smoking weed on a daily basis and he wanted lots of toys that I had to pay for. I was against the new four-wheeler.

One night at work, Eric called to say he had found a great deal on a four-wheeler and blah, blah, blah. I said, "Well, I really don't think this is a good idea. However, I will leave it up to you." His response was, "I already have the paperwork for the loan. I'll be right over to get your signature."

That was the exact moment I knew it was over. Not that I didn't know that before. This was truly the time my switch flipped completely off without question. It was that exact moment in time when I was finally sure I was done. I had tried to let him make an adult decision based on our marriage and my desire to have children. He knew how I felt. I had made that very clear. He also knew we were already up to our necks in debt. He had pretended my opinion mattered all the while having the paperwork in hand. Any ounce of hope for him ever changing... like the love switch... flipped to OFF.

Eric came to the dealership and I begrudgingly signed. He left as happy as a clam. I sat in my office wondering how and when I would leave him and where I would go.

I still enjoyed work. Brent and I would sneak upstairs to the accounting department to grab kisses. It started to get noticed. Keep in mind, we hadn't slept together. I did love making out with him. I grabbed every one of those kisses that I could.

71 | It's Time

A weird thing happened. My friend Jackie invited Brent, along with some others, over to this new salesgirl's house. Who was I to protest? I was not invited.

The next day I discovered Jackie's big plan. She must have been jealous. She said bad things about me, her good friend... things she clearly hoped would make Brent reconsider. She decided she knew what was best for him, and that didn't include me.

He told me he went to this gal's apartment. At first, there were several people there. Next thing he knew, he found himself alone with car girl who was wearing only a robe. As the flashing neon sign went off in his mind, he quickly exited the situation. This did not make car girl happy, and it didn't make Jackie happy either.

Brent told me the whole story along with the details of Jackie warning him to stay away from me. What a bitch! I had never been anything but nice to that girl. She was supposed to be my friend. And I had to keep working with her while pretending I didn't know the horrible shit she had done to me. I found out later she had done something similar to her very best friend. This gal had some real self-esteem issues.

Brent received other warnings. I get it. I'd had an affair that was not well hidden. I never left Eric. I'd had the very handsome boy from New Jersey stop by, causing quite the stir. What would make anyone think I would leave Eric this time? I'm sure that plenty of labels were being slapped on me on a daily basis.

But they didn't know I had found my soulmate in Brent. They didn't know I was petrified of Eric. We were basically roommates. I didn't have sex with him. I wouldn't say, "I love you." I avoided being alone with him at all costs. And yet, he wouldn't leave. I knew I was going to have to be the one to do it, no matter how scared I was. Either way, it didn't matter if I ended up with Brent. I knew it was over with Eric. I had to find the courage.

I had become quite close with Lisa, the gal I worked with at the dealership. I told her everything. She was sympathetic and understanding without judgment. She made me an offer. She had met a nice man from York and had started to date him exclusively. Her lease was up in Lancaster and she was looking to move to York to be closer to her shiny new boyfriend. She asked if I wanted to get an apartment with her.

Meanwhile, Brent was living with his parents but was offered in-law quarters from his godparents. He was going to move there in July. This was in York as well.

Lisa and I decided it would be important to find a place that either of us could afford by ourselves should the other move out. She could potentially move in with her boyfriend, and me? Well, I was super unstable and didn't really know what the fuck I was doing.

It didn't take long for Lisa to find a nice two-bedroom apartment in York. We set a time where she and I could go and look at it. I trusted her. However, it was nice she was being so considerate.

The apartment was in a big complex on the lower floor. You had to walk down steps. It had two nice bedrooms, but I realized I didn't even have a bed. There was a small kitchenette, a nice size living room and one bathroom. The downside was there wasn't a washer and dryer. We would have to do our laundry in a shared laundry facility for the whole building. However, it was the right price for both of us. We would split everything down the middle and move in August 1st.

It was also time for a new car. I had been working on my spiritual stuff and creating a list of things I wanted. I had always wanted a red convertible. My whole life. One day at the dealership, a man traded in an immaculate, red Mercedes C230. It had this hard top that when you hit a button, it would pop up and slide into the trunk.

While I had been around cars for most of my adult life, I really didn't fawn over any of them. I thought some were fun, however I really just wanted something safe and reliable. But this was different. I took that Mercedes convertible for a ride with the top down, and I'd never felt so cool in my life. I turned the radio up and drove that sweet ride several miles down the road. I was hooked. The good news was that Jacob was still quite nice to me and helped me lease it inexpensively. I thought of it as my "I'm finally leaving Eric for good" gift to myself. I deserved it.

I had been thinking up ways to tell Eric I was leaving. I certainly kept my distance from him. One day I said I had to get away, and I was going to go for a ride in my new car. You'll never guess where I was headed. Okay, you probably will. Brent had moved into his apartment and I wanted, no needed, to see him. I needed to be reminded of why I was leaving Eric.

Keep in mind, that while I believed Brent to be my soulmate, he was not so convinced. But I did want to be reminded of what it would be like to be with a man who was responsible and kind to me. Someone that wouldn't call me names. I wanted to feel like a hot commodity. I was 31, had a good paying job, no kids and was pretty cute. If Brent didn't want me, I was sure there would be plenty of other offers out there or in North Carolina.

Those were the things I told myself as I drove to York, along with all the questions I had. Was this a mistake? Would I end up alone? Would I finally find happiness? I turned the music up louder and let my hair fly as I drove those forty minutes with the top down.

I must say I was a bit nervous. More than a year after our first "friend" date, this was where we were landing. He appeared calm and collected and super handsome. We sat on his living room floor. There was very little furniture in his new place. My intentions were just to see him. It did not take long for the making out to start.

One thing led to another, and before either of us knew what was happening, it happened. Wow! So wonderful! I was in love with my best friend.

The question was... was he in love with me too?

72 | Really Scared

I drove home knowing for sure that I had to leave Eric. I also knew I needed to do it for all the right reasons, and not just for Brent.

I found my courage, especially since I had already signed a lease with Lisa. I told Eric I would be leaving that same day. The tears came and then anger. Once again, I packed my clothes and makeup and headed to York to my new apartment, my new roommate and hopefully my new life.

Eric called me every day at work. He did a lot of begging. But it was gone. I had nothing left for him. He was not convinced. In my new routine, I would work all day. I'd receive a daily call from Eric trying to convince me to come home. I'd leave at 9:00 and drive to my new apartment and shave my legs and put on pajamas, then head over to Brent's apartment about fifteen minutes away. We would hang out, go to bed and have sex. I'd sleep over and get up early the next morning, drive to my new apartment, then shower and get ready for work. I did this almost every day.

The only time it was different was when Brent had his kids every other weekend and Wednesday nights. During those times I would hang out with my new roommate and sometimes her boyfriend and his friend. I tried to keep busy as these were tougher times for me. I wanted to spend every minute with Brent, but we decided to wait before telling his kids we were seeing each other.

As I said, Brent had made it clear to me that he was an emotional mess. Not because of his soon to be ex-wife, but because of his children. He really suffered with sometimes overwhelming guilt. I did what I could to reassure him and listen to him and be his friend as I had always been. Still, sometimes he would go into his "cave" where he was completely emotionally unavailable. When that would happen, I would be devastated.

One night after work and after several weeks of our routine, he said he needed some time alone. *What? What do you mean?* He was in his "cave." I hated that fucking cave. I'm not generally a patient person and I want what I want. And in general, in my life when I want something—I mean really want something—I usually get it. I can be very persuasive. He was not budging on this.

I wanted to see him so badly. I ached to see him. I needed reassurance that he still cared. Nope. He was not moving on this. He tried to say that everything was fine. I didn't understand. He was breaking the routine. I asked myself, "What have I done?" I had left the security... not really... of my house. I was sleeping on a futon... at least in my own room... in a two-bedroom apartment where I had to do my laundry with the general public. I know a lot of people have to do that. I just wasn't used to it.

Unfortunately, Lisa was not home to cheer me up, since she was spending the night with her boyfriend. There I was all alone for the first time since I could remember and I was going to have to sleep in that two-bedroom apartment by myself. I couldn't stop crying. I literally got on my knees and prayed to God that if Brent was not the one for me, please to give me strength to walk away. That was going to be my new prayer. I couldn't handle not knowing for sure that he loved me. It was going to be a long night. Actually, I was so emotionally exhausted, I fell asleep pretty quickly.

I was getting ready for work when a knock came at my door. I took a look in the peephole and guess who was there. It was him, Brent. My heart started beating quickly. What was he going to say to me?

To my delight, he gave me a big hug and kissed me. He explained again that he just needed some time to himself the night before. We went into my bedroom. On that futon, for the first time, he told me that he loved me. On this day, he was once again my soulmate.

73 | The Day America Cried

Our routine continued as it had before—work, quick stop at my apartment, head to Brent's, get up early, go back to the apartment, get ready to go to work, and repeat.

I continued to have sessions with my spiritual counselor. I needed clarity more than ever. She talked to me about possibly volunteering in my community. I had never done that type of thing. Not that I didn't want to, but I just had never found the time. She suggested an agency in York that provided daycare for children during crises. It sounded right up my alley. Plus I needed something to do during the times when Brent had his kids, so I called and scheduled a meeting.

It was another 2:00 P.M. start to my workday so I had time beforehand to go and meet with the director of this organization. I hadn't turned on the television. I went to the appointment and met with the director. She was delightful. She showed me around and told me all about the place. What they do for children is amazing.

I noticed they had the television on, and there seemed to be something newsworthy. I left feeling excited about the opportunity to support my community and to help children. I went back to the apartment since it was still too early to go to work. A knock came on my door. It was Brent. "Have you looked at the news? The World Trade Center's been destroyed!" It was September 11, 2001.

A bit later I walked into the showroom and customers were standing around the television crying. I finally got a look at the news. My heart was hurting. The dealership decided to close as most businesses did that day. Brent said he had to see his kids. I understood completely.

I drove that thirty minutes home with virtually no traffic. It was eerie. For me, there was a great sadness in the air I could not escape. When I got to my apartment, the phone was ringing. It was my mom. Since one of the planes crash-landed in Pennsylvania, she was worried that it was near me. I could hear the relief in her voice when we spoke.

After a couple of hours, Lisa and I decided we couldn't watch any more news. Instead we watched *The Wedding Planner*. Since that day, I have never been able to re-watch that movie.

The phone rang again. I was hopeful it would be Brent. But it was Eric. "You have to come home." Why? "Because of this attack in New York." I assured him that I did not have to come home because of that. "Yes, you do," he said in his angry bully voice. I hung up.

Brent called me later. His kids were all good. But nothing would ever be the same after that day.

74 | You Just Can't Hide Love

Some people at work knew about me and Brent. Others suspected. Still, we continued to keep it on the down-low for the moment.

I decided not to tell Eric where I lived. One night at closing, I was walking to my car with a young sales guy. He climbed into his car but as I was getting into mine, Eric flew into the parking lot, blocking my car so I couldn't back out. Where was that sales guy? He'd seen what happened but just left! My heart started thumping. What was Eric going to do?

I nervously got out of the car and tried my best to seem stern, all the while shaking like a leaf. Eric begged me to come home again. I stayed strong. I don't think he could tell I was really scared. After what seemed like a lifetime, he got in his car and drove away. I breathed a sigh of relief. I was going to kill that sales guy for leaving me like that. What if Eric had gotten violent? I wouldn't have expected the sales guy to defend me... but at least he could have called the police.

By the time I got to Brent's apartment that night, I had to let out the tears of fear. He was also pissed at the sales guy, who knew the whole situation. Brent did have a talk with the other sales people about the possibility of Eric showing up in the future, and he coached them to call the police if needed. Luckily, it never came to that.

One morning as per my usual routine, I arrived at my apartment to a phone ringing off the hook. I answered. It was Eric. "Where have you been?" he said, once again in his angry, bully voice. "Here," I answered. "No, you haven't," he accused.

Wait. How did Eric know that? "What do you mean?" I asked him. He told me he knew I hadn't been home because he'd been cruising around my parking lot and didn't find my car.

Oh no! How had Eric found out where I lived? "Don't you fucking worry about it," he deflected. Then he hung up on me, just to call me back repeatedly. I cried and begged him to leave me alone. It was torture.

I had to keep answering the phone because I didn't want the ringing to wake Lisa. Finally, I took a peep in her room and realized she must have spent the night with her boyfriend. One last call from Eric led me to say, "I'm not talking to you anymore today." With that, I hung up, then got ready for work as quickly as I could, being ever so cautious on the way to my car. I think he somehow knew about me and Brent.

I wasn't the only one getting unannounced drop-bys. Apparently Brent's soon to be ex-wife showed up at his apartment and asked to use the bathroom. For whatever reason, while she was in there, she looked in his trash can and found a used condom. Reality hit her. Brent was moving on.

Another night when Brent decided to visit his kids, his ex was acting really strange. Brent had great intuition. He found a young man hiding in the bathroom shower shaking with fear. That cat was out of the bag.

Although everyone at work had suspicions about me and Brent, it was still not confirmed. There was a station across from the dealership where we all got gas. A creepy, weird man worked there. I had actually done paperwork for his new car when I worked at the previous dealership, so he kind of knew me. He was nice and polite... until one night Brent was right behind me in line at the pump. I filled my car and left. When Brent went into the gas station, creepy weird guy told him, "I'd like to wear her ass as a hat." Brent was not happy, but defending me would let another cat out of the bag. What he really wanted to do was punch the guy in the face.

Per Brent's divorce agreement, visitation with the kids would include alternating holidays. Thanksgiving would be with his ex. I knew it would be tough for him, so I offered to make Thanksgiving dinner for just the two of us—a beautiful turkey with all the fixin's. After dinner we sat down to watch TV when we heard a car and then running, and then a knock on his door. It was his kids! His ex had decided it was a good idea to just drop by without calling.

Neither of us knew what to do. I hid in the bathroom and prayed no one had to go. I sat there hearing little voices, remembering my red Mercedes was parked right in his driveway. No one asked about that. Brent did a great job of giving hugs and kisses and they finally left. His ex never came inside, although I'm sure she knew I was there.

Once that happened, we both had enough of hiding. We decided to tell the kids. We picked a weekend and I came over when the children were there. His oldest was pretty excited since she and I had already bonded at bring-your-daughter-to-work day. Brent had two girls and two boys—ages 9, 7, 4 and almost 2. I know. I'm a saint, right?

75 | Divorce, Family, and That Fucking Cave

I officially started the divorce process, much to Eric's anger and sadness. He was ridiculous. He wouldn't even let me have the cat. I was actually okay with that as I thought it would be unfair to separate our cat and dog—they were buddies. But then Eric wanted me to pay "child support" for the animals. Are you fucking kidding me?

Eric called my mom. As she had done in the past she said, "Eric, it's too late." He had the nerve to say to her, "Do you know she bought a Mercedes?" My mom's classic reply was, "She's paying for it, isn't she?" He had no response to that. He would not dare try to bully her.

I had to make arrangements to collect my belongings. I was owed so much more than I took. I just wanted out. But as Mom would say, "You can always get more stuff." I picked a time when Eric wouldn't be home. Brent's dad let me use his giant van so I gathered all my clothes, that same china I had carried with me since I was 16, and my hope chest. I wanted the microwave, since Mom had given it as a Christmas present, but I couldn't carry it by myself.

Eric even wanted to keep the photo albums. I had no fight left in me. I wanted to be free of that marriage. Sometimes I think I should have fought harder. After all, I had paid for most of the stuff we owned.

Brent was more than generous in his divorce agreement. He gave his ex everything, along with a large check every month. Some of the money was for the kids and the rest was spousal support since she didn't work. He left with a television and DVD player plus his personal items. It's amazing what you will sacrifice for your kids and your sanity.

That year Brent would have the kids late Christmas Eve and Christmas morning. That meant he would be responsible for all the gifts. He made a good living and was determined to make it an amazing holiday. I was excited to help buy presents. He actually sent me and Lisa with his credit card to go shopping for the kids. It was awesome!

I spent that Christmas in North Carolina, but first Brent gave me some lovely and thoughtful presents. My favorite was a sapphire ring, as sapphire was his birthstone. It was a lovely Christmas for us both.

Brent would still sometimes go into his "cave." I couldn't understand. He was normally so loving, and then he would be emotionally just gone. During those times, I would torture him with questions like: "What's wrong?" and "Do you still want to be with me?" I know this drove him crazy. However, he was driving me crazy. Was he in or out?

I used my prayer: "God, if he's not the one, please give me the strength to walk away." Then Brent would come out of his "cave" and be my best friend and lover once again.

Brent introduced me to his parents and they were wonderful and welcoming. I never once felt judged. So it was time to take Brent to North Carolina to meet my mom. We would drive down and stay with her and Nelson. Mom decided the whole family could come together instead of me and Brent needing to drive around to everyone individually.

As Southern folks do, we held a pig pickin', also known as a pig roast. Basically, you cook a full pig on a barbecue spit outside, typically served with collards, mashed potatoes, homemade biscuits and of course, beer.

Brent didn't seem intimidated to meet my whole family at once. My mother asked him when he was going to make me an honest woman. He remained calm. I found out later that he promised her he would never hurt me.

At one point my uncle was sitting beside me. When he stood up, Brent took his place. Being the joker he is, my uncle said, "Would you step in my grave if I got up out there?" Everyone just laughed.

After the beers started flowing, my new stepfather asked Brent if he wanted to go frog gigging. Brent had no idea what he was talking about. I immediately said, "No, he doesn't want to go out into the swamp at night on a non-motorized boat with a flashlight and pole with a large two-prong fork on the end while one of you shines a light and the other stabs a giant frog to bring back and cook." Meanwhile Brent was nodding, "Sure, I'll do that." No, no, Brent. You don't want to do that. Even after a few beers.

My family really liked Brent. Mom was so glad to see me happy for the first time in ages. I think my dad would have approved. I believe he would have thought Brent was the first guy I dated that was actually smart enough for me.

76 | Routine and Change
at the Same Time

We spent that year with me staying every night at Brent's. After being around the kids more often, I even stayed over when they were visiting. Still, I was paying monthly rent on the apartment with Lisa, as well as splitting utilities. There was talk of moving in with Brent. Okay well, I talked about it. But Brent wasn't ready.

At work, the gossip quieted down after everyone knew we were seeing each other. Brent had taken a lot of shit from management in the past about me. That seemed to be quieting down also. However, the sales manager was a complete dick to me. He was friends with Eric, plus I had turned him down for a date years before.

The owners of the dealership planned to purchase another franchise at the southern end of the county, and they offered Brent the position of general manager. That's a super big deal to become GM before the age of 30. That hardly ever happens unless it's a family-owned business. It would also be good for us at work so people wouldn't think Brent was showing favoritism toward me. I wasn't happy about not seeing him all day, but I was thrilled for his opportunity to build a dealership pretty much from the bottom up.

I was a really good finance manager. There may have been negative labels people assigned to me, but in this one area they couldn't say anything bad. I was considered one of the best in Lancaster County. I was also bored at my job.

As you know by now it's not good for Reesy to be bored. There wasn't anything else for me to learn. I was at the top. There was also the long hours. I worked twelve-hour days and every other weekend. With Brent working at a different location, I was no longer entertained during slow times.

In addition, the sales manager became increasingly not nice. He clearly no longer liked me. What was I going to do? As a people-pleaser it was painfully difficult. But where could I go to earn the kind of money I was making?

Around that time, Lisa had been seeing her boyfriend for over a year. Our lease converted to a month-to-month basis and she wanted to move in with him. That would leave me paying the full rent plus utilities—all while spending every night with Brent. Even so, there was no talk of us moving in together.

As a finance manager, bankers came to talk about giving them business. Sometimes they would buy lunch. The more I thought about my unhappiness at work, the more I started thinking about these bankers. They got off work every day at 5:00 and they didn't work weekends. I wanted to be a banker. Wait—I didn't have a degree. What does a banker earn?

77 | I Won't Let It Stop Me from Trying

I started checking the "want ads" in the newspaper for a job in banking. There it was: Wachovia was looking for a licensed financial specialist. That's someone who opens checking accounts, does loans for people and sells certain investments. It did not say anything about a degree being a necessity.

Meanwhile back at the dealership, my friend-not-friend Jackie was not performing so well. She would make mistakes and just wasn't approachable to the sales guys. As karma would have it, she got fired. Once she left, I never heard from her again. Good riddance.

I sent my resume to Wachovia and received a call for an interview. I was so excited! Could I really get out of the car business? Most who stay for a couple of years rarely ever leave.

The bank job was in York which meant a shorter commute, plus less chance of running into Eric or Jacob. In my lifetime, I'd had six interviews—McDonald's, the department store, car dealerships, and the law firm. This interview was very different.

I would learn later that it was called "behavioral interviewing." You are asked a question about a scenario such as: "Tell me about a time when you had to overcome a sales objection." Then you had to answer in a "S.T.A.R. response." S—describe the situation. T—task you were faced with. A—the actions you took. R—the end result. If you missed one of the S.T.A.R. parts, you would lose points on the interview. Thank goodness I was quick on my feet and had examples for each of the questions.

I left the interview feeling pretty good. There was one slight problem. The pay would be salary plus commission, however, there would be three months of training plus ramp-up time before commissions would start... and the base salary was not anywhere near what I was making. I would barely be able to pay my rent and utilities.

Remind me why I was doing that in the first place? I stayed every night with Brent and never visited my apartment except to change clothes. Maybe I wouldn't even get offered the job.

The decision didn't take long and the call came. I got the job! I was going to be a banker! I would have normal working hours. I would only have to work every other Saturday until noon. Also noon would mean 12:00 P.M. rather than whenever the last customer leaves. I was excited. Except the salary was going to be a problem.

78 | Finally Some Really Good Moves

Brent was excited as well. He was so happy for me to get away from all those labels and what people would say about me and about us. He even asked me to move in with him. Hallelujah!

I gave notice to the apartment complex and arranged a storage unit for my little bit of furniture, including a few things Lisa had kindly left for my use. There wasn't enough room at Brent's apartment for everything. Not that we had a lot. He and I started our life together with a television and DVD player, dishware he bought me for my birthday, and our personal items. His godparents already had a bed in the apartment. We would have to buy plenty of things, but it didn't matter. I was psyched!

Finally, I was feeling some security with Brent. Or was I? A little voice whispered in my ear, wondering if he really wanted me to move in, or if he had caved to the pressure. I pushed that voice way down and thought it would all be fine. He loved me.

The October moving day came and Lisa and her boyfriend helped us get everything where it belonged. I had been at the new job for about a month. My perception of being a banker was not exactly how I'd imagined it. I had pictured bankers sitting around in a branch office, waiting for people to come in and open a checking account or ask for a loan. While that is somewhat true, I was about to find out just how much bankers have to "sell."

In my role as a Licenses Financial Specialist, I would be meeting with clients to open accounts—checking, savings, money market. But I'd also be processing loan applications for home equities, lines of credit, personal loans, auto loans and eventually small business loans. The biggest deal was getting my Series 6, Series 63, and life insurance investment licenses, which each required passing an exam. I wasn't afraid of the tests as I'm a pretty smart chick, but it was a job requirement. Three attempts to pass these tests, and otherwise... no license, no job. No pressure!

Wachovia offered fantastic training—three months for the regular stuff and another month for the licensing exams. I was determined not to fail. In reality, as per most of life, failure really wasn't an option. I would make this work. I would have to travel to Reading, PA, each day, a little over an hour ride, with mileage reimbursed. I would spend two weeks learning certain tasks, then work with a mentor at their branch to practice what I'd learned. Pretty smart, right?

It was fascinating to me. They made a big deal out of online banking and direct deposit. I didn't care. If they said they were the best thing since sliced bread, then I was saying they were the best thing since sliced bread. They called these items "sticky products"... because once customers have these items, it makes it more challenging for them to switch banks. Hence, they "stick" to the bank.

Once out of training, you earn commission on all the products and services you sell to your clients. Wachovia's business philosophy focused on relationship building and I was great at that. Each time we needed to complete a C.N.A.—Customer Needs Assessment—a six-page document filled with financial questions to ask every client in order to determine the best products and services for that person. Again, right up my alley. I did exactly what they told me to do. I never questioned it. I was going to do it the way they taught me.

I enjoyed learning all this new stuff, and it seemed I was pretty good at it. The trainer was a lady—one of the toughest I ever met. I thought there were tough ladies in the car business, but this gal was no joke. Her wrath was ugly, embarrassing newbies and making them feel like assholes. Of course, I never suffered her wrath because I did what I was told.

Even though I had an hour commute both ways, I still got off by 5:00 every day, sometimes earlier. And I'll never forget the first bank holiday—Columbus Day in October. I asked the trainer skeptically, "Are you sure we don't have to come here Monday?" She laughed. I couldn't believe it.

Once loan training began, I really excelled. After all, I had been lending money for over ten years in the car business. I already knew about reading credit reports, debt-to-income ratios, and how to speak the language. I only had to learn the Wachovia way.

Then it was time for the licensing part. Wow! I took online training from home, followed by practice test after practice test. Sort of like the classes and preparation for the S.A.T. in high school. Only you don't really pass or fail the S.A.T. This was not only pass or fail, it was have a job or not have a job. And just for fun, the test questions loved to fuck with you. By fuck with you, I mean let's just throw in a backwards ass question and screw with your mind to see if you were really paying attention. Other than being able to do this from home, it wasn't exactly super fun. Still I soldiered on and learned the material. Practice test. Practice test. UGH!

79 | Better Labels and Success in Banking

This training was set up in tracks. That meant I started with a group of sixteen people who had my same job in different parts of central Pennsylvania, and would complete the full training with the same people. That's presuming they all made it.

The environment was the polar opposite of the car business, but not as stoic as the law firm. It was also like a clean start for me in a new town where no one knew my past. I would have to change my potty mouth though, as I wasn't hearing any "f" bombs. At least at first.

When you are in training with the same people for three months you begin to get to know them. Our group had to make a one-week trip to Charlotte, NC, for regulatory training. I will say this—a lot of bankers like to drink alcohol. Sadly, for me, drinking usually brings the potential to vomit, be way too friendly and embarrass myself. I also needed all my brain cells for this very boring training. I was going to need to be careful on this trip if I wanted to reinvent myself and strip off all those old labels.

After class, groups of us would meet for dinner. Most would go out afterward for adult beverages, but I went to my room to study. Was I becoming a goody-goody?

One gal in my training class intimidated me. She was outspoken and driven, determined to be successful. She was from the "coal" region of Pennsylvania. Sometimes she would seem nice and then other times she would just hammer the shit out of someone. While a little scary, I thought she was kind of cool. It was clear we shared a lot of the same drive to be successful. She also didn't have any previous banking experience. I thought we might make good friends.

The last night, this lady invited me along with her and another gal to dinner. After dinner, she convinced me to join them for a drink. We strolled around Charlotte and found a lovely bar. After a few drinks we decided to head back to the hotel.

As we were walking, my new (scary) friend asked, "Are you really this nice?" *What?* Apparently she had labeled me way differently than what I had dealt with before. I had consumed enough alcohol to tell her that I was rather frightened of her. So funny.

Turns out, she was a super person who would do anything for a friend. And the best part was that she would "f" bomb it with me. A real person. Someone I could relax with during all of this training and stress of passing the licensing tests. We became fast friends. I had so mislabeled her. What was I doing labeling anyone anyway? Hadn't I learned what it was like to be labeled as something you aren't?

For weeks after the NC trip, I sat in our (yes, *our* apartment) taking practice test after practice test. Again, with those fuck-with-you multiple choice questions. It was brutal. My test date was December 15th and I had done nothing but study. No Christmas shopping. Nothing. Study, study and more study. After all, my job depended on it.

I had to go to a Sylvan Learning Center to take this test. I could only bring a pencil and paper into the room and we were not allowed to leave once the test began. That could be a problem for my nervous bladder. But I was as ready as I was ever going to be. If I failed, I would get two more opportunities... and a big delay to start earning commissions.

I went into that testing room and sat down in front of a computer. I started the exam. At the end, you push this horrible red button and have to wait for twenty seconds. It was the longest twenty seconds of my life. I didn't even realize I was holding my breath.

I passed! I was good to go! YAY me! This gal without a formal education, from a tiny little town in North Carolina, and labeled all kinds of things had passed her Series 6 investment license! Suck on that, all of you who ever thought I was less than smart!

80 | Apparently I'm Pretty Good at This Banking Stuff

When you are new to the role, you are generally placed at a smaller branch location. Even though I had excelled in training, I was still placed at the smallest location in York. This detail was important because the smaller the branch, the less traffic; the less traffic, the fewer opportunities walk in the door; the fewer opportunities, the greater need for cold calling.

Make no mistake... a banker is a salesperson. Wachovia invested a lot of money into our training, and we would be held accountable. Every day, I had to get on a checkout call and report the number of loan applications I had processed that day. *Are you fucking kidding me?* Nope. Every Monday morning I had to be on another conference call to discuss tactics for how I was going to reach my numbers. I had never had official goals before. This was way different than I expected.

The good news was I had always been a natural salesperson, and now I could actually build relationships with clients—clients who came to me for financial advice. That felt really good. I also had a great team at my branch. The team is critical for referrals. Part of the tellers' contribution to branch sales and success was to spot opportunities for the financial specialist. Once my team saw I was a hard worker and would actually call their referrals, we began to crank out the loans, which at that time was the bank's most lucrative product. And if you did your Customer Needs Assessment, as trained, it was not that difficult to find other opportunities to sell useful products and services. I became very good at the C.N.A.

An odd thing I found in banking was that not everyone had the same mentality as I did. I know, big surprise. These employees would "push back" on things that were part of their job. Not everyone completed a C.N.A. on every client. *What?* We were told in training to do one for every client. They even made us create a "value statement" to memorize and say to each client about why we were doing it. Some of my peers rebelled. Not me. I figured Wachovia had done the research and this worked, and since I had never been a banker before, I was going to do it unless the client refused.

Another example of "push back" was when a client entered the bank, we were supposed to say, "Welcome to Wachovia." This was to be said every time with every customer. We were even rated on this. Wachovia used Gallop polling to determine our customer service quality. The first question was: "Did someone from the staff welcome you?" I was amazed at how some would decide for whatever reason they didn't need to say it to everyone. My mentality was so different. My experience was so different. I had never decided to not do what my employer asked. This job would be no exception.

I found success quickly, recognized as a "Rising Star" and invited to a dinner. I received kudos on conference calls. I received notes and emails of gratitude and congratulations from my direct supervisor and my supervisor's supervisor. I was in heaven. I was successful and being recognized for it... and all I was doing was my job. Though I had never worked harder in my life. It was a far cry from the afternoon crossword puzzle while waiting for a customer at the car dealership. I was busy the whole day.

It didn't take long before one of the largest and most successful branches in York had an opening for a financial specialist. Their branch manager wanted me badly because she'd heard all the good things I was doing at a branch that had never been successful in the past. I wanted to earn more money and have more opportunities. It was done! I moved to my new branch less than a year after starting.

It was extraordinary! I had a much larger, more aggressive team, and way more walk-ins, so less cold calling. I quickly rose to the top. Out of 100+ financial specialists across Central Pennsylvania, I was in the top ten! I had made it! I was earning commissions, and building great relationships with clients who would return to me again and again for assistance. The best part was I was getting recognized for my performance. I loved it!

81 | I So Love This Man and Still I Need More Counseling

I was really in love with Brent. It was so different than any other relationship. There wasn't any yelling. I remember spilling something on the carpet. I froze. In my past, Eric would have freaked out on me. Brent was calm and acted like it was no big deal. This was all new to me.

Periodically, the guilt would hit him and he would go into his "cave." I would then obsess over asking him a million times if he was okay and what was the matter. I know this drove him crazy and yet I couldn't help myself.

The pattern was the same. Things would be great. We would be laughing and having fun and then he would have a moment. He'd come out of it after a day or two. My obsession to make sure everything was okay took a toll on me. I also wanted more. Of course, I did. I wanted to marry Brent. He once said he wasn't sure he would ever marry again. He always said he loved me and was loyal. But I'm a strong believer in marriage. I needed to know I would never lose him.

His kids were great! We still got them every other weekend and one day each week. I made home-cooked dinners, then we would watch movies and hang out. I was in love with them too. From the beginning of getting involved with a man with four children, Mama said to me, "Remember Reesy, you are committing to the kids as much as you are to Brent." I never felt an ounce of doubt. I loved his children.

I continued my spiritual journey and became friends with my counselor. I was learning so much about the exchange of energy between people and how that can impact you. Have you ever been in a great mood and then you talked with someone... and after that conversation was over, you felt terrible? That was their negative energy impacting you. I became increasingly better at the classes. I had a knack for it. My intuition was strong.

I started to notice an odd thing during some of the classes. As the students would break into groups to practice, often the "issues" would deal with others in the group. I found this unusual considering these folks didn't see each other on a regular basis. In fact, the majority of them only saw each other at these classes four or five times a year.

When I was dealing with my "issues," it often involved negative energy around my involvement with Brent. I didn't feel I was doing a good job of energetically protecting that relationship. Usually afterward, I would be in the best of moods having dealt with all of my shit. But something was brewing.

The teacher becomes the student. The student becomes the teacher. Sometimes there is envy. During several moments in my life, I just knew when everything was about to change. My counselor and I were sitting in a restaurant one day, actually working on her energy. My small still voice gave me an answer that she was energetically in a "box." Boxes keep you stuck, and sometimes those boxes also have labels on them—labels that can be positive or negative.

As I made this statement to her, she got an odd look on her face like... *How did you know that?* I learned she had been working together with the creator of the practice about the topic of boxes. How could little ole me possibly have such a connection? I knew that moment would change our relationship.

After that, we no longer had the same closeness. I didn't understand then. I truly believe it was hard for her seeing me know something that she didn't think I could know. I was reaching new levels and maybe outgrowing her.

And to top it off, during the classes, it was often her energy negatively impacting my relationship with Brent. How could this be? Was there no one I could trust?

82 | Does a House of My Very Own Mean Commitment?

As the kids grew, the apartment felt smaller and smaller. When they would come over for the weekend, we would set up foam cushions in the living room for them to sleep on. When it was warm, we could get them outside, but in cold weather we were stuck. We had to start looking to buy a house.

The good news was that Brent's ex started living with another man so his monthly check to her had been greatly reduced. The other good news was that because I worked in banking, I could get discounts on a mortgage. We began our quest.

Periodically, I would mention marriage to Brent. His response was always the same. "I don't want to be with anyone but you. Buying a house is just as much of a commitment as marriage," he would say. "I'll be signing a thirty-year mortgage with you." While I was happy about buying a house together, I knew deep inside that was not going to be enough for me. I wanted the security of being married. I craved it.

We found a lovely four-bedroom home in North York in our price range. It wasn't huge, however, it had the bedrooms we needed, two and a half baths, a two-car garage and a nice yard. It was located behind an elementary school and a township building so no one was going to build behind us. It was also brand new. No one had lived in it before. It had good energy.

We made our offer, got the financing and moved in November 2004.

I loved owning a house with Brent. We had so much more room for the kids. We did need to buy a lot of furnishings, most all of it financed. However, it was what we had to do in order to create a home for the kids and for us.

We had also started a new family tradition. Every May we would take the kids out of school for a week and go to the Outer Banks for a family vacation. My mom, her husband and my beloved Aunt Jane would join us. It was awesome.

I still wanted more. I wanted to be married. I wanted a baby. My biological clock was ticking. Loudly.

83 | Love Me or Not.
Either Way I'm Going to Be Fine

Every Easter there was a spiritual class held in Lancaster, which was much more convenient since I could come home every night. As had happened the last couple of times, negative energy came out toward my relationship with Brent. As that class came to a close, I gained more clarity and came to two very tough decisions.

First, I would stop taking classes for a while—until others stopped attacking my relationship or until I was strong enough to protect it. Second, I was going to have a big talk with Brent. He was either going to end the weird uncertainty, or I would walk away. God had given me the strength to do so.

The class ended Sunday afternoon. I came home with such determination to have this conversation. I would not falter. I went and got two beers, one for him and one for me. I asked him to sit down because we needed to talk. Unlike previous conversations, I didn't cry. Not one tear. He knew something was different. I was calm, cool and collected. I loved this man. With determination and God on my side I began the conversation.

I told him how much I loved him and how he was my soulmate and best friend. I also said that I could no longer take his "cave" time. I needed his full commitment. I explained that didn't necessarily have to mean getting married. It did mean that he could no longer do this back and forth stuff. I told him I was prepared to either sell the house or let him buy it by himself. I also told him that should he not be ready for that commitment, I would be moving back to North Carolina and starting over. I just couldn't do this any longer.

I sat on that couch with my beer and stated my thoughts clearly and concisely. He looked at me and knew I meant business. All other conversations had involved crying and begging. He knew he was about to lose me if something didn't change.

As sad as it might be, I had reached my tipping point. I needed Brent to be fully present with me and love me with his whole heart. I had found my worth through all the spiritual counseling and self-reflection and self-love. I loved this man completely and I deserved that love back.

I saw the look on Brent's face change as I talked through my options. This was in no way an ultimatum for him. Well, maybe, kind of. It was really more of a wakeup call. I watched his face go from "is this going to be another crying session" to "wow, I'd better get my shit together."

Good news. He got his shit together. From that point, things changed. While Brent still needed his "cave" periodically, it had nothing to do with how he felt about me. I saw his commitment level shift. He began to realize that we were soulmates. I could both feel and see the difference. He finally let go and allowed himself to fully love me.

I was so happy. I was hoping for an engagement ring in the near future. I'm sure you may be thinking, *"Holy shit, Reesy. How much do you want from this man?"* My answer is that I wanted everything I deserved. I deserved a man who loved me with his whole heart. A man who wanted to spend the rest of his life with me. I deserved the love of my life. I truly believe in love and marriage, even if I hadn't done it very well in the past.

Let me also say that I do not believe love is all you need. Love is certainly the key component. But there is so much more. If you want a lasting relationship you need to love the good and the bad. I also think you need to like the person. There is a difference. You can love someone, yet not like them very much. Because of our situation of getting to know each other as friends first, I knew I not only loved Brent, but I liked him too.

Another key to a lasting relationship is having things in common. Plenty of people say opposites attract and perhaps for some that is true. It definitely had not worked for me. I believe you need to be with someone who shares similar interests and ideologies—particularly around humor, entertainment, raising children and financing. Brent and I had all of these key elements. As best friends, we had the strongest foundation for a long lasting relationship.

About a year or so later, we began to discuss marriage a little more. Brent even took me to jewelry stores to find out what kind of ring I liked. My heart swelled.

We had planned a trip to the Dominican Republic for November 2006. I was so sure that he had already bought the ring. I just knew he was going to ask me to marry him before the trip.

It was Friday night of the weekend before our departure. I was really getting psyched. I asked what he wanted to do and he said, "Why don't we go and look at rings again?" *What the fuck?* He should have already had my ring. I tried to look cool and calm but I was boiling on the inside. Was he just trying to pacify me?

In my nicest voice I said, "I'm going to give myself a pedicure." I'm positive I sounded irritated. I went upstairs to our guest bathroom, lit a candle and put together all the stuff I would need.

I was sitting on the edge of the tub soaking my toes when he came in. My back was against him. He got on his knees behind me and said, "I want to be with you forever." My heart melted, of course. I couldn't stay mad at him. I said, "I want to be with you forever too." I turned to hug him.

That's when he repeated, "No, I want to be with you forever," and there on his knees he held out a little green box... "Will you marry me?"

I didn't know whether to cry because I was so happy or punch him in the face for pretending we still needed to shop for rings. I decided on a romantic kiss and tears of joy! It was the tipping point I will never forget.

The ring was elegant and near perfect by jewelry standards. It was a round single-carat solitaire with "hearts and fire" as a descriptor as it sparkled so beautifully in the light. It was mounted in platinum. I loved it! He had actually picked out the diamond and helped to design the setting, mounted high atop four prongs. It was so sparkly. I couldn't stop smiling.

As you have learned, I am not the most patient person, especially when it comes to something I really want. It's part of my charm. Or maybe not. Since we had started our family tradition of going to the Outer Banks every year, we thought it would be nice to get married there. Of course, I wanted to do it the very next May.

Brent wanted to wait. I'm sure he thought, *"Woman, aren't you ever satisfied?"* He won that one. We would not be getting married that May. Maybe the next. I had to be satisfied in the moment. And I was. I was engaged to my soulmate and I was going to marry him.

84 | I'm a Super Star

Things at work were going really well. I was at the top of my game. I had totally drunk the Wachovia kool-aid and was doing exactly as they taught me. Per my normal "Type A" personality, I wanted a promotion. Of course, I did. My supervisor was leaving. Her role was called Sales Leader. She managed all the licenses financial specialists in the York region. I wanted that job.

I posted my application and was granted an interview. It didn't go well. During conflict, their language was to say, "I would like to give you some feedback," which really meant, "I'm going to tell you all the ways you just fucked up."

It was tough to hear and yet it was helpful to understand the type of answers they had been looking for. They promised I would be given leadership opportunities in order to develop stronger examples for the S.T.A.R. interview process. The challenge was that this job position did not come along very often. Especially in York. And I wasn't moving.

Eventually another regional leadership position became available for a Service Leader, covering the York and Harrisburg market. The job was to manage the Financial Center Managers to ensure operational soundness, customer service standards and—right in my wheelhouse—sales referrals from the tellers and Financial Center Managers.

I thought it was a great role for me as I had witnessed so many opportunities where this particular area could be improved upon. I prepared for the interview. As they had promised, I had been given more opportunities to lead initiatives, conference calls and other types of things, giving me plenty of examples for the upcoming interview.

The other good news was that my direct supervisor would be someone I really liked and knew. He was the one who had reached out to give me the original "feedback" from the previous leadership interview. I would be interviewing with two Regional Directors and their boss. Whoa! Lots of management there. I would also have to drive to Reading for the interview. I was sooo nervous!

Did I mention I have a nervous bladder? I tried not to drink very much before the hour and fifteen-minute drive. I also made sure to go to the bathroom right before the interview.

I went in to face these three people. They were all trying their best to get me to relax. The S.T.A.R. questions began. And they were tough! There were no positive questions. What did that mean? There was no "Tell me about a time you did something great." It was more like "Tell me about a time when you tried something and it didn't work." "Tell me about a time when someone disagreed with you" and "What did you do?" I had to think really hard. I had prepared. I had examples. Now I had to make those examples work with these questions.

Oh no, I really gotta pee! After five questions, my brain and bladder were about to explode. Reluctantly, I asked if I could please use the restroom. I returned quickly to the daunting conference room. They asked one more question. Just one more. *Oh no!* Had I fucked this up by going to the bathroom?

They thanked me for my time and I left feeling like I had completely bombed. This was the opposite of how I had felt leaving my last leadership interview. I thought I had nailed that one, but clearly I had not. I just knew another inevitable "feedback" call was coming.

I drove home in tears and feeling like I'd sucked the big one. In fact, I thought it was probably the worst interview I ever had.

Then I got the call from my would-be supervisor. He was his normal nice self. Before he could say anything I decided I needed to give him "feedback" on how terrible I thought the questions were... how there weren't any positive questions.

Right in the middle of my rant, he said, "You got the job, Reesy." *What?* I felt like such an asshole, and at the same time so excited. The new role would pay more and allow me to grow professionally. I was in shock.

"Of course, I'll take the job! Thank you so much!" I will always be thankful to him for getting me this opportunity. I was sure he was my tipping point. He believed in me. We would later laugh about my interview pee and my rant.

Life became even more amazing! I was engaged to my soulmate and landed a regional well-paying leadership role. I felt sure I was leaving all those negative labels behind for a happily-ever-after future.

85 | You Gotta Hear About the Wedding

Brent and I decided to get married in May 2008 in Corolla, Outer Banks. There was much to do as we would be planning and paying for the whole thing. At that time, the wedding industry in the Outer Banks was different than in non-destination wedding areas. Meaning, a lot of people wear many hats. As an example, our minister was also the cake maker. Our caterer was also the day-of-wedding planner.

We would need to go down early to get everything set up. I made as many calls as I could from Pennsylvania. I did, however, want to meet these people in person. After all, this was the last time I would ever get married. I actually told my older brother that if for any reason, this didn't work out, he was to stop me from ever doing it again.

Brent and I decided we would rent a big, beautiful, ocean-front home and invite only our immediate family and closest friends. The house was gorgeous. It was called "Sunrise, Sunset," named for the giant windows on opposite ends of the home from which you could see the perfect morning and evening views.

We met the photographer and had engagement pictures taken on the beach—super fun! Since Brent had let me pick out everything else, when we went to meet the minister/cake lady, I told him he could absolutely pick what kind of cake he wanted. Chocolate with peanut butter icing was his favorite.

This lady was so very nice. She had a calmness about her that I really felt. We talked about our ceremony. I didn't want the whole "obey" thing in the ceremony. I did want to make sure and invite God.

Then it was time to try the cake. Brent explained what we wanted. She said she would gladly do that. However, her most requested cake was key lime. She thought we should at least try it. I'm really not a fan of key lime, but she was quite convincing. Apparently she soaks the cake in lime juice and gets orders for this cake from all over the East Coast.

She gave us the chocolate peanut butter one first. Yummy! Then she gave us the key lime. It was like an explosion of deliciousness in your mouth. I've never tasted a better cake. It took only one bite for Brent to say, "This is it." It would be a smaller three-tier key lime cake with white icing and seashell decorations.

Next we met with the caterer/day-of-wedding planner... and yeah, she does the flowers too. Ideally we wanted to get married on the beach. Weather would determine if that could actually happen. In case of rain we needed someone's help in quickly changing things to indoors. I wanted simple roses. The wedding party was just me and Brent and the kids, so I requested flowers for each of us and our moms. We also hired a guitar player and the great photographer who had taken our engagement pictures.

It was set. We would be getting married May 11, 2008.

I drove down with our friend Jeanine two days early just to relax and get ready. My best friend Dayna met us as well. My stomach was doing flip flops. I think it was my nerves. I mean I had two terrible marriages. I couldn't go through another one. In my heart I knew Brent was the one. Apparently, my heart wasn't telling my stomach it was going to be okay.

The rest of our family and friends arrived and we met at the house. It was lovely but the weather wasn't being cooperative. We had vacationed there every May for six years, and this was the coldest and rainiest. I didn't care. We could get married in front of those big windows facing the ocean.

My day-of-wedding planner was to arrive by late morning. This was especially important since it seemed we would be getting married in the house instead of the beach. Furniture needed to be moved and things needed to be arranged.

I was in the master bedroom with the girls. The ceremony was slated for 4:30. At noon, I asked Dayna to go see if the day-of-wedding planner/caterer/flower person had arrived yet. Dayna returned with a glass of wine saying, "She'll be here any minute."

I did my makeup and Jeanine curled my hair. It was getting late. I asked Dayna to check again. She returned with yet another glass of wine. "She's on her way."

Finally, I knew something was up. This woman wasn't coming. Brent had not been able to get ahold of her. The guys were setting up the living room.

The wine could not contain my anger. Where the fuck was this lady? I had given her a large deposit. She had our food, my flowers and was supposed to be helping. How would we be able to get married?

The lovely minister lady arrived. *Okay Reesy, calm down. The minister is here so you can still get married. You may not have any flowers. You can still get married. There may not be any food. You can still get married. You can order pizza. These are your closest friends and family. They will understand.*

The photographer arrived and came into the master bedroom and started taking pictures. This helped to take my mind off of the caterer/flower/day-of-wedding planner. Where was she?

Around 3:30, just an hour before we were to be married, the lovely minister lady came in. Keep in mind I had about three glasses of wine by then. She took me by my hands and said in her most kind voice, "We spoke with the caterer/flower/day-of-wedding planner lady and she is on her way right now."

Without hesitation, fueled by the wine, I said, "Oh really? She should be on the road with her kidney hanging out since she isn't here." I know that was mean. But she was fucking up my wedding day. The sweet minister lady kept her calm look on her face although I could read a bit of the shock in her eyes. Bless her heart. (That's a real bless her heart, by the way.) I probably scared the shit out of her. *Bridezilla* was a label that came to mind. In my defense, it was my wedding day and this lady was nowhere to be found.

It was almost 4:30 and she still wasn't there. I decided and Brent agreed, we would go ahead with the ceremony. I wouldn't have flowers. That was okay. And if she never showed up, we would order pizza.

I had decided to walk down our makeshift aisle by myself. Mom told me later that she wished she would have stood up and walked with me. Her health was not so good at the time though. It was still sweet that she wanted to do that.

There in front of those beautiful windows showing that amazing ocean stood the most handsome man I know. His tux was basic black pants with a white shirt and cream vest matching my ivory wedding dress. The boys wore the pink vests and the girls had on matching pale pink tea-length dresses. It was breathtaking.

Chairs from all over the house were set into two sections creating the aisle. My dress was simple but elegant—ivory and sleeveless with a short train and a simple veil.

We stood there in front of our closest friends and family. The minister began. The ceremony, too, was simple and beautiful. There in Corolla, Outer Banks, North Carolina, at 4:35 P.M. I married my soulmate.

In addition to the minister, I had a vase where Brent and I and each of the kids emptied a little sand from the beach, symbolizing our unity as a married couple and family. I still have that vase with that same sand in it.

What I didn't know was at that exact moment, the caterer/flower/day-of-wedding planner was knocking on the basement door. One of Brent's best friends went to the door and told her it would have to wait until the ceremony was done.

I was overwhelmed with happiness. Then the caterer/flower/day-of-wedding planner gave my bouquet to my friend Dayna for pictures. She told her she wanted to talk with me. My sweet Dayna warned the lady against that. "I don't think that's a good idea." It wasn't. I didn't even want to stay in the same room as that woman.

I had another glass or two of wine and my anger at her subsided. I did notice there was food we hadn't picked. Thankfully it was more expensive food. Was she trying to make up for her mistake? What had happened really?

I found out later that she had overbooked herself. Some of that food was from the wedding she had done earlier. What an asshole.

As it began to get dark, my new husband came to me and said, "We have to get in the basement. There's a tornado." I laughed. He said, "Honey, I'm not joking. We have to go." Oh my goodness! Was this real life? The day had been far from perfect and yet perfect all the same. Now I was going to be stuck in a basement with the caterer/flower/day-of-wedding planner lady and not cuss her out or punch her in the throat? All of which she deserved.

Thankfully, we weren't touched by the tornado and in a short while we went back upstairs.

I had made it. I was married to my soulmate. I had a great new job! I had stripped all those negative labels. Wonder what they would say if they saw me now. Not that I know who "they" are. Still I wondered what "they" would say. I had been through a lot. I had made a lot of bad decisions. I was a poor girl from a tiny town without a formal education. Yet, there I was leaving that all in the past.

I had found my happily-ever-after after all.

86 | Perspectives

Is your perspective your reality?

Is what we believe really true? It can be. Or we can choose to change our mind, thus changing our reality. As I have learned, if you want your world to change, you have to change.

I took the opportunity to explore whether my "labels" accurately represented what others thought of me. I reached out to those who knew me well as a teenager, and some who knew me from a distance. I know... scary, right?

I sent messages to each of my three sweethearts—Greg, Teddy, and Paul. I promised not to be offended. At least I would try. I asked for open and honest responses. I gave them the out that if they weren't comfortable, I would understand. Both Greg and Teddy replied.

I also asked Ruth Ann, our cheer captain in my junior year, and another classmate, Melissa, after we reconnected at our 30th high school reunion. She recalled a particular pair of really cool purple jeans that I had worn in school. Little did she know they were ones I had paid for myself.

Another part of Melissa's response took me off guard. She said because I was popular and a cheerleader in school, she didn't really get close to me. As an adult, I've often been told how approachable and friendly I am, but I realize it might not have always been that way. I probably missed out on a lot of really great friends because I was so busy people-pleasing and keeping things going at home.

Each of the other responses took me a bit by surprise. Teddy apologized for the grief he caused me. He shared that he has struggled with fidelity for a large part of his life because of some traumatic sexual things that happened to him at a young age.

Over time, he has learned to be faithful and true, because, as he says, "It's a lot less work." I get that one.

Greg's response was emotion filled. I believe he knew more about who I was than any other boy I dated. He remembered me as the spunky, curly-haired girl who worked the front counter. I was sassy... not mousy and shy like a lot of the girls he went to school with. He said I was the outgoing, cheerleader type, however, once he got to know me he found my sweet side. This was interesting to me that he perceived "spunky, cheerleading type" as a negative label.

Now for the ladies who only knew me peripherally. Ruth Ann was, and still is, one of the kindest, sweetest women you could ever meet. She described me as jovial with a smile that was warm and inviting. She also mentioned my loyalty and generosity, and said we went through a challenging time in cheerleading that I don't quite recall. However, she remembered I displayed enormous amounts of love and forgiveness.

Ruth Ann recalled our famous cheerleading party at my house, and how I did my best to try and take care of everyone. She also said I was "taken advantage of at times" by people I trusted to be loyal... "and yet, you never let that stop you from loving everyone and sharing your beautiful spirit." I think she saw way more than I saw in myself.

I asked Ruth Ann if she thought of me as "wild." She replied, "Wild at heart," as a means to create fun for others around me. She mentioned how popularity dictated a lot of my decisions. Then Ruth Ann said the only thing that made her sad as she reflected was that she believed I lived in the shadow of one or two close friends when I truly deserved the limelight.

Wow. She saw past stereotypes and labels and saw my true spirit. No wonder she received a top award out of the hundreds of girls at summer cheerleading camp. Ruth Ann was always able to remain true to herself without allowing outside influences to shape her into anyone other than her authentic self. If I had a "do over," I would definitely spend more time with her.

After speaking recently with Melissa, she and I had a lot in common in regard to our home life. We both struggled to fit in, often trying to be something we weren't, or what others thought we should be. Being a teenager is not for sissies.

Melissa shared a memory of a dance we both attended. I was with a cute boy while she came with a girlfriend. She thought I had such a glamorous life and she wanted that too. Apparently, I did a great job of hiding all the not-so-glamorous stuff.

We had algebra class together but Melissa thought wanting to be my friend might have made her seem aggressive. She felt she could be clingy. Just like me, Melissa stuck many labels on herself.

She remembers me as the girl others wanted to be. This was shocking. *Even I didn't want to be me!* Melissa also said she thought I couldn't and wouldn't want to be everyone's friend... because some only want to be friends for *what* you are, versus *who* you are. That is some deep, true stuff right there. I regret not getting to know Melissa better in school.

So is perspective reality?

How many opportunities in life do you get to actually find out what people honestly think of you?

While there were some labels and misunderstandings, I was grateful for the truth, kindness, and positive impressions each of these people shared.

How many opportunities did I miss to make a positive impression on someone? Many.

Today I do what I can to share a smile with someone who is frowning or to compliment someone who seems sad—no longer as a people-pleaser, but because it makes me feel happy. When you can make others feel better, laugh more, or just spread happiness, ultimately you're also helping yourself.

87 | What It's Really About

I hope that as you read my life's lessons you've been able to learn from my mistakes. I hope it made you laugh. Maybe cry a little.

As you may recall, I wanted to be a motivational speaker. You can probably tell I like the spotlight, but what I love most is to inspire people... to make a difference in someone's life.

My first cheerleading tryout was at the age of 14. Whether on the football field, basketball court, competition, coaching as an adult, teaching aerobics, or leading a group of bankers, I have and will always be a cheerleader. That comes with lots of labels, some positive but most negative—stuck up, slutty, dumb, goody-goody, and the list goes on. According to Merriam Webster's dictionary a cheerleader is:

> *cheerleader*
>
> : a person who is a member of a group (typically a group of young women) who shout out special songs or chants to encourage the team and entertain the crowd during a game in sports like American football and basketball

In that same definition, a cheerleader is also:

> : a person who encourages other people to do or support something

Cheerleading saved me from a not-so-great home life. It was my retreat. I never minded the practices or the games, or having to work at McDonald's and fundraise in order to afford it. It made me feel special. From being "Rookie of the Year" my freshman year, to winning state championships and being named co-captain, my most favorite cheering memory was in my senior year, when we played one of our long-term rivals, the Bath Pirates (my high school sweetie's school).

We had never beaten them at football for as long as I could remember, though our cheer squad did beat them every year at regional competition. Nonetheless we cheered our hearts out on the sideline... and that Friday night in the fall of 1986, we whooped them. The score was insane... like 67 to 0. That's right, zero!

When that final buzzer went off, I have never seen or felt such pure, innocent excitement. Some of us cried tears of joy and ran onto the field to hug our dearest football guy-friends. It was exhilarating! Except for my high school sweetie, as it didn't make anyone from Bath very happy.

I hope every cheerleader out there loves cheering as much as I did, and realizes that they are true athletes. I hope they understand how deeply they inspire the team and the fans, and most importantly, I hope they also feel inspired knowing they don't have to cower under anyone else's labels.

As a self-proclaimed cheerleader of life, I know that inspiring someone can make all the difference for both parties. One of my favorite adult cheerleading stories—not where I dress up in my old uniform and put my hair in ponytails for my hubby (and not that I haven't done that)—was when I was a Regional Manager for a bank, managing over 24 branch locations. I had to hold a lot of conference calls, lead a lot of initiatives. One day I had to inspire my employees around whatever initiative was the hot item of the time. Afterward, one of my managers called to discuss further tactics to reach our goals. She said, "You make us believe we can do it." That was when I understood that the need for cheerleaders never goes away. Helping others see who and what they are truly capable of—if they just start believing—is life-changing.

Throughout my story, I mentioned the many, many labels that were self-inflicted, or stamped on me by others like a scarlet letter.

I've done some things I'm not so proud of, and I've also done things I feel great about. I struggle with being my harshest critic.

It started when I was 5 years old after my grandmother told me it was my fault that my father was having a nervous breakdown. I lost my childhood innocence, labeling myself as responsible for everything that went wrong.

Another self-inflicted label was feeling unworthy and not good enough... not good enough for my grandmother (who was clearly a psycho), not good enough for Paul, not good enough for Teddy not to cheat on me, not good enough to keep Greg adoring me, not good enough for my father to keep a job so I could go to college, not good enough for that football coach to let me be on the homecoming court, not good enough for "as good as I can get" Todd, not good enough for Eric to put me first as a wife and partner. That unworthiness label deeply embedded into my being.

These labels led me to become a people-pleaser. I wanted—no, I needed—to be liked by everyone. And if someone didn't like me, I would do whatever I could to change that opinion, often sacrificing my own needs and happiness.

I'm not asking for pity. I could have sat and stewed in those labels, allowing them to overtake me and permanently make me someone I wasn't. Instead I worked hard to remove them. Every now and again, they try to show up. I have to strip them off again and remind myself who I really am—the person I've become, the true authentic Reesy.

It's not always easy. With the support of my sweet husband Brent, family and amazing friends, I am reminded that I am worthy. I also remind myself that God said I am worthy, so who am I to say anything different? I must also thank my spiritual counselor for the classes that first taught me to strip off those labels.

To anyone who ever labeled me or made me feel unworthy, I say, *"Fuck off!"*

There are two groups of people—the labelers and those walking around carrying those labels. But in reality, even those who label others are looking for a way to feel better about themselves, probably because of the self-inflicted labels they're suffering under.

If you've been walking around with labels that clearly are not who you are, know that you have a choice. It may not feel like it at the moment, but you can decide whether to wear those labels with shame and let them define you... or you can strip those fuckers off! Every single one. Do not—and I repeat, *do not*—allow them to define the person you truly are. Say no to them. Even if this means shouting, "No! That is not who I am!"

Perhaps you stand up and imagine those labels stamped across your body. Then envision yourself physically ripping off each of them, one by one. Or maybe you write them down on little pieces a paper... and then burn the papers.

Do whatever you need to do to get rid of them. I prefer the whole "fuck off" method, but that may not be for you. Whatever your way, find it and get rid of them, because as long as you let these labels define you, you will be destined to fulfill them. I believe you don't want that. I sure didn't.

It may take therapy and counseling, but it's worth the work.

For those who spend time judging others, thinking you know who they are and what they are about, I hope you take my lessons to heart as well. The next time you start to judge a book by its cover, think again. Your actions have way more consequences than you imagine—especially if those labels are negative and incorrect. You can't know what's happening in someone else's life. They may be acting or doing certain things because of extraordinary circumstances. So just stop that shit. If not, I promise it will come back to you ten-fold in a negative way. Think of it as doing your future self a favor. Remember the whole "Judge not, lest ye be judged." Yeah well, that shit is so true. It may take 50 years for that negative karma to come back to you, but it will... and you are not going to like it.

Teachers, when you look at a young person, consider the question behind their questions, or behind their silence. I can almost assure you there is one. Perhaps that kid is not a smartass. Perhaps they have above-average intelligence and really need your inspiration. Take a moment before you respond to really think about what and why they may be asking their question. Your response can make a difference for the rest of that person's life.

When it comes to the label "wild," which my less adoring fans labeled me, I believe wild is different than "slutty"—although that could have been stamped on me somewhere along the way as well. Perhaps you replace "wild" with noticing this is a person who isn't afraid to speak their mind. Perhaps what you are seeing is immature leadership skills, perhaps fearlessness, a search for some level of control and security that's missing elsewhere.

For me, I wasn't afraid to say what was on my mind because I had other things to be afraid of. I had to worry about my mother's abuse of alcohol, my father's inability to keep a job, how I was helping to pay the bills at home at a time when I shouldn't have even had to give that a thought. I wasn't afraid to speak up. I wasn't afraid to ask questions when things didn't make sense. I simply wasn't afraid outside of my "duties" I had at home. I was also searching desperately for happiness and acceptance. What others may have seen as "wild" was just me trying to find my way... trying to be more than what everyone thought I was.

Okay next, "slutty" and "home wrecker." It's true, I was super boy crazy. A lot of my closest friends have been male, and for a large portion of my life I worked in a predominantly male industry. I did not, however, sleep around. I longed for security and the kind of love that lasts forever. I watched my friends find long-term boyfriends, get married, and have children. Truth be told, their fairytale romances didn't all work out, but I felt lost. I wanted someone to love me so badly that I sacrificed some of my morals along the way—for which I've asked forgiveness.

Anyone's transgressions are between them and God. It does not give us the right to attach labels. We can't know exactly what happened, and we certainly shouldn't trust the rumor mill. It's up to each of us to get to know someone, and to offer help when they find themselves in difficult situations.

I believe most affairs happen because one or both parties are unhappy. Sadly, instead of seeking our own inner happiness, we look for it in someone else. Many thought I should have stayed with Eric, because they saw the flowers and gifts, but they didn't see the physical and emotional abuse. When tempted to pass judgment, opt for kindness instead.

As for labels like "pretty but dumb," "prissy," and "Southern women are not so smart"... what in the world makes anyone believe those preconceived notions? Some folks may like pink and looking their best, but that doesn't make them less intelligent. They may not want to dig around in the dirt, but they can clean their own toilets. And Southerners may speak slower and with a different accent, but they're just as bright and twice as nice.

I replaced "wild and out of control" with "outspoken and determined." I decided to love from my heart and not just my body. I could have felt sorry for myself and stayed stuck in terrible situations. Instead I used my strong will and mind to achieve more. I married my soulmate and I became a regional manager with the fourth largest bank in the nation. I didn't get there because I'm just another pretty face.

I had to dig deep and find my authentic self. I'm courageous, intelligent, loving, kind, charming, God-loving, romantic, prissy-and-proud-of-it, willful, spunky, and a cheerleader. Replace the labels others stamped on you with new ones that inspire you to become your best self. You truly can be anything you want to be. You just have to start to believe you can.

If you want your world to change, you have to change. It's easy to place blame on your childhood or various circumstances that have dragged you down. Instead, take a moment to gather your courage. Close your eyes and imagine who you most desire to become. Make a list of all those great things inside of you. Then write down all the things you want to become—no matter how far out of reach they may seem. Read that list every day. Slowly you will start to notice the changes. The most important lesson is *never* to let anyone tell you who you are or what you are capable of. You were not created for mediocrity.

Although painful, I now thank those people who labeled me—good, bad, or ugly.

My grandmother taught me that even though you can have a black heart, others can still love you. My parents may not have been the best providers, but they always made me feel loved. The football coach who kept me off the homecoming court taught me that through perseverance I could find my own spotlight. The teacher who wouldn't answer my smartass question taught me to be more patient with my stepchildren's questions. Those who underestimated my intelligence helped fuel my ambition to be successful. Those who treated me as "less" so they could be "more" gave me the desire to become the best person possible.

I'm grateful to my daddy for thinking I was the greatest thing since sliced bread. My mother taught me that I deserved better. Many teachers saw past the smart-mouth, sassy teenager to inspire the intelligent gal who was just trying to fit in. And my dearest friends stood by me for years, thinking more of me than I ever thought of myself.

I'm indebted to the special loving relationships of my life. Each one taught me a new lesson—some good, others not so much. But without the difficult lessons, I would not have known what it's like to find a real soulmate.

I thank all those employees who looked to me for leadership and believed I could help. I also thank the assholes for teaching me what type of leader I did not want to be. I also thank my therapists, spiritual counselors, and those I met along my recovery journey.

I'm ever grateful to my soulmate, Brent, who has shown me the love I always dreamed of but never thought I deserved. He gave me hope when I didn't think I would ever be happy again. He is the love of my life, my rock, and what makes my world slow down when needed. He still makes my heart flutter.

I thank God for this most amazing journey called life. I hope I will continue to learn and work every day to become a better person, and my authentic self, where the true beauty lives.

Lastly, I thank you, the reader. May you find the courage to strip off the labels that have been holding you back, so you can start the journey to become the very best version of yourself—the you that you were always intended to be.

Acknowledgments

While I have thanked many people in this book, I wanted to give a few more shout-outs to the amazing support I have received in my journey of writing this book.

First and foremost, I want to thank God. I know He's been with me every step of the way.

I want to thank my best friend since third grade, Dayna Parr McAdams. She has been my biggest cheerleader for most of my life. She always believes in me.

I would like to thank my publisher/writing coach/confidante and best of all friend Demi Stevens. She was amazingly patient with me during this over three-year process. She could have said many times this just isn't happening. Instead, she was always there gently helping me do this amazing thing.

And of course, I want to thank my almost perfect husband, Brent. He is my rock. He is my soulmate. He never stops believing and encouraging me.

About the Author

REESY NEFF lives in York with her husband Brent. Her four stepchildren are all grown and living on their own. She has an amazing granddaughter that is simply the apple of her eye. Being a Nana is the best job she has ever had.

After 15 years in banking, Reesy started her own business. Omega Ecycles is a recycling company for end-of-life electronics. Her goal is to make a greener world for her grandchild (and hopefully grandchildren) and future generations.

Reesy volunteers in her community. She and her husband are big movie buffs. She also enjoys playing golf, line dancing, reading and spending time with her family. She loves taking the whole family to the Outer Banks in North Carolina for vacation every year in May. The beach will always be her favorite place to go. And of course, her favorite thing to do is to be someone's cheerleader!

Made in the USA
Las Vegas, NV
29 September 2021

31386747R00168